THE WOMAN WHO TOOK POWER IN THE PARK

The Woman Who Took Power in the Park

MARY ROBINSON

LORNA SIGGINS

with an introduction
by MARY MAHER

MAINSTREAM
PUBLISHING

EDINBURGH AND LONDON

First published in 1997 by
MAINSTREAM PUBLISHING COMPANY (EDINBURGH) LTD
7 Albany Street
Edinburgh EH1 3UG

ISBN 1 85158 805 1

A catalogue record for this book is available from the British Library

Typeset in Adobe Garamond
Printed and bound in Great Britain by Butler & Tanner Ltd

Contents

Acknowledgements

Whatever about midnight oil, a lot of tapers were burned on the other side of the Atlantic for this book. A Boston-based literary agent, William B. Goodman, lit them back in year zero, and it was his determination and faith in a journalist with little obvious background in political writing that resulted in the final product. Mary Maher of *The Irish Times* was a constant source of encouragement, information, advice and reassurance, while Arthur Reynolds and Dermot Somers read the drafts and asked all the hard questions.

I am indebted to the editor of *The Irish Times*, Conor Brady, who must have a library of book credits to his name, for his support; also to Don Buckley, day editor; Dermot O'Shea, pictures editor; Eric Luke and all Dermot's photographic staff, who are named in the photo credits below; Mick Crowley of photo production; John Gibson, John Vincent and Esther Murnane of the *Irish Times* library; Shay De Barra of the RTE library; and Mick Slevin of the former Irish Press Group.

I am most grateful to Ann Lane, the President's personal assistant; Bride Rosney, special adviser to the President; Jonathan Williams, literary agent; Judy Diamond, editor; Helen Litton; Adrian Glover, Hayes and Sons; Dermot Brangan, Consulate General of Ireland, New York; John Paget Bourke; and to all those who agreed to be interviewed, including members of the Bourke family, close friends and colleagues of President Robinson, now UN Human Rights Commissioner. The lunch and hospitality provided by her father, Dr Aubrey Bourke, in Ballina, County Mayo, will never be forgotten!

Fergus Finlay of the Labour Party, who published a book on the presidential campaign of 1990, and Michael O'Sullivan, who wrote a biography of the President in 1993, were generous with time and information, as were Maol Muire Tynan, Fintan O'Toole and the many colleagues in *The Irish Times*, *Irish Independent*, *The Irish Press*, *Sunday Tribune*, *Sunday Business Post*, *Sunday Independent*, *Phoenix* and RTE who recorded

Mary Robinson's career over the years. Last, but far from least, thanks to Cian for his good timing. I owe an immeasurable debt to some very close friends – lieutenants all – who fed flagging spirits. Thank you: you know who you are.

Credits: I am grateful to the Harvill Press for permission to reproduce the last stanza of Paul Durcan's *Backside to the Wind* on p.148. My thanks are also due to the following for permission to reproduce photographs: Dr Aubrey Bourke and John Paget Bourke; the President's office; *The Irish Times*; *The Irish Press*; Pacemaker, Belfast; Denis Minihane, *The Examiner*.

INTRODUCTION

by Mary Maher

She said when she launched her campaign that she would change the role of the Irish presidency. No one really believed her.

Her most ardent supporters asked each other in discreet mutters what she could mean. The post was largely ornamental, circumscribed – and quite properly – by the Constitution. It just wasn't possible to stretch these particular parameters. But it wasn't a bad slogan. For most of her supporters, the point was the campaign, a spirited gesture, a challenge to the old order. A dignified loss with something up to 40 per cent of the vote would be a triumph.

Her opponents sneered at the presumption. 'Dangerous nonsense,' the then Taoiseach, Charles Haughey, declared.

Seven years later, the role of the Irish presidency is so dramatically changed that it is difficult to see what added dimension her successor could give to the position, or indeed to remember clearly what it was that her predecessors did in their time.

Most significantly, it is difficult to imagine ourselves, the Irish, as we could have been in the 1990s without Mary Robinson in the Phoenix Park. She found a way to change the presidency that represented what we had become in a way we had not yet realised. She did it simply, going where politicians had never been especially welcome and presidents never seen, bringing the most marginalised in Irish society home to the presidential residence at Áras an Uachtaráin.

She lit a single candle for the immigrants of every generation, and with one powerful symbol fanned the imagination and memory of the millions of people of Irish descent throughout the world. Then she walked out on that world stage, into the poorest and most neglected communities and the centres of power, becoming herself a powerful symbol of what we are today, a symbol of the real Ireland.

When she announced that she would not stand for a second term, Fintan O'Toole wrote in *The Irish Times*: 'The most unlikely aspect of her presidency has been the way in which a political persona forged in the white heat of some of the most bitterly divisive campaigns of recent decades has come, somehow, to represent in the Republic of Ireland a national consensus.'

It is this unlikely aspect that is the subject of this book, and Lorna Siggins is uniquely well placed to take on the task of exploring it. She, too, is from the west of Ireland, and as one of that generation of women who followed Mary Robinson's, she has been a witness to the years of turmoil and tumultuous change in the latter half of this century. In her richly descriptive and detailed profile, Lorna Siggins traces the forces that shaped the shy girl from Mayo into a champion of civil rights, an advocate for women's equality, a tireless public servant and, finally, Ireland's first citizen.

CHAPTER 1

The Long Shadow

The story could well start in Allihies, a little west Cork community whose copper-miners had long since migrated across the Atlantic to build new homes for themselves in Butte, Montana.

Allihies had decided to call a conference on 'coastal communities'. Eily Kelly, the postmistress, and a local committee of lobster fishermen who also ran sheep on the craggy hills, agreed that the event could not be a flop. The village, population 600, was too important to suffer such an indignity.

Somebody, perhaps one with a vacation home in the area, might have suggested the conference in the first place over a pint of Guinness in the local pub. There had been a long-running controversy over the handling of grants to Ireland as a member of the European Community, and the resulting impact on isolated places like this. The future of such peripheral areas had been ignored by the civil servants responsible for apportioning the Brussels money in the warm offices of the national capital. A conference might get a few of them down to see what life was really like on Ireland's Atlantic seaboard.

But who would come to open it? Who would drive 250 miles from Dublin to hear the views of a small community? Why, pregnant women from Allihies had to book into lonely hostels in Cork city for weeks before their due date to be near the maternity hospital; home was *that* remote.

Easy, said a Dublin voice at another meeting in the pub: look for a speaker with rising ambitions. He might be able to get someone with a bit of a profile himself. Just a few days before, the European barrister and former Dublin University senator Mary Robinson had declared her nomination for the Irish Republic's presidential election. There was considerable surprise and excitement. The seven-year post had become vacant for the first time in fourteen years.

Dr Patrick Hillery, the incumbent, had held the presidency for two terms. The ruling party, Fianna Fáil, had nominated its Minister for Defence, Brian Lenihan, and he was expected to romp home in the plebiscite of November 1990. One of Fianna Fáil's most senior politicians, Lenihan was a 'glad-hander' – a master of the Tammany Hall political school at which many of his party colleagues had been willing pupils. But he was a little special: charming, articulate, witty, loyal and one of the most popular politicians in the Dáil. There was a lot of public sympathy for him also, for he had undergone a liver transplant in the United States not long before.

Dick Grogan, a journalist with *The Irish Times*, did approach a friend, former attorney general John Rogers, a kingpin in the Mary Robinson campaign. Rogers agreed; and for various 'symbiotic reasons', in Grogan's words, the idea worked. Mrs Robinson spoke in a community hall originally built for former employees of the copper-mines. The village had never before been visited by a president, or a presidential candidate. The closest it had come was when Eamon de Valera, then leader of the new Irish republic, had visited the nearby fishing port of Castletownbere in 1938 to receive back Berehaven dockyard, one of four naval bases maintained by Britain under the 1921 Anglo-Irish treaty.

Michael McNally, John O'Leary, Eily and other committee members stood discreetly at the back of the hall as Mary Robinson spoke about peripherality, and the need for people to express their ideas and their 'sense of place'. She could identify with this sense of place, and she could identify with the frustrations. One of her abiding childhood memories in County Mayo, she said, was of going out in a fishing boat and watching crabs being thrown back overboard. The same lucrative crabs now fetched high prices on the European market. 'The skippers couldn't sell them then,' she said. 'Thankfully, that has changed, but we still have underexploited riches from the sea. Brussels doesn't understand the language, and so it has to come from you, yourselves, here,' she told the fishermen, touching on anger over the government's acceptance of a harsh European Community policy that had extended generous rights in Irish waters to other member states. The real need to listen, understand and value a traditional way of life and environment did not necessarily mean 'stopping the clock' on progress, she said. Instead, such values should be built into 'careful, considered development' that was not part of an arbitrary set of policies thoughtlessly imposed on the community.

The presidency could lend a moral influence to certain issues, she said. It could help to empower local groups which felt they no longer had a voice. Villages like Allihies were dismissed as being on the periphery, but to those who lived there, there was nothing peripheral about it or any other 'remote' seaboard community. The centre was wherever you were.

She spoke with passion; she spoke to no script. There was resounding applause. Afterwards, a fisherman who was very active in the constituency on behalf of Fianna Fáil touched the elbow of this *Irish Times* reporter. He was lost for words. A woman whom he had remembered as a chubby-faced, earnest, polo-necked Dublin academic, and who was identified with minority issues and apparent 'losers' was going to get his vote . . .

The serious but radical constitutional barrister and mother-of-three, in her late forties, already wore a public face as a representative of the Seanad or upper house of the Irish parliament. 'Wheeled out when there was a debate on a question nobody could understand', she was 'definitely not somebody you'd want to go out with at night for a couple of drinks', according to one campaign colleague.

She was not a socialiser; nor was she particularly concerned about appearances. She was slightly awkward, formal – some would say shy. The story went that she once had her unravelled skirt-hem mended by a woman she was representing in a landmark case in the European Court as they travelled by taxi to the court in Strasbourg. A 'pre-natal bluestocking', one acquaintance crudely put it.[1]

Six months later: a chilly exhibition hall, a dark November evening, a south-central Dublin suburb. Intermittent shouts from small groups of people clustered around black boxes. By the time Brian Lenihan, ever the statesman, arrived at about quarter to four in the afternoon, the result of the 1990 Irish presidential election was all over, bar the final counting.

Ruairí Quinn, director of elections for the Labour Party's candidate, was euphoric. 'Historic, this is historic,' he said. It represented a 'sea-change' in Irish politics. This was a time when 'all political parties would be taking a closer look at themselves'.

In burst the colourful senator and university lecturer, David Norris, of no particular political persuasion. Clasping the hand of a beaming politician from the right-of-centre party, Fine Gael, he couldn't resist crying, 'The west's awake!' It wasn't the Dublin result that he was so excited about, he told me. It was what had happened on the other side of the island, out in the Atlantic. Mary Robinson, his former fellow scholar at Trinity College, Dublin, and one-time colleague in the Seanad (Senate), had topped the poll on the Aran Islands – bastion of that image of a conservative Ireland, envisioned by Eamon de Valera. It was unthinkable.

'Out there', images of a national icon were not exactly being smashed. De Valera, a man with a reputation even greater at home than the 'beatified' US president, John F. Kennedy, had left few physical statues to topple. He had been Ireland's best known leader internationally as the architect of the new Irish Republic. Fifteen years after his death, however, public attitudes to his legacy were changing.

It was a legacy which had shaped twentieth-century Ireland and which would determine the role of those leaders who were to succeed him. In the words of Tim Pat Coogan, one of his biographers, the 'Long Fellow' had cast a 'long shadow' that still fell over Irish life in the 1990s:

> Quite simply, the history of Ireland for much of the twentieth century is the history of de Valera. As befitted a man who sometimes seemed to model his actions on the Roman Catholic doctrine of Three Divine Persons in One God, his tangible legacies are three also: the Irish Constitution; the largest Irish political party, Fianna Fáil; and the second-largest Irish newspaper empire, the Irish Press Group, founded, as was so much of his political strength, on Irish America. His intangible influences can still be traced in the divisions between the leading Irish political parties, Fianna Fáil and Fine Gael, and in attitudes towards Northern Ireland, Church-State relationships, the role of women in Irish society, the Irish language and the whole concept of an Irish nation. Any one of his visible creations would have been an achievement beyond the powers of most men. The three, taken together, must be accounted a rare feat indeed.[2]

De Valera had been Taoiseach – Prime Minister – and, later, President of the Republic for which he had fought in 1916; for which he had been imprisoned by the British; and over which he had waged a bitter civil war. It was he who had defined the job description of a post he held himself for two consecutive seven-year terms – from 1959 to 1973, the year when, coincidentally, Ireland joined the European Community. Under his 1937 Constitution, the Irish presidency was designed as a non-executive head of state. The post would symbolise sovereignty, and a complete break with the British Crown.

Opposition politicians were not so convinced during the debates on the draft Constitution in June 1937. De Valera was drawing up a little dictatorship for himself, they charged. His ministerial colleagues laughed at such claims. One cabinet member reportedly told an American diplomat in Dublin that it was to be a sinecure – little more than 'shaking hands with visiting golfers'.[3]

And that, for many years, was what the successive incumbents did. In the two decades before de Valera retired as Taoiseach and became President, he was preceded by Douglas Hyde, a 79-year-old academic who was the agreed candidate in 1938. A west of Ireland Protestant and an Irish-speaker, he symbolised both nationalist and Anglo-Irish Ireland.

Hyde was 85 when he was succeeded by Seán T. O'Kelly – de Valera's Tánaiste (deputy prime minister) and the first president to be elected by a plebiscite. O'Kelly was also the first to have to work with a government comprising former opponents in politics, and was to find that his office was restricted: at one point, a proposed state visit to the United States was blocked.[4]

It was only after the tenure of de Valera, the third president, that the office became controversial. Ironically, the architect of the 'guardian of the Constitution' had been a great 'disturber' in Irish political life. As Coogan has pointed out, de Valera's insecure background – shaped by his mother's dispatching him at the age of three with an eighteen-year-old uncle to Ireland, where he was reared by relatives – contributed to his insatiable desire for power. It also affected his attitude towards women. Yet the 'Long Fellow' had few visitors to the president's residence and former vice-regal lodge, Áras an Uachtaráin, in Dublin's Phoenix Park.

Not so his two successors, both of whom tried to make the presidency a more active appointment. Erskine Childers – son of the revolutionary author of the classic *The Riddle of the Sands* – clashed with the government on a number of issues after he was elected fourth president in 1973. In contrast to his predecessor, Childers travelled extensively around the country, urging people to protect the environment, stop drinking and smoking and live a healthy life. He also appealed for an end to violence in the North during a St Patrick's Day broadcast in 1974.

Childers threw open the doors of Áras an Uachtaráin to some 2,000 visitors in his first year in office, and was certainly the first Irish president to be photographed in a canoe in County Wicklow. The gesture was intended to help sweep away the stuffy image of the office. Although Childers threatened to resign over government opposition to his concept of a presidential 'think-tank', he never did. He was the first to open a debate on the presidency, but was quickly disillusioned, according to broadcaster and historian John Bowman. His widow, Rita, has told of a shopping trip to a stationer's to buy 'the largest felt pen on the market'. Her husband wanted to write 'overruled' on all those memoranda he was advised by government officials to jettison.[5]

On his sudden death in 1974 Childers was succeeded by another agreed candidate. It might have been the first woman: Rita Childers had been proposed by the leaders of the two main political parties because of her outstanding contribution to the office during her husband's term. However, her planned nomination was revealed to the press and the Fianna Fáil leader, Jack Lynch, withdrew his support, believing that he had been set up.[6] Lynch went instead for another non-political figure, Cearbhall Ó Dálaigh, who had been Chief Justice and a member of the European Court.

Ó Dálaigh was a constitutional lawyer with a broad range of cultural interests and a facility for languages, including Irish and Chinese. The

Chief Justice was not prepared for the 'political' responsibilities, however, according to historian Jim Duffy, and suspected that the Taoiseach, Fine Gael leader Liam Cosgrave, was not abiding by the Constitution in his treatment of him. Cosgrave briefed the President on government policy only once every six months and failed to tell him of a planned declaration of a national emergency. He may have regarded Ó Dálaigh as politically naïve. At one point, the President had offered to substitute himself as hostage when Tiede Herrema, a Dutch industrialist based in Ireland, was kidnapped.[7]

The tensions came to a head in September 1976 when President Ó Dálaigh exercised his constitutional right to refer a piece of legislation, the Emergency Powers Bill, to the Supreme Court. Although the court found that the bill was constitutional, and Ó Dálaigh signed it, his action made waves in Anglo-Irish relations. British politicians, with no constitution of their own, queried his decision. In Ireland, government frustration was articulated publicly by the Minister for Defence, Patrick Donegan, who departed from a prepared script at a military function to describe the soldiers' supreme commander as a 'thundering disgrace'.

Such was the outcry that the Defence Minister tendered his resignation, but it was refused by the Taoiseach, who told him to apologise to President Ó Dálaigh instead. That meeting never took place. A 'no confidence' vote in the Dáil or parliament, tabled by the opposition, was defeated. Ó Dálaigh submitted his own resignation, after less than two years in office, to 'protect the dignity and independence of the presidency as an institution'. He and his wife retired to live near Sneem, County Kerry, and visited China as guests of the government the following year, 1977. On 21 March 1978 Ó Dálaigh died suddenly at home after a heart attack and was buried in Kerry after a state funeral.

Not surprisingly, there was no appetite in the country for another presidential election, and the former Fianna Fáil minister and European Commissioner, Dr Patrick Hillery, was the agreed nomination. He served two terms, and there are conflicting views on his contribution. He kept a low profile and did, indeed, play golf. He entertained political allies in Áras an Uachtaráin. His low-key approach intensified 'popular apathy and indifference' to the presidency, in the view of one commentator; yet in many ways Hillery had no choice but to retreat, while also restoring dignity to the office and ensuring that it would never be used to test 'constitutional stability'.[8]

Hillery was not beyond controversy. In 1979 he publicly denied rumours that he and his wife were to separate. In 1980 he attracted criticism for his decision not to attend a remembrance service for Ireland's dead in two World Wars. The following year he declined an invitation from Queen Elizabeth II to attend the Prince of Wales's wedding.

In 1982, following the collapse of a coalition government comprising Fine Gael and Labour, Dr Hillery's 'political neutrality' was tested when he came under pressure from former Fianna Fáil colleagues to decline to dissolve the Dáil as he was empowered to do. The Taoiseach was Dr Garret FitzGerald. The Fianna Fáil leader, Charles J. Haughey, whose leadership had been under threat in the weeks before, could then have formed a government and quickly called an election, uniting his party behind him. Hillery angrily dismissed the telephone appeals from some of his former cabinet colleagues, and granted the dissolution.

This may have been Hillery's most significant contribution to the credibility of the presidency.[9] In 1990, as an election was planned to select his successor, he played a part in the outcome. To what extent he did so is still being debated, and depends on the strength of other influences, such as a changing Ireland in a Europe which could not abide by some of the edicts spelled out in de Valera's 1937 Constitution.

That Constitution reneged on some of the promises made to all citizens in the 1916 Proclamation of the Republic, such as the recognition of Irish women as full citizens, and other statements of equality. In the early decades of the twentieth century, women had played an active political role in the struggle for Irish independence. This fact was largely written out of history in 1937. One female academic described the tract at the time as 'not a return to the Middle Ages' but 'something much worse'.[10]

It would be up to a woman, Mary Robinson, to try and restore the balance. Unlike de Valera, her west of Ireland background was secure, happy and privileged. Like Erskine Childers, she believed in a certain kind of democracy. Like Cearbhall Ó Dálaigh, she was cultured, educated and an expert in constitutional law. And she was to shatter moulds and reshape them around her own experience and commitment to social reform, like that contemporary of de Valera's, Eleanor Roosevelt, widely described as the most influential woman of her time. Although she was the powerless spouse, Eleanor Roosevelt was able to use the American presidency – albeit as First Lady – in the 1940s on behalf of causes that she believed in, rather than 'letting it use her'.[11] Her power was that she had no power. The same would be said of a non-executive head of state when Mary Robinson followed suit.

CHAPTER 2

The Right Stuff

Mayo's Moy river rises in the Sligo hills on the Atlantic seaboard and cuts down to the cathedral town of Ballina in the shadow of Nephin mountain. Lining the banks from dawn onwards, still figures await their quarry. There is a particular lilt to the ripple of these waters. The Moy is one of the finest salmon and trout rivers in Europe.

Within a line cast of St Muredach's Roman Catholic cathedral and the nearby Augustinian ruins is the famous Ridge Pool. Here, decked out in green waistcoats and waders, royals and celebrities differ little from locals as they wait for a flash of silver among the rocks. They talk of bait and fly ties, and grumble about falling catches due to pollution and poaching. Many in the market town once fed off the river; poorly paid netsmen toiled in the non-tidal waters above the weirs to trap fish for sale to Liverpool.

Ballina itself – Béal an Átha or the 'mouth of the ford' – holds its own place in Irish history: founded less than four centuries ago as a flax and linen community, it subsequently became a shipping port, receiving an unexpected visit by a thousand Frenchmen in 1798 – two years after a similar attempt by the new French republic to liberate Ireland from British rule.

'Irishmen . . . recollect America, free from the moment she wished to be so,' read the proclamation issued by General Jean Joseph Amable Humbert, leader of the expeditionary force which landed in Killala Bay on 22 August of that year. 'The contest between you and your oppressors cannot be long. Union! Liberty! The Irish Republic! – such is our shout.'

The shout was short. The contest lasted just over a fortnight. Having initially defeated the British at what is now known as the 'Castlebar races', the French were finally outnumbered after being chased through five counties. Humbert surrendered and was sent back home. Lord Charles Cornwallis, head of the English administration in Ireland, showed no such mercy to the Irish volunteers.

One of those caught up in the fray was a Dr Patrick Barrett of Ballina whose son, also Patrick, was an officer in the local yeomanry corps and a volunteer with the Franco-Irish army. With a price on his son's head, the doctor was an obvious scapegoat. He was sheltered for a time in a house, since called Amana, although its occupants, the Jones family, were loyal to the British Crown. He was arrested, taken to Castlebar, and court-martialled on charges of collusion with the French. A local tinsmith gave evidence that he had seen Barrett casting bullets from a mould. The doctor was hanged in Fair Green, Ardnaree.

A century and a half later, Ardnaree – Ard na Rí, the 'king's heights' – was where Mary Bourke and her four brothers played as children. Amana was their grandparents' home. Complete with stables and a walled garden, it stands close to the town's eighteenth-century Protestant church of St Michael's, where many Bourkes and their kin lie buried.

It was typical of the emerging Irish middle class in the nineteenth century that the Births, Marriages and Deaths registers should cross religious divides. There were practical reasons for this, reflected in Ireland's complex history under British rule. From the time of Henry VIII, English influence in Ireland was maintained through the Crown's representative in Dublin, rather than through the Gaelicised and very independent Norman lords. Political tension was exacerbated by the Reformation, which forced Norman and Gael to forge a common identity through Catholicism.

Colonisation reached a zenith during the reign of Elizabeth I. Power and wealth was vested only in those with land, who in turn swore loyalty to the Crown. Thus, before Ireland lost its parliament by an Act of Union in 1800, the Irish parliamentary representatives were mainly Protestant stock, whose families had been rewarded for past military service with tracts of property. Others were established Irish families who supported the Crown.

The seventeenth-century Penal Laws were designed to ensure that this 'ascendancy' class maintained its influence untramelled. Catholics and dissenters were prohibited from owning land and from holding public office. Under one statute, a Catholic was not allowed to own a horse worth more than five pounds; if offered that sum for a horse of his by a Protestant, he was bound to accept. Hence, the definition of an Anglo-Irishman by Brendan Behan as 'a Protestant with a horse'.[1]

Still, with growing urbanisation, a Catholic middle class did emerge in the eighteenth century in towns like Ballina. Trade was the basis of its economy, making the most of links with Irish people overseas, and a road and canal network at home. Moneylending was another form of income. By the time an Irish bank was founded in 1783, some 10 per cent of the capital came from Irish Catholics.

By 1730 the worst of the Penal Laws was over, though the legacy lived on and was not given formal relief on the statute books until Catholic emancipation in 1829. Little use was made of some of the more heinous Penal Laws, such as the Protestant right of 'discovery' of Catholic-owned land. Many of the recorded cases tell of friendly Protestants who turned the land back to Catholic owners.[2]

Mary Bourke's father, Aubrey, had been reared in Amana as one of a family of seven. He was not a child of the Anglo-Irish 'big house'; rather, his family were what some might now call 'Castle Catholics' – a euphemism for the comfortable class which had identified itself with the British administration in Ireland from the period of Catholic emancipation onwards.[3] In time, he would pass on to his own children the story of Dr Barrett, who was hanged in front of the house 'in his fashionable morning coat, knee breeches, silk stockings and low shoes fastened with golden clasps'.

'We were fascinated by the horror of it all, especially the idea of the suspended lifeless body wearing shoes with gold clasps swinging to and fro,' his daughter would write many years later. 'There was quite a lore and superstition surrounding the place where the tree once stood.'[4]

Originally of Norman stock, Bourkes, Burkes and de Burghs became chieftains who were 'more Irish than the Irish themselves'. Some were landed gentry, rewarded through service to the Crown. As the historian Roy Foster has pointed out, the term 'ascendancy' for the upper caste in eighteenth-century Ireland did not equate strictly with descendants of colonists, rewarded through military service, or with the 25 per cent of the population which was Protestant at the time. He defines it as Anglicanism, a social élite which was 'professional as well as landed, whose descent could be Norman, Old English, Cromwellian or even ancient Gaelic'.

This élite was not, therefore, comprised solely of one ethnic group, nor one religion; but the golden circle dominated law, politics and society, through the Irish House of Commons, and held an ambivalent, often resentful, attitude to England which would produce the sort of savage social comment articulated by Jonathan Swift, or the support for independence sought by activists like Theobald Wolfe Tone.[5]

In 1815 a John Bourke of Heathfield House, Ballycastle, County Mayo, married Elizabeth Paget, another member of the Mayo landed stock, related to the Paget earls of Uxbridge and marquesses of Anglesey. Secure in family wealth, she chose one of the traditional routes taken by the ascendancy class for her sons: the British army. Of the four in the military, two became generals.

William Orme Paget Bourke, Mary Bourke's great-grandfather, was a captain in the 18th Regiment of Foot or Royal Irish Regiment, one of the oldest independent garrison regiments raised in Ireland.[6] He commanded the last British regiment in Australia. But it was his brother, Lieutenant-General Oliver Paget Bourke, who brought military 'honour' to the family, as reflected in a tablet in St Michael's Church. Having obtained his first commission as an ensign in the British Army in 1835, he served with the 17th Regiment in Afghanistan and Baluchistan in 1838–39, and in the Crimea. He was in command of his regiment during the Siege of Sevastapol from December 1854 to February 1855. As colonel, he served as exon or officer of the yeomen of the guard with the Queen's Royal Bodyguard, and was promoted to the rank of major-general in 1873. He retired as a lieutenant-general, and died in Dun Laoghaire (then known as Kingstown) in County Dublin in 1880.

Another brother, Paget John Bourke, served as a captain in the British Household Cavalry and part of the Royal Bodyguard for Queen Victoria, while a cousin, Sir James Paget, who graduated from Trinity College, Dublin, was Queen's surgeon. Victoria favoured her Bourke bodyguard, giving him a diamond ring for one of his three marriages. He in turn wore a black band on his arm after her death. He had an apartment in Buckingham Palace in addition to his residence in Regent's Park, London. His full uniform is still with the Bourke family.

William Orme Bourke's marriage to Jane Morrogh in 1856 was mixed. As befitted the tradition, girls were reared as Protestants and boys as Catholics. The Morroghs were of the Cork Catholic gentry; a set of rosary beads given by the British Catholic monarch, King James II, to one of Jane's ancestors, Thomas Morrogh, High Sheriff of Cork, was, until recently, said to be in the possession of the senior branch of the family, now living in Argentina.[7] On his retirement from the military around 1870, William took a house near Bonniconlon, outside Ballina.

William's son and Mary Bourke's grandfather, Henry Charles Bourke – known as 'H.C.' – was born in Bonniconlon about two years after the return from Australia. When he was still very young, his parents moved to the midlands, latterly to Athlone, County Westmeath. Educated at Trinity College, Dublin, H.C. became a well-known Mayo solicitor. His wife, Eleanor Macaulay, came from a medical family and had for a time contemplated becoming a nun.

H.C. and Eleanor lived for horses. H.C. kept racehorses and hunters, while Eleanor, or Nellie as she was known, was featured in *Tatler* when she became foxhound master of the North Mayo Harriers. She was one of the first women in Ireland to do so, in 1914. Her husband, who had close ties with the pro-Treaty political party,[8] Cumann na nGaedheal (which merged to form Fine Gael in 1933), also had land and cattle. What he paid tended to set the local price of oats.

'Neither castle nor cabin' was how the early-nineteenth-century diarist and former resident of Amana, Elizabeth Ham, described the house in which the Bourkes lived in Ballina – then a garrison town, with a busy shipping trade supplying the bonded stores lining the Moy quay. The house was the first of its type in Connacht.

> The walls were very thick, the windows small and well defended with iron bars. The roof was thatched, and supported by four immense beams of oak that went into the ground, and met at the top . . . two rows of lime trees bordered the lawn to the road which was considerably lower and it was all open when we first went to live there, but my father built a wall next to the road and filled the ground up level with its top, so we had nothing on appearance between the house and the broad Moy, that here ran shallow and rippling, and was crossed by salmon weirs just above. It was a lovely spot.[9]

Amana was a 'happy, amenable' home, remembers John Paget Bourke, Mary Bourke's cousin. He spent many summers there and remembers his grandparents as being religious people with a passionate interest in all things equine. 'Pater', as his grandfather was called, was a 'tough, dictatorial little man', who studied form, placed bets most days, and decreed that there be silence in the house when the racing results were read out on the radio. The couple had a large garden, and 'Mater', his grandmother, grew her own vegetables, kept chickens, made jam – 'all in the middle of town'. They had several servants. Picnics on Enniscrone beach were 'expeditions' which took some days of planning, with hampers being prepared, and tables, chairs, awnings and panama hats all packed into the car. He remembers a daily rosary; such was his grandmother's affiliation to the Catholic faith that his grandfather did not tend his relatives' graves in the Protestant churchyard until after her death.

H.C. Bourke was 'devilled' or apprenticed to his uncle, Robert Paget Bourke, a man known to be 'skilled with his fists'. He set up his own practice subsequently, and represented the law at a turbulent time. Home rule had been promised but not delivered. The political leadership provided by Charles Stewart Parnell, a Protestant landlord, had collapsed with his sudden death in 1891. Mayo, which had experienced some of the worst effects of the Great Famine of 1845–47, was also the wellspring for one of the biggest mass movements in modern Irish history.

It is not only the magnitude of the fatalities, with over a million people dying between 1845 and 1890 and some two million emigrating; the fact that the Famine received tacit support from an Irish middle class has marked it as one of the taboo subjects in the country's history.[10] Recent work by historians on the 150th anniversary of the first potato blight of 1845 has helped to explain some of the issues, such as the intellectual response among decision-makers who felt it presented an opportunity to 'accelerate Ireland's economic and social development'.[11]

When the potato blight struck, the British government viewed it as a natural disaster, an act of God, as was so poignantly explained by Cecil Woodham-Smith's classic book, *The Great Hunger*. The £9.5 million spent by the British government on famine relief in Ireland was half the amount paid in compensation to slave-owners a decade earlier, and a seventh of the amount spent on the Crimean War ten years on. The government's response fuelled a growing nationalist sentiment in Ireland and it also established a firm power base for the Catholic Church, which became synonymous with the cultural void left by the Famine.[12]

In the poor lands of the west of Ireland, the population had become almost wholly dependent on the potato in the late-seventeenth and early-eighteenth centuries. The boglands of Mayo provided turf, the beaches seaweed, sand and 'shore food'. 'Rundale villages, powered by the potato, acted as a mobile pioneering fringe; the spade and the spud conquered the contours.'[13] When agricultural prices halved after the Napoleonic wars, and the linen industry was hit by new technology, a series of wet summers created the conditions for economic distress – and ultimate collapse.

In certain areas it was the survival of the fittest, with farmers and shopkeepers exploiting their weaker neighbours, and landlords packing off the destitute to America in aptly named 'coffin ships'. The Repeal Party of constitutional nationalists, led by Daniel O'Connell – who had championed Catholic emancipation and who helped turn Irish politics into a personality cult with his widely attended public addresses – was in favour in principle of radical action, such as a prohibition on continuing exports of Irish grain to Britain. But O'Connell became ill, and political alliances compromised his party's response. An assertive revolutionary movement seeking land reform, known as Young Ireland, would take the nationalist high ground. Still, land reform and tenant rights would dominate Irish politics for the next half-century, with the Famine proving to be a watershed.

H.C. Bourke was a constitutional nationalist who 'retained a certain sympathy for the Empire', according to journalist Michael O'Sullivan. Getting an accurate picture of the events of the time depends greatly on whom one speaks to in Ballina, he notes.[14] In the early years of the twentieth century, shortly before independence was obtained, Amana was raided by the IRA for guns and cars; or, perhaps, Amana was raided by the British Black and Tans.

H.C.'s granddaughter would confirm the latter version. 'My father used to tell us the story of the day the Black and Tans drove into Amana and ordered . . . H.C. Bourke to give them cars,' she wrote in 1993. 'My grandfather refused but it was useless and the armed Black and Tans searched the outhouses, found the cars hidden under hay and drove off with them. Often, during these times, my father together with his brothers and sisters would be woken at night and told to lie on the bedroom floor . . . to avoid crossfire.'[15]

A profile in 1974 in the Dublin periodical *Man Alive* may have been unfair when referring to the family's spiritual home as 'far from Ireland', and its services to the British Empire being more noteworthy than those in Ireland.[16] A look at the genealogical roots of any established Irish family can reveal divided loyalties and pragmatic decisions that reflected turbulent times.

For instance, an uncle of H.C.'s wife, Eleanor, was a member of the Irish Republican Brotherhood and the Mayo Land League. Tom Augustus Macauley was sentenced to ten years in Mountjoy jail, Dublin, as one of six people alleged by an informer to have planned to kill a landlord's agent in a case known as the 'Crossmolina Conspiracy'. Yet Eleanor's sister, Muriel, married Joseph Sheridan of Spencer Park, Castlebar, who was to become Chief Justice of Kenya and president of the Court of Appeal in East Africa. Sir Joseph also chaired the Masai Riots Claims Commission of 1918–19.

Adopting an expedient approach to an uncertain political situation, H.C. appeared at courts which had been set up by the nationalist party, Sinn Féin, as an alternative to the British judicial system in the years preceding independence. This created difficulties with the authorities and resulted in some charges against him associated with 'causing disaffection'.

Paget, the eldest child of H.C. and Eleanor, maintained the family's links with the British Empire. Palestine, Kenya, Cyprus and Gibraltar were among his postings as a judge. He married an Irishwoman, Susan Killeen, a daughter of the Clare County registrar and one of the early girlfriends of the Irish revolutionary, Michael Collins. There was a flash of glamour about Paget's proposal, coming by telegram from the Seychelles, while the engagement ring was the famous diamond originally given to his uncle by Queen Victoria.

Paget, Mary Bourke's uncle, was identified as a target by resistance movements in both Palestine and Cyprus, and was under military protection. He was knighted at Buckingham Palace, at a ceremony attended by his mother and his brother Aubrey. After he returned to Dublin he was kidnapped in April 1975, but was held in captivity for less than a day, in what was believed to have been a case of mistaken identity. The target was thought to be the British ambassador to Ireland in a bid to force the release of a republican activist, Dr Rose Dugdale, who was on hunger strike in Limerick prison.

Aubrey was one of two doctors in the Bourke brood; his elder brother, Hal, was a general practitioner in England before retiring to France. Two other brothers, Roddy and Denis, became an RAF officer and an actor respectively. Roddy Bourke subsequently pursued business interests in Australia, while Denis, who left Trinity College for the West End of London, also went into business and emigrated to South America. Two girls, Ivy and Dorothy, became nuns – the former after a Trinity degree, the latter straight from school.

The seven children had a governess, Mrs Wall, and at the tender age of ten Aubrey de Vere Bourke was sent to boarding-school in England. Home visits were rare – Christmas, Easter, the summer holidays. Like the aforementioned Dr Barrett, Aubrey undertook his medical training in Edinburgh. It was, he remembers, a very anti-Catholic city and he even witnessed priests being stoned by Protestants.

Mary Bourke spent the first years of her life in a three-storey house across the river from Amana, overlooking the Ridge Pool. Still the largest residence on Emmet Street (formerly Victoria Terrace), it is marked by a weathered brass plate. 'Bourke' is just decipherable. A smaller plate advertises a medical practice. The doctor's dispensary is largely unchanged on the ground floor: shelves stacked with books and medicine bottles, weighing scales in the corner, a chart for eye tests. Two large photographs on the wall reflect family history -- one a portrait of Aubrey Bourke when he was chairman of the United Drug Company, the other a portrait of his daughter shortly after she had been elected President of Ireland.

Upstairs, where Dr Bourke still lives, is a photographic gallery spanning generations. It is his 'boasting wall', his grandchildren quip. There are sons and brothers on college rugby teams; there is his brother Paget and his wife, meeting Princess Elizabeth and the Duke of Edinburgh in Nairobi in 1952, shortly before the coronation. There is the 21-gun salute from 21 grandchildren for the doctor's 75th birthday in 1989. The 'political humour' section is upstairs – several photographs of his daughter with the then Tánaiste and leader of the Labour Party, Dick Spring, during and after her presidential election campaign.

There are also photographs of his late wife, Tessa O'Donnell from County Donegal. A daughter of Hubert and Winifred O'Donnell, Tessa was one of six children, four of whom went into medicine. She grew up on the Inishowen peninsula, a dynamic character, an extrovert and a keen hockey player at University College, Dublin, where she too studied medicine. The O'Donnell children were privileged; they did not live in student digs, but in a large house in Dublin's fashionable Merrion Square, a short walk from the old college premises. When she qualified as a general practitioner, Tessa worked for a time on Donegal's Arranmore island, but it was in Dublin that she met Aubrey Bourke.

Aubrey had worked in England after completing his medical training, but returned to Ireland when the Second World War broke out. 'The only option in England then was to go into the armed forces and, as I was thinking of getting married, I came home.' Working in maternity in Dublin's Coombe Hospital – 'great experience, with endless raw material under appalling conditions' – he met Tessa, who was working in Temple Street Children's Hospital at the time. It was natural that the couple should return to his family fiefdom of north Mayo.

Aubrey Bourke took up practice in their new home, the large Georgian house on Victoria Terrace, while Tessa reared the family. 'She loved her medicine and was very good at it, but patients would call and ask for me. Few trusted a woman,' her husband told me.[17] It was very frustrating for her, he acknowledged, because she was a 'very, very strong lady' and a forceful character, who was to have an enormous influence on her children's careers.

Tessa rapidly became part of the world of hunt balls, dances, suppers with relatives and friends, and wild, windy walks on Enniscrone beach on the Mayo-Sligo border or by Foxford in Drummond wood. But the west of Ireland to which the couple returned in 1939 was not a healthy environment. Tuberculosis was one of the biggest problems, with babies being fed on untested milk. Dr Bourke recalled: 'If you could give someone time to tell their story, you were on the way to helping them to accept their sickness, and fighting it. Essentially you removed the fear.'

'A family's not right till there's a Mary in it' was how Tessa spoke before their third child and only daughter was born.[18] The children learned how to ride, and played round the stables at Amana, which was 'always filled with the sound of rushing water from the salmon weir' below.[19] They had a nanny, Anne Coyne, from Knockmore near Ballina, and a maid. They were sent to a private preparatory school run by Miss Claire Ruddy across the Moy at Ardnaree. 'Private' was something of a misnomer, according to Dr Bourke and his son, Henry, given that most of the children of Ballina's professional classes attended at a fee of about five pounds a year. Some parents never paid, Henry recalled. There were only two teachers, with forty children to a room, and it was both co-educational and inter-denominational.

Miss Ruddy ruled with the proverbial iron fist. One of her canes had a shepherd's crook at the end, which, Henry remembers, was used 'reasonably liberally'. She insisted that her Roman Catholic pupils attend a children's Mass at eleven o'clock on Sunday mornings. When young Aubrey Bourke attended another service with his parents one Sunday, he was 'whacked' the next morning at school.

Life for the Bourkes was comfortable, in contrast to the desperate poverty experienced by small landowners, struggling to eke out a living on blanket bog, further west of Ballina. Yet they were not sheltered from reality.[20] Neighbours remember the future president as a small girl in a six-gun cowboy outfit, who was 'a tomboy and great fun', and who could acquit herself well at football with the young lads in the street.

The nearby Moy Hotel, once owned as a townhouse by the Bourke family, had hosted luminaries like Maud Gonne and the playwright George Bernard Shaw. Claire Ruddy, private tutor, was in the Maud Gonne mould, according to one of her students who recalls her as a nationalist and a woman of independent mind. Dorothy McKane, a Ballina pharmacist and one of the last to attend the school before Miss Ruddy's retirement in 1969, remembers that she was very attached to the Irish language and to the classics:

> We all had a very good grounding in Irish, and she put quite a republican bent on history, too. She had lived through the civil war period, so everything was quite black and white. She was an excellent teacher, if strict, who didn't tolerate fools gladly. But anyone who wanted to go to college went there, and we all retained a great affection for her. We would go and visit her in the nursing home in her later years. She left a mark on me. I was with her in hospital when she died.[21]

If Miss Ruddy helped to influence it, there is evidence of an emerging sense of social justice at this early stage in a little girl. Mary's brother Henry recalled how she insisted on regularly swapping roles during games of Batman and Robin. Another brother, Adrian, remembers how she was 'as wild as a March hare', very good at cricket, rounders and horse-riding, though he and Henry 'probably dismembered her dolls'.

Adrian, now a successful Mayo-based solicitor, cites two indications of a strong independent streak in his sister, and a capacity for leadership. On the first Sunday of one August, his father took the three youngest children out on a medical call to Pontoon, County Mayo. While waiting outside the house in the car, Mary had a look at a nearby hill and decided that it should be climbed. Although Adrian was only a toddler, she took both brothers up the rise, and their father emerged from the house to find them playing cowboys and Indians and leaping from rock to rock.

'The old man let out a roar,' recalled Henry. They were taken home,

Mary and Henry were 'whacked' and she was sent to bed with no lunch and 'certainly no ice-cream'. Henry did get lunch and dessert. Adrian, the baby, was saved by the intervention of his mother, but was consigned by his sister and brother to being the 'Indian' for a month in retribution.

On another occasion, there was a foray to the cinema in town. They asked their mother's permission. She was told that the film was probably a Roy Rogers western or a Laurel and Hardy comedy. In fact, it was not quite so harmless, but was a version of *Dr Jekyll and Mr Hyde*, according to Henry. Some way through it, the lights went up, the reel spun to a halt and there was an announcement. Mrs Bourke was present. Would her children go to the foyer? She had obviously looked up the cinema listings in the local weekly paper, and had not liked what she read. They were taken to a local ice-cream parlour and treated to a banana-split each. Mary was 'glowering and resentful', her younger brother recalled.[22]

There was also a pragmatic streak in Mary, which some might describe as a mite ruthless were it not for the fact that a girl among four boys must often have had to fight her corner. 'When we were children, we made our First Confessions. Like many other novice penitents, I had no idea what to confess, and my first real memory of Mary consists of explaining this to her outside the church doors,' Henry wrote in *The Sunday Tribune* in 1990.

> She saw a safety-pin on the ground and without hesitation solved my problem by telling me to pick it up and confess to the priest that I'd stolen it. My confession went down a treat, and since then I've been inclined to take her advice on all important matters. That she can be persuasive I have never doubted, since the time a few days later, after my first Holy Communion, she urged me to swap a half-crown that had been given to me by my grandfather for three old pennies on the basis that three was better than one . . .[23]

Her father and grandfather provided role models. 'From my earliest years, I could see him taking an elderly person out and talking to them in a particular way,' she would note of her father later. 'He is an old-style GP and a lot of his medicine is listening to people and having time for them and finding the words which mean more than prescribing a drug. My grandfather was a lawyer and he was very passionate about justice for the small guy, the tenant, the person who is inarticulate.'[24]

Her brother Henry has elaborated on this:

> It is not easy to describe, especially today when values seem very much more material, the atmosphere that nurtured us. The fact

that we were relatively comfortably off was relevant only in that our parents instilled in all of us at an early age that we therefore owed more to society. There was no question, for example, that we should live anywhere except above the surgery in Ballina. What if anyone should need a doctor in the middle of the night? The patient, no matter who it was, was king and I believe it was this attitude that played a major part in moulding Mary's overriding belief in the dignity of the individual.[25]

Her father's aunt, Mother Aquinas, had been provincial for the Sisters of Jesus and Mary at Gortnor Abbey on the shores of Lough Conn near Crossmolina, County Mayo.[26] Right up till her death in her nineties, Mother Aquinas was an integral part of a Bourke family Christmas which was still marked, even after Mary's own marriage, by a trip to Gortnor for midnight Mass. 'And afterwards Mother Aquinas would put on a smashing tea and we'd be there till two in the morning, eating sandwiches and cakes; it was a real beanfeast,' Dr Bourke remembered. 'The children would be sent home with something in their pockets, and we'd be begging her, as provincial, to let the nuns have a late sleep in the morning . . .'[27]

CHAPTER 3

We Expected Anything of Her

A middle-aged nun stands at the foot of a stairwell, talking to two little boys. Fresh-faced, in grey socks and sandals, the boys are perhaps nine and seven. Not from the city. 'We're Adrian and Henry Bourke.' Their sister, Mary, is about to enroll as a new pupil in the nun's school.

The young girl has already gone ahead with her parents to visit the dormitories. Tall and thin, she has freckles and black hair cut short. By the way Mary moves, the nun knows that this is a girl who 'lives with boys'. She had greeted this new pupil with some interest. The girl's aunt had entered the Religious of the Sacred Heart in England, and was working with the missions in India.

One of the small boys turns to the nun, hesitantly, a question on his lips. He gestures to his sister. 'Mary's a girl now, isn't she?'

It is an innocent memory, and one which is as vivid for Sister Joan Stephenson, former mistress of studies at Mount Anville girls' secondary school in Dublin, as if it happened yesterday. The small boys were genuinely concerned that the 'family rugby', as the nun called it, was going to suffer. Two older brothers had already been 'lost' to school teams at Clongowes Wood College, County Kildare. Having had more than a passing interest in the game herself, the nun tried to offer some consolation.

Now in her eighties, Sister Joan Stephenson played more than a passing part in Mary Bourke's life as a boarding-school pupil at Mount Anville. Run by a French order founded by Madeleine Sophie Barat, it was, and still is, a successful girls' second-level school, regarded as the finest for young Catholic women in the Republic and equivalent to the Holy Child in Killiney, Dublin, or Jesuit-run schools for boys such as Clongowes and Belvedere. Situated in one of the capital's middle-class southside suburbs, it commands a fine view across Dublin Bay.

Mary Bourke was only ten years old when she left the shelter of Ms Ruddy's private school in Ballina to board over 150 miles away from home on the outskirts of an unfamiliar city. Most girls from the Ballina area who were bound for post-primary education were sent to the local school run by the Sisters of Mercy. The order had been active in the area since 1851 – when, coincidentally, their first house was that once owned by the unfortunate doctor, hanged at Ardnaree. The Mercy sisters were to play an integral part in Ballina life from the late nineteenth century. They ran an orphanage, where boys were taught net-making and other skills, and took over the workhouse and district hospital. Their girls' secondary school, St Mary's, opened in the late 1880s.

But, in keeping with her background, Mary Bourke was to be sent instead to an establishment which would prepare young women for third-level education – if they had the ability. Her grandfather had decided that she should be sent away. He had found her up a tree one day, and decreed that she must go to boarding-school to tame her spirit. When her father told her that she had a place in Mount Anville, she 'jumped down a whole flight of stairs' in the house in Victoria Terrace. 'She was so delighted! And she loved it when she went.'

Sacred Heart rules were strict, and the teaching was unorthodox. Young women were to be seen and not heard, of course. Bells sounded for prayers, breakfast, for a conversation period, for silence, and for class. One former pupil recalls that if the regulations were strictly adhered to, there was only time for three chats of twenty minutes a day. Visitors could talk to the girls but only in the parlour.[1]

There were separate uniforms for winter and summer, and a white dress and white gloves were worn on special occasions. Writer Mary Rose Callaghan, who shared a room with Mary, remembers the obsession with ceremony and formality which ensured that the young charges lived in something of a cocoon. She recalls asking if she could do embroidery on a Sunday, and 'the wrath that that brought down on my head'.[2]

The demands of the state curriculum were met, but the school was determined to ensure that its young women were given a wider appreciation of the arts and humanities. Sister Stephenson, who was born a daughter of a lawyer in Carrick-on-Suir, County Tipperary, and brought up in Wimbledon when her father died, had been educated at Mount Anville herself and entered there as a nun. She held a good degree in English and French, but also taught religious education, philosophy, psychology, ethics, logic, English literature, Latin and history. When she became mistress of studies, she dropped some of her subjects to spend more time on administration and attending to the welfare of the pupils.

The Mayo girl was a good 'all-rounder' with a fine intellect, but a little too young to be top of the class. 'She would have been in the top ten, rather than the top three as is widely quoted,' Sister Stephenson recalls.

Mary was ambitious, but to a point. 'In so far as she was competitive, she was probably more worried about how she compared to her brothers at Clongowes.'

Mary Rose Callaghan says she was influenced by night-time stories read by a teacher, Mother Alexander, who was charged with showing the new girl the ropes. Mary Bourke 'didn't like being told what to do!' She also recalls 'how bright she was': clever enough to move up a class.[3]

Active and good at games, particularly hockey and baseball, Mary also received private coaching lessons in tennis. 'As she was approaching 12 to 14, I suppose I saw a more reflective person emerging,' Sister Stephenson observes. 'She was genuinely thoughtful, didn't have many close friends. Yet she had a compassion that was unexpected. I remember one day witnessing her comforting a little boy in the Montessori school who had hurt his knee.'

Arts were her forte – French, which she was keen on, and literature. She also showed good historical judgment. She was not a head girl, but nor was she a rebel. She was a 'blue ribbon' or prefect and was also a Child of Mary with the school's sodality. This spiritual 'honorarium' was much sought after, as were the school prizes which Mary Bourke picked up each year. Her teacher was struck by her anxiety to please her parents at all times.

The nun does not recall young Ms Bourke's prominent involvement – recounted frequently in newspaper profiles – in a campaign to restore the school's subscription for the liberal daily newspaper *The Irish Times*. The publication was still considered to be an organ of the Protestant ascendancy, and was reputedly 'banned' for a time at Mount Anville. Sister Stephenson says the subscription, for sixth-year pupils, was only cancelled after a series of 'attacks' on the Archbishop of Dublin, John Charles McQuaid. Pamela Kerins, Mary's future sister-in-law who was three years below her in Mount Anville, does remember that there was a protest, and that the daily delivery was resumed.

Morning Mass was at 7.30, after the first bell at 6.50 a.m. A 'lie-in' on Sundays meant 8.30 a.m. Mass. Every weekend, a conduct record was read out to the whole school. 'Notes', as it was known, could be a nerve-wracking experience, as each girl was expected to walk across the polished hall floor to collect a card which classified the week's behaviour and academic achievement as 'very good', 'good', 'fair' or 'indifferent'. There was no 'excellent', Pamela Kerins remembers. Each name and result was read out loud; the five nuns present for the ceremony included the Mother Superior. Pupils knew what to anticipate by the card's colour – pale blue for 'very good'; yellow for 'indifferent'.

There was a hidden objective to all this, claims Sister Stephenson. 'It taught the pupils proper deportment, and how to appear at ease in public.'

Mary Bourke might have scored 'indifferent' once a year, if that. The former mistress of studies only remembers one 'row', when a group of pupils went missing from their dormitory after midnight one summer. They were found in their pyjamas in a separate day-school building, having climbed in by a window which was out of view. They were not eating cream buns, cooking sausages or talking about boys; they were reading Shakespeare's *As You Like It*. There was method in their madness. 'They didn't want to take up games time with study, and thought they would get a bit of extra work in at night.'

Prune-eating competitions and such like were far more Mary Bourke's style than any show of outright disobedience. Boyfriends were for the older girls: *she* had too much to do. She had an 'ordinary tomboyish dislike' of being tidied up. The blazer was lived in, often covered in dog hairs, according to the nun, and her appearance could be a mite unkempt. Yet Sister Stephenson remembers doing a double-take one evening, when 'unexpected style' greeted her in the corridor. It was Mary. The make-up was a little slapdash, but 'at least she had discovered it existed!'

Though the child was not religious, she was, in the nun's view, deeply attached to the essentials of the faith. Her grandparents and parents were daily Mass-goers in Mayo. 'She had a very keen interest, expressed in religious education class. There was a spiritual giftedness in her. And she had a great desire to learn about the mysteries.'

She recalls another occasion when pupils were washing their hair during a free weekend afternoon. Mary Bourke wanted to play tennis. She was only about eleven at the time. 'She shot out, rubbing her short hair.' The nun knew she hadn't washed it but let her go. Mary came to her later and asked her if it was possible to 'act a lie'. She could not live with 'the thought that she had deceived someone', Sister Stephenson believes.

For all its merits, the education was 'terribly enclosed', according to another past pupil and former minister in government, Gemma Hussey.[4] She was a few years above Mary Bourke, but recalls a 'tall, freckle-faced girl with a cherubic face and long legs' and a 'lovely, puckish grin', who was 'full of brains and sporting prowess, almost irritating in her excellence'.[5] Gemma was not made a prefect, because she was told that she didn't 'subscribe 100 per cent to the school's ethos'. Similarly, Gemma did not become a Child of Mary because, as the Reverend Mother told her, 'it is the opinion of the nuns that you are a flirt'. This was a mystery. She was to discover, after she left, that some boys whom she had met at parties during the school holidays had been sending her letters which she had never received.

Pamela Kerins also confirms that school life was very sheltered. The girls never got out, beyond trips home at Hallowe'en, Christmas and

Easter, or day-trips to the homes of fellow pupils living close by. 'Away' matches in hockey or netball and occasional visits to the theatre represented the only 'release'. The 'big adventure' was to buy chips on the way back in the taxi, Pamela Kerins says. In baseball, 'we used to hit the ball as far as possible so it would take a long time to fetch'. Drama did not take great priority, compared to sport, but there were 'wishings' where a select group had to perform a set piece. Mary Bourke was always winning prizes, her fellow pupils recall. 'We knew she'd do well. We expected anything of her.'

Gemma Hussey believes that some pupils reacted to what was regarded as a very authoritarian church, and this contributed to the 'revolution' of the 1970s and 1980s among her generation. When she met Mary Bourke again many years later, she was seeking her advice, as a 'new girl' in the Seanad. 'Mary said that it would be best if I didn't know the rules, because that way "if you break them, you can plead ignorance".'[5]

As far as her brothers were concerned, Mary Bourke had broken the rules herself. She had done the unthinkable – produced first-class school reports. Oliver and Aubrey, the two older brothers, were tearing up theirs if they could get away with it; Henry and Adrian, the two youngest, weren't performing much better. Yet their sister was actually working! And, as Adrian remembers, this 'new polished product' was returning home during school holidays, wearing skirts instead of jeans, with 'Henry and I looking askance at her'. Mount Anville, he says, 'was the making of her and she was the making of it'.

John Paget Bourke, her cousin, also noticed the change. The tomboy he knew, who was 'not intellectual' but was well able to hold her own on any front, and with whom he had spent summers on Enniscrone beach, had become polished. 'Not that she was ever one for sitting on the lawn with her head stuck in Dickens or Dante,' he says. 'If Cowboys and Indians was going on, she wanted to be one or the other. She was always full of bounce.'

Now, however, she was also winning scholarships to the Yeats Summer School in Sligo. She was probably one of the youngest students to attend the lectures on the poet, and did so for three successive summers, sleeping on horsehair mattresses in Sligo Grammar School. She was enthralled by writers and poets like Denis Donoghue and Brendan Kennelly, and wrote some poetry herself.

Mary Bourke was to maintain her association with Mount Anville after she had left for a Paris finishing-school. When she became engaged, her future husband, Nicholas Robinson, met her teachers in Dublin. That he was a Protestant would not have been an issue with the liberal Mount Anville nuns. They were well used to mixed marriages. Many of their pupils had received a dispensation from the Archbishop to study at Trinity College, Dublin (TCD) – up until then a Protestant university and subject to a Catholic Church 'ban'.

Founded by Elizabeth I in 1592, TCD was modelled on the residential colleges of Oxford and Cambridge. Its graduates were obliged to subscribe to the Oath of Supremacy as an act of loyalty to the British Crown. Catholics were unable to take degrees before 1793, while fellowships and scholarships were reserved for members of the 'Established' – Protestant – Church of Ireland until 1873.

After Catholic emancipation in the late nineteenth century, many eminent Catholics were sent there to study, but it was clear that the Irish university system needed to be expanded. During the ensuing debate on how this was to be done, the attitude of the Catholic Church towards Trinity began to harden. Three secular colleges at Belfast, Cork and Galway had been proposed: such was the alarmed response that the first Catholic national synod in Thurles, County Tipperary, in 1850, decided to found a Catholic university.

The rift widened in the post-Famine period, from 1850 to 1875, when the Church became most closely associated with the nationalist movement. Antipathy was to translate into an edict from many bishops to the effect that it was a mortal sin for Catholics to attend Trinity, even though the Taoiseach, Eamon de Valera, had been registered as a student for a time. The 'ban' earned some form of legitimacy in 1928 when the Chief Justice asked the Archbishop of Dublin, Dr Byrne, for guidance on whether Catholic minors who were wards of court might study at the university. His lordship felt that they should not.

Just when enlightened parents were starting to ignore it again, the ban was renewed. In 1956, a synodal statute passed at the Catholic training college, St Patrick's, in Maynooth, County Kildare, forbade 'under pain of mortal sin' Catholic youths to frequent Trinity, and conferred on the Archbishop of Dublin the power to decide 'in what circumstances and with what guarantees against perversion' attendance might be tolerated.

The statute came into force in 1960, and resulted in a fall in Catholic admissions to Trinity from 25 to 17 per cent, though it picked up again later that decade. However, in what one historian describes as a 'chillingly vigorous defence' of the ban, the Archbishop of Dublin, Dr John Charles McQuaid, reminded his flock in February 1967 that, contrary to popular belief, there had been no relaxation of the laws.[6]

The Paris finishing-school was carefully chosen by an ambitious mother. It would give her only daughter time and space to develop the sort of intellectual freedom that she might not enjoy in a convent. (In some social circles, it was also a selling point for a good marriage.) The four boys would be well groomed at Clongowes Wood College, alma mater of the captains of Irish industry. Mary would have her corners rubbed off at Mlle Anita Pojninska's on Rue de l'Amiral d'Estaing in the 16th arrondissement.

She would have met compatriots: this and similar establishments were frequented by the young upper-middle-class Irish Catholic girls of the 1940s and 1950s, at a time when the so-called Protestant ascendancy was trying to gather two pennies together for its young women at home. On her first night, when she was feeling somewhat homesick, she also felt a little gauche; staying in the Sacred Heart convent in rue St Dominique, near by, she was confronted with a half-carafe of wine which had been brought to her by a nun at dinner. Soon, though, she was enjoying Parisian life, including arthouse cinema – sometimes at ten o'clock in the morning; it felt 'quite scandalous', but stimulating, she was to remark later.

Patience Ryan, a contemporary who is now living in Dublin and the United States, has described Mary as a detached, clever pupil, who engaged in intellectual argument and was 'quite brilliant'.

> The nuns were in awe of her, I remember. There were about twenty of us, some French and others who had been to Sacred Heart schools elsewhere. We each had our own room. I was just 16 and had been to school in Rathnew, County Wicklow, so I was a bit younger than Mary – and in awe of her too. I went to the Sorbonne and Mlle Anita's. Others went to one or the other or both.
>
> We came back to the convent for lunch and dinner, and had wine at both, but you took water with your lunchtime wine. There was an antiquated system of coded bells, which meant that you knew if a phone call was for you just by the number of rings. Once a week the nuns would convene a discussion group, which Mary tended to lead. I didn't understand some of her concepts, which seemed way ahead of most of us.
>
> She was quite religious, not in terms of saying the rosary, but in a quiet, spiritual sort of a way. She wore these white gloves, and flowery dresses, and was very serious – and very attached to her grandfather. He died that summer that she was there and she was quite devastated.[7]

The feminist movement had not hit Ireland at the time, but some of the students were making the most of a new wave of liberation. Mary Bourke was uncomfortable with what she may have regarded as promiscuous behaviour but she was what some might have described as prim. She studied a lot.

She returned to Ireland with a love of French language and literature.

'A year in France completed the metamorphosis from tomboy to young woman,' her brother Henry has observed, 'and I still have this crystal-clear memory of the moment when it occurred to me that this distinctly feminine creature, who spoke fluent French along with some Italian and Spanish, who could intelligently discuss art and literature and current affairs, was lost forever as Batman – or Robin!'[8]

Sister Joan Stephenson, who was never so convinced of the benefits of such finishing-schools for pupils still in their early and mid-teens, was sure that the girl from Ballina was going to pursue a literary career after Paris. Her ability to write English was matched by her grasp of history. Her interest in literature had been very apparent in her last two years at school, and she had begun to write poetry in France, some of which she showed to the nun back in Dublin.

But Mary Bourke was destined for a profession. Over an apocryphal 'glass of sherry', her parents received a dispensation from the Archbishop of Dublin, Dr McQuaid, to allow their daughter to sit an entrance exam to TCD. Like her grandfather, Mary was to study law.

'His love of law in the real sense . . . she got that from him,' Dr Bourke says. 'They were always such good friends. He used to talk to her as if she was an adult, from the time that she was very young, and she has never forgotten that.'

In fact, there was no sherry at the Archbishop's palace, the doctor says. He had received permission from the local bishop to allow his two older boys to study medicine at TCD.

'But when Mary was going, Archbishop McQuaid was at his worst with these Lenten pastorals blasting the university. TCD needed a recommendation from the head of whatever school she was at. Mary went to her principal in Mount Anville and she wouldn't give it. It was vital at the time. She was told that the nuns had been forbidden by the Archbishop to do anything that would encourage any Catholic to go to Trinity.

'This had to be in in a couple of days, and I was a busy doctor and hadn't time to move. I went to the local bishop, Dr O'Boyle, and he laughed and said I was in trouble. He told me I must go to Dr McQuaid myself, but that I must not say, under any circumstances, what my business was when I got there. Otherwise, the Archbishop wouldn't see me.

'So we drove to Dublin. Tessa sat in the car with the rosary beads, and I was greeted by a chaplain who said the Archbishop had to go out somewhere in an hour. I said that I *had* to see him. He vanished, I sweated, and he came back. He asked me again about my business and I said it was very private, and I had left patients in Mayo. He went off again. Eventually, I was taken to a lovely study to see his lordship. He couldn't have been more courteous.'

Explaining his dilemma, Dr Bourke told the Archbishop that his father and brothers had studied at TCD, he had two sons there, and that he wished his daughter to take the course in legal science there if she passed the entrance exam. 'I said that my sister Ivy went to Trinity and that she was now a Sacred Heart nun in India. He asked me if I had considered breaking that tradition, but I said no. He then asked who the principal of Mount Anville was and produced this letter. I took it out to the wife in the car, drove out to Mount Anville, and showed it to the principal. I tried to smuggle the letter then into my newspaper, but she wanted it. It was an absolutely nerve-wracking experience, and I literally had to say that people were dying back at home, just so I could get an audience in the palace. It made me grow up a little bit,' the doctor told me.

When his two youngest sons, Henry and Adrian, applied to study law, Dr Bourke 'didn't go near anybody'.

Religion apart, there was also discrimination against women in the TCD of the 1960s, even as the sexual revolution, rock'n'roll and the so-called 'permissive society' gathered pace across the Irish Sea. The university had begun accepting women students in 1904, and initially facilitated the conferring of female graduates from Oxford and Cambridge who were not eligible to collect parchments from their own universities, until 1920 in the case of Oxford, and 1947 in Cambridge.[9]

Yet women staff were not admitted to the Trinity Common Room until 1958, and to what is known as the 'High Table', where academics dined, until 1965. Initially, they were associate members and paid a half subscription, which permitted them to use the premises until 5.30 p.m. There was only one woman on the college board, Frances Moran, when Mary Bourke registered in 1963.

Although there was accommodation on campus, women were not allowed to apply for rooms on the same terms as men until 1972–73. In fact, until the mid-1960s, when it was extended progressively towards midnight, there was a curfew after 6 p.m. – though this 'six o'clock rule' became 7 p.m. in the mid-1950s. Many who required lodgings lived in Trinity Hall, a residence three miles out in the southside suburb of Dartry which had been built originally as a hostelry for the many women travelling over from Oxford and Cambridge to receive their degrees.

Mary Bourke did not have to walk out south to Dartry; she could even nip home at lunchtime. In a pragmatic move, her parents had acquired a Regency house at the back of the college: 21 Westland Row was where one Oscar Fingal O'Flahertie Wills, son of Sir William and Lady Speranza Wilde, had been born on 16 October 1854. A year later, Sir William, an aural surgeon, had moved with his family to a more imposing mansion on Merrion Square. During her own college days, Tessa O'Donnell had shared a house bought by her parents in Merrion Square and knew it was an arrangement that could work very well.

Nanny Anne Coyne, known as 'Nan', was sent east to Dublin from Mayo, along with Victorian furniture, ensuring that the house, with its heavy velvet curtains and grand piano in the sitting-room, would not be the typical TCD undergraduate's chilly room or dingy flat. The college authorities were initially unhappy with this independent arrangement, Dr Bourke recalls. The door was always open, though the doctor believes that he may have fed half of TCD and UCD. It was 'Wilde house' in more senses than one, he says.

Sweeney's grocery shop and newsagent, which still stands across the street in Westland Row, kept a tab which was settled up every so often on Tessa Bourke's visits to Dublin. Every morning, Nan Coyne would set out five glasses of milk at the top of the stairs; all five Bourke students would dash down, glass to mouth, leaving each at the door at they vanished. Tessa's children were regulars in the local hostelries, the Lincoln Inn and Kennedy's or Kenny's — at least the male family members were, for 'the sister' had other things on her mind, according to one brother who remembers how four young men 'tramping out of the house' one night for a pint felt the lash of her tongue as she returned from the library. 'We scarpered out into the street like four small boys.'

Independent senator and former TCD lecturer in English literature, Dr David Norris, puts it most succinctly. He had entered college as an English student, and was also elected scholar, on the same day as Mary Bourke. Of the five Bourkes who came to Trinity, two came to play rugby, two came to party and one came to study, in his view; they did 'just that'.

'They were all successful at it,' the senator says. 'They were all talented people, both socially and intellectually, although Mary was the one who was academic. Aubrey and Oliver, the two older boys, were soft, amiable, decent, sporty, rugby types. Henry and Adrian were the party-goers, the rakes, who had a good time, were good fun and quite sharp-tongued.' One night, the lads filled the bath with every available type of alcohol; a visiting US academic passed out in it, fully clothed.

In the early 1960s, the college was to a large extent cocooned from the radicalism beginning to infect third-level institutions in Europe and America. Indeed, with a high percentage of British and Northern Irish students, many regarded it as being cocooned from reality: University College, Dublin (UCD), founded by the Catholic bishops at the end of the previous century, appeared to be making a much more significant contribution to national life, though UCD students tended to think that their TCD counterparts were getting 'sex on demand'. Until the mathematician Albert Joseph McConnell became provost in 1952, with the support of

Taoiseach Eamon de Valera, Trinity reflected what historian J.V. Luce observes as the ghetto mentality enveloping the Protestant community in the Republic. The college in the centre of Dublin had, Luce says, taken on 'a striking resemblance in social terms to the Big Houses of the countryside – each symbolising a ruling caste in the aftermath of its power'.[10]

'Direct action' in the 1960s had been inspired by the response in the United States to the Vietnam War, and resulted in violent protests on many university campuses. The restlessness spread to Europe, and in the mid-1960s the London School of Economics found itself at the centre of controversy over its appointment of a president with South African links. Trinity's turn came in 1968 – ironically, as Luce notes, at a time when the board was moving to meet student demands for a greater say in the college's administration.[11] A small group of students belonging to the Action Group on Southern Africa, a subsidiary of a Maoist organisation known as the Internationalists, picketed a visit to the college by the King and Queen of Belgium. This provoked a hostile reaction among other students. In the mêlée, the Garda Siochána (police) were called, scuffles ensued, and there were allegations of garda brutality.

But by that time, Mary Bourke had graduated. During her years there, TCD student politics was essentially concerned with greater participation in college affairs, through the Student Representative Council (SRC) which preceded the more radical students' union. Both Adrian and Henry Bourke served as president and chairman respectively of the SRC, while their sister was secretary from 1965 to '66. Indeed, as SRC president in February 1969, Adrian Bourke proposed that the two senior student representatives should be granted sabbatical leave from their studies, and be given a modest salary with expenses to cover their term of office.

The majority of TCD undergraduates were conservative, interested in having a good time, making useful contacts, and obtaining some sort of a degree. The college had about three thousand students then – a quarter of the number on the roll now. Student societies received modest subsidies from the college, in the knowledge that their role transcended mere recreation. Aspiring lawyers and politicians in cavalry twills, tweed jackets, cravats, hand-made shirts and shoes could make their mark in the college's rival debating societies, the 'Hist' (historical) and the 'Phil' (philosophical); language students and bored medics tended to join Players, the amateur dramatic group with its own theatre; and distinction in field sports, or rowing on the Liffey, helped to fill out curricula vitae for those young men with an ambitious eye on the professions. The annual end-of-term Trinity Ball was a very elegant affair, which carried its own eight-page programme and a hired seamstress, who was available for repairs to gowns in the Elizabethan rooms.

Senator David Norris, who socialised with the boat club, remembers that the Bourkes had a certain social standing and would never have regarded themselves as inferior to the 'English immigrants' with their sports cars and 'Gatsbyesque' parties in Connemara angling lodges. He attended some of the family's parties at Westland Row, which were semi-formal affairs with uniformed porters on the door to guard against gate-crashers, and Nanny Coyne acting as the chatelaine.

Mary was, he remembers, 'distinguished from very early on' because of her broad range of very human interests which extended beyond an 'arid, legal' landscape. She was stimulating and interesting company, but also reserved. She didn't act in college, but was to join a small theatre group called the Focus in Dublin where she took Stanislavsky Method classes. She was asked to 'think of becoming something very familiar', she recounted later. As she was studying law, her most familiar object – and the one she tried hard to become by closing her eyes – was her briefcase.[12]

Norris remembers that there was quite a lot of prejudice from fellow students against her then, which was to continue in the Law Library after graduation. Here was this 'intelligent, attractive woman from a secure social background, who was extremely clever and ambitious,' he says. 'This was legitimate for men, but not for women, who would have been regarded as intellectually aggressive if they had behaved in this way. Mary wouldn't defer to men simply because they were men but would pursue an argument right to its conclusion.'

Having won a scholarship in her second (or senior freshman) year, her next challenge was to become auditor of the Law Society. The election was her 'first great coup', according to Henry. She took part in debates, dis-tinguishing herself by winning the coveted Benchers' Trophy. She also served as editor of the student law review, *Justice*, from 1965 to '67.

On one of her rare nights out – given that the Sacred Heart order was cloistered – Sister Joan Stephenson was invited by her former pupil to attend the auditor's inaugural address on 3 February 1967. The keynote speakers, as the nun recalls, were the British judge Lord Devlin and Professor H.L.A. Harte of Oxford, both of whom were published authors on the concept of law and morality. Sister Stephenson judged Professor Harte to be 'totally pagan in outlook' while the judge, a Catholic, seemed to be 'more Christian'. The latter's thesis was that 'if society was constructed of bricks made of individuals, it was no service to this society to have a man drunk in his study every night'.

The inaugural address was provocative – in fact, not just a keynote speech on the night but a hallmark in Mary T.W. Bourke's career. Her father, who had read it before she delivered it, 'nearly', in his own words, 'had a canary'. 'It was all about how contraception, homosexuality and law must be kept apart. Mary was advocating contraception or divorce, but the law was the law and must be kept separate, she maintained. I nearly had a fit. I got in touch with a man I knew very well, Canon McDonald in Easky, County Sligo, who later became our bishop. I told him I wanted to see him badly; he told me to come over.'

The canon gave him a whisky while he read the text. 'He said there was nothing wrong with it and explained that she was giving this as a student . . . I was never so relieved in all my life. I remember that the boys, Henry and Aubrey, said that they didn't think Mary knew what the pill was. Perhaps she didn't – she was *that* innocent! And yet she could deliver this lecture in a legal sense.'

'Remarkable' is how the Revd Enda McDonagh, professor of moral theology at St Patrick's College, Maynooth, has described the text. He was invited by the new auditor to speak at her Law Society inaugural, but was unable to attend. He read the speech, however, and kept it. 'It was very brave, very courageous, very different, and a student speech as well,' he says. 'Other voices were articulating similar ideas – Labour Party members like David Thornley. But this struck at the heart of the matter in a very clear way, and set a pattern for what was to happen in the next twenty-five to thirty years.'[13]

Addressing the effects of non-criminal law in enforcing morality in Ireland, Mary Bourke questioned the special position afforded in de Valera's Constitution to the Roman Catholic Church. Whereas Irish law did not attempt to enforce Catholic morality in relation to adultery, prostitution and drunkenness, it did place an embargo on divorce, homosexuality and birth control. She submitted that the prohibition on granting a divorce should be deleted from the Constitution, and the law relating to it should reflect 'the public opinion of the times'.

She criticised the designation of suicide as a crime, referring to recent prosecutions for attempted suicide. Homosexuality should be legalised, if public opinion so desired, she said. As for the restrictions on contraceptives, these represented a 'legal infringement on the freedom of non-Catholics in this country'. However, in relation to abortion, she doubted if legislation such as the Medical Termination of Pregnancy Bill, then under consideration in Britain, would ever reach the Irish statute books.

Referring to the effect on law of a country with strong Christian principles, she noted that the Republic's 'healthy Christian climate' had not caused any notable change in attitude towards imprisonment. Was locking people up morally justified? Ireland, she submitted, should take a lead in reformulating its policy of imprisonment for non-violent crimes.

'If a man's watch is stolen, and the thief apprehended by the police, under due process of law the thief may well end up in prison,' she said. 'However, if the victim were asked his opinion, he would demand the return of his watch, but hardly that the culprit be locked away and segregated from society for a definite period. Rather, the average man would prefer to see [the thief] fined as a deterrent for this crime against property, thus letting "the punishment fit the crime".'

At least the extensive use of the suspended sentence in Ireland was an encouraging factor, she went on. Quoting George Bernard Shaw, she said that the time had come when morality was something which could be discussed freely in Ireland without – even unconsciously – giving offence. She concluded by talking about Dora Russell, author of *The Right To Be Happy*, who was 'not impressed by external devices for the preservation of virtue in men or women'. Marriage laws, the police, the army and the navy were 'the mark of human incompetence', Russell wrote.[14]

Dr Bourke, who was present, recalls how 'stunned' the retired Supreme Court judge and former TCD senator, Kingsmill Moore, was. 'He said that he would like to live long enough to see what she would do.' From that time on, her parents felt that 'nothing was impossible' for their only daughter.

In Sister Stephenson's view, her former pupil had backed the 'pagan' Professor Harte. 'I was dying to get a hold of her afterwards to tell her that she was wrong. But I didn't. It was the only time that I saw her perhaps a little dazzled by the world about her. Yet she looked absolutely beautiful in a smart dress, black hair shining, in the midst of all those wizened old men.'

He sat at the back of the lecture room, doodling and drawing cartoons. She sat near the front; she was a year older than him. Nicholas Robinson was third in a family of four boys from a middle-class Dublin Protestant home, descended from coopers attached to the Guinness brewery. His grandfather had run a coal business. His father, Howard, was an accountant with the City of Dublin Bank and a prominent member of the Masonic Order. His mother, Lucy, had studied art and was related through her mother to a well-known Dublin sculptor. She died when Nicholas was only ten, and he was sent to board at Mountjoy School in Dublin city centre.

In college, he began to date his classmate, Mary Bourke, the girl who sometimes wore silk gloves to evening debates. When she took her finals, she secured first-class honours. He scraped through with a third-class placing. She won a scholarship to Harvard Law School in Boston. Through his family connections, he had been offered an apprenticeship with the prominent Protestant legal firm, Matheson Ormsby Prentice, in Dublin but thought he might go to London to try his hand at cartoons.

He was known to be clever, but 'didn't kill himself', David Norris remembers. Urbane and as distinguished as Mary Bourke in her own way, Nicholas Robinson took an 'Olympian view of life'. But if he enjoyed himself, he was also regarded as very reliable and stable.

After the finals, there was little time for idleness. Within a day of the last exam, Mary Bourke was on the plane to Boston, over a week late for the start of term. Nicholas Robinson was late arriving at the house at Westland Row to bid her farewell with a single red rose. Nanny Coyne accepted it instead.

CHAPTER 4

Direct Action

The year: 1967. American troops launch Operation Junction City, the biggest assault of the Vietnam conflict. The Rolling Stones are in court in Britain on drugs charges. The French president, Charles de Gaulle, rebuffs Britain's latest efforts to join the European Community. Israel triumphs in a six-day war against the Arabs. The Beatles release *Sergeant Pepper's Lonely Hearts Club Band*. Race riots sweep through American cities. 'My boys' is how US President Lyndon Johnson – 'LBJ' – refers to his troops in Vietnam, amid growing opposition to the war at home. A peaceful rally at the Lincoln Memorial and Pentagon turns violent, and the novelist Norman Mailer is among 250 people reported to have been arrested.

Race was *the* issue across the Atlantic as a young Mary Bourke left a snug – some would say smug – Dublin university behind to take up a Harvard fellowship. Twelve months later, Trinity College would discover the meaning of 'direct action'. In the meantime, foreign news reports carried accounts of US paratroopers being despatched to restore order in the streets of Detroit, after some of the worst scenes of turmoil since sporadic rioting began over the race issue. Ironically, the July 1967 Detroit violence broke out when police were called to a rowdy party at an illegal drinking shop, known as a 'blind pig'. The party had been held to welcome back a black soldier from Vietnam.

This was just three years after LBJ had signed the Civil Rights Act of 1964. It was regarded as the most sweeping civil rights legislation in US history. Determined to complete the work undertaken by his predecessor, John F. Kennedy, LBJ made a television appeal in which he called on all US citizens to help 'eliminate the last vestiges of injustice in America'. The new law prohibited racial discrimination in employment, places of public accommodation, publicly owned facilities, union membership and federally funded programmes. 'Let us close the springs of racial poison,' the President, himself a Texan, had said.

Cambridge, Boston, 23 April 1967: here a campaign for peace, initiated by civil rights leader Martin Luther King, would eventually prompt Senator Eugene McCarthy to make a bid for the American presidency and result in President Johnson's decision not to stand again.

Harvard would ravish the heart. It was founded in 1636 to educate the religious and secular leaders of the new Massachusetts Bay Colony, and had become a university, the oldest in the United States, by 1780. Over more than three centuries, the campus running down to the banks of the Charles River has produced six US presidents, 33 Nobel laureates and 31 Pulitzer Prize winners. It still likes to think of itself as handpicking world leaders, who will go out and 'sell America'.

Many of the young movers and shakers would have sat chewing pencils, gazing out onto Harvard Yard below, listening to the droning of a noisy fan in the oak-lined Widener Library. Three centuries before, the college's open common was where the university president was permitted to 'graze one cow'. Now the fiefdom extends over more than 360 acres, with about 460 buildings in the Cambridge-Boston district, among them, Radcliffe College, dedicated since 1879 to the advancement of women; Massachusetts Hall, built in 1720 and the oldest Harvard building still standing; Memorial Church and Memorial Hall, the latter being one of the country's finest examples of Ruskin Gothic architecture and built to commemorate the Harvard men who fought for the Union in the American Civil War.

Grey squirrels still chase acorns among the high oaks in the yard, but much has changed at what one trendy Boston guidebook terms the 'WGU' – world's great university. The chapel, founded by intolerant Puritans, is now used in ecumenical harmony by rabbis and pastors, and the university itself is much more accessible to the average US citizen through a number of fellowships. Fees, however, are still regarded as horribly high.

Just north of the Yard stands Langdell Law School, which has been described as the 'gatekeeper of American legal education'.[1] Established in 1817, it adopted the Socratic method of teaching by open dialogue, now widely applied, and its thousands of alumni can be found in the US Supreme Court, the White House and the corporate boardrooms of US cities. During its early years, it was a 'clubby, chummy and decidedly male place', according to lawyer and Harvard graduate Eleanor Kerlow.[2] It had student societies such as the Pow Wow Club, Lincoln's Inn, and its first dean, Christopher Columbus Langdell, christened his group of loyal students 'Kit's freshmen'. During the industrial revolution, it was a 'beacon of reason', Kerlow writes, 'instilling in its students a sense of endless promise, fair play and public service'.

The Langdell Law School had its controversies: the Pound-Frankfurter row in the 1920s between its professor, Felix Frankfurter, and the law school dean, Roscoe Pound, over Hitler and over Roosevelt's progressive New Deal; a clash in the appointment of three Jewish candidates; and the Joseph McCarthy years of the 1950s, when the school's very values were called into question.

One of those lecturers touched by the activities of the US Senate Subcommittee on Internal Security during the McCarthy era was Dean Erwin Griswold, who was still a major influence when Mary Bourke registered in 1967. Griswold advised two brothers not to take the Fifth Amendment when they were called to the subcommittee to testify, since to do so would imply guilt – in this case, that they had both been involved as undergraduates in a radical organisation.

Griswold was to oppose McCarthy publicly later on, championing the right not to incriminate oneself. His views laid the foundation for defining the rights of criminal defendants. His sense of justice reflected the ideals of a school he would shape as dean for 21 years, until he was appointed US solicitor-general; and this school shaped a 'moral force' – Watergate special prosecutors, labour law experts, graduates who served in Washington at the time of Roosevelt's New Deal. Many of the students who would become, as Eleanor Kerlow puts it, 'lieutenants' in the post-Second World War government of Dwight Eisenhower, JFK's New Frontier and LBJ's Great Society, were 'steeped in the tradition of Harvard law'.

Archibald Cox, best known as the Watergate special prosecutor and one of the law school's finest professors, preceded Griswold as solicitor-general in the early 1960s. He has described Griswold as one of his mentors, part of a group which 'taught, instilled, exemplified a love of the law and the role of the law'. Writing in the *Harvard Law Bulletin* in 1992, Cox expanded the point: such mentors 'taught that there is for each time and place (but also therefore, by implication, at all times and all places but always different) an ideal fitness of things that correspond to those beliefs, and that we ought to do what we can to make that fitness prevail.' Such mentors, he said, believed that 'judges and academic scholars had an obligation to pursue that goal, putting aside all private predilections, commitments, self-interest, and using only the most disinterested and detached reason they could bring to bear'.[3]

Not everyone would share Cox's view. In April 1968 the college newspaper, the *Harvard Crimson*, reported that a secret club within the law school, known as the Choate club, had refused to invite Griswold to become a member. Griswold, by then solicitor-general, refused to comment beyond saying that the club had been widely known about for many years. It was said to be the only club on campus in which a single student could block a faculty member's admission.

Langdell Law School is perceived in recent decades to have lost its way. The atmosphere changed in the late 1970s and early 1980s, Kerlow recalls, attributing this change to *The Paper Chase* television soap factor. Books and television shows by and' about lawyers 'glorified the rigour of legal training and the power of the professors, and students themselves became self-conscious, even giddy, about the spoils that would come to them from positions as associates and partners at Wall Street law firms.'[4]

During the civil rights movement and anti-Vietnam War protests on campuses throughout the US, a record number of law students registered at Harvard. Deemed for too long a male preserve, it was becoming more open in the 1960s to participation by women and minority groups on the faculty and student bodies. Lead stories in the *Harvard Crimson* convey some of the atmosphere: if not quite as lively as Berkeley or Columbia, it still made its contribution to the mid-1960s' boycotts and demonstrations over Vietnam and civil rights. Students were being threatened with the draft.

By February 1968 its Graduate Student Association Council, traditionally one of the university's most apolitical 'sherry party and beer blast' organisations, had decided to hold a referendum on Vietnam. Four Vietnamese students on campus had decided to 'risk death' by issuing an anti-war statement, the *Harvard Crimson* reported, while the conservative law school faculty took out an advertisement in the *Wall Street Journal* opposing the university's policy towards the war in South-East Asia which was signed by 60 per cent of staff and just under 50 per cent of law school students.

For a young Irish woman in her early twenties, the atmosphere in Cambridge and around Harvard Square must have been intoxicating. She was not the stereotypical Irish, straight off the plane and looking for the friend of a friend who would know about digs and a waitressing job. Nor was she part of the Boston Irish mafia which had dominated city politics. Her fellowship was awarded before her outstanding final results from TCD – a first-class moderatorship and a first-class LL.B, coupled with a first-class barrister-at-law degree from King's Inns, Dublin. She had spent 'one night on the town celebrating' after her last exams, and had taken a plane to Boston the next morning. 'Even so, I was ten days late for term and in Harvard that really means something.'[5]

Professor Arthur von Mehren, Joseph Story Professor of Law Emeritus at Harvard, had convinced Mary Bourke that she should go to America. They had met at an extraordinary session of the Hague Conference on Private International Law in April 1966. The young Irish barrister had volunteered her skills in law, English and French, as an official note-taker and was appointed a *secrétaire rédactrice* at the conference. She had mentioned that she was interested in studying in the United States; von Mehren happened to be a member of the Harvard law school graduate committee which would vet applications.

Not as distinguished as the Juris Doctor (JD), the master of laws (LL.M) is one of three degrees Harvard offers; it is regarded as a valuable addition to the curriculum vitae of a lawyer with a basic degree who wishes to study the US legal system. Many LL.Ms have become Supreme Court judges all over the world, and some have become high-ranking government officials in justice and finance.

Geographical diversity among the students is one of the features of the LL.M class, according to von Mehren. Applications, therefore, can become something of a lottery, but there has been a steady flow of participants from Ireland since the 1960s. There is no set programme, apart from a stipulation that one common law course be taken. Otherwise, each student designs his or her own course of study.

Mary Bourke took six subjects: conflict of laws, the prediction and prevention of harmful conduct, an introduction to urban legal studies, international transactions and relations, legal aspects of the European Common Market, and the civil law system – a course taught by Professor von Mehren himself. He describes her choice now as 'rather interesting': four subjects were international, and two had an urban and sociological thrust.

Von Mehren recalls a 'very attractive person', exactly the type sought by Harvard for the LL.M. She was always 'very charming', spoke well and communicated with others, having been both liberated and stimulated by her year in France before university. She was, he says, 'an individual you liked to be with', who was reliable and level-headed, who studied hard but was not dull.

She spent quite a bit of time getting to know the Boston area and was one of two Irish participants on that course in 1967–68, the other being Fergus Armstrong from Sligo, now a partner with a Dublin legal firm, McCann Fitzgerald. He had studied law at UCD, and had co-edited the legal journal, *Justice*, with Mary Bourke for a time. He took up his Harvard fellowship with the help of an endowment from a perfume magnate.

Though Harvard and Trinity, with their Elizabethan quadrangles and rubrics, had so much in common, the two campuses could not have been more different. The coffee-houses and bookshops of Harvard Square were alive at a time of great ferment in American political life, when Johnson was endeavouring to deliver on the Kennedy legacy through his Great Society programme of broad social reform. Indeed, Harvard was an extension of the Kennedy 'Camelot', and was closely associated with Democratic politics.

Part of LBJ's reform involved a tax-reduction act to stimulate economic growth. His civil rights legislation included a voters' registration act, giving black people the franchise. However, amid racial tensions, the legislation was proving impossible to implement. The death of two blacks in Mississippi confirmed the liberals' worst fears, and many black Americans shied away from registering. The US Student Non-Violent Co-ordinating Committee (SNCC), founded in the early 1960s, was sending observers to voter registration rallies as a measure of support.

Graduate students, many of whom had taken time out from pressurised new careers, were not among the radicals in Harvard, according to Fergus Armstrong and Glen Floyd, now head of his own law firm in Durant, Oklahoma, and a contemporary of Mary Bourke's on the LL.M programme. Dress was 'New England-style' – tweed jackets, suits, skirts. 'We all had two degrees at least and had been around for a while, teaching or practising law or whatever.' Mary Bourke was part of that group – 'one of the brightest', who enjoyed taking on the lecturers on particular points of law. 'She was a very serious student, but she was also just a delightful person to be with,' Floyd recalls. 'We were a very conscientious group of people – people who went back out across the world to become leaders in whatever we chose to do.' One is now professor of international law at the University of Berne in Switzerland; another is associate professor of law at the University of Auckland in New Zealand; yet another is a professor at the University of Manitoba in Canada. 'And Mary is the one who became president . . .'

She took rooms in one of the university's student residences, Wyeth Hall on Massachusetts Avenue. Her father, who visited her at the time her TCD results came out, relates how she had told fellow students in one of the introductory sessions that she was 'going to have a damn good time'. Certainly, there was little time to feel homesick, though she may have felt a lump in the throat on seeing copies of Irish newspapers, including the local Mayo weekly, the *Western People*, in the Square. Yet she was struck by the degree to which her fellow students were prepared to take responsibility for the future of their respective countries. The approach to law she found 'much more open and questioning'.[6]

In March 1968 President Johnson took the nation by surprise when he announced that he would not be seeking re-election. The following month, John F. Kennedy's widow, Jacqueline Bouvier Kennedy, was among the mourners at the funeral of the civil rights leader, Martin Luther King. Dr King had been due to speak at the 1968 Harvard Commencements, on the invitation of the class committee, in a bid to ensure that both Vietnam and the civil rights issue were dealt with during the ceremonies. It was the first time that the university's senior class had invited its own speaker independently.

Gunned down in Memphis, Tennessee, on 4 April by an 'unknown white assassin', King had risen to national prominence in 1963 through his famous 'I have a dream' speech and his leadership of mass protests. A disciple of Gandhi and a theology graduate, he had anticipated his own death. Black riots broke out in all the big American cities on the news of his death. Such events were to cast a binding spell over an insular Irish conscience.

Social values were being questioned; everything was 'up for examination', including the values of a legal education and the legitimate use of marijuana.[7] The academic year was intense, but life in Cambridge would not have been complete without occasional visits to the theatre. The Brattle still stands off Harvard Square, though now it has been converted into an arthouse cinema. Every one of the dozens of colleges in Cambridge and around Boston had a drama group. The university's Hasty Pudding Theatricals started its 120th annual production. Mary Bourke feasted on plays, and remembered it a year later as 'a great theatrical bonanza'.

Fergus Armstrong recalls that there was far too much pressure to study to take full advantage of Harvard student life. 'We had an assignment every night,' he says. 'Given that instruction was by the Socratic method in open theatre, one never knew when one was going to be picked on and one had to know one's stuff. We were very stretched, slightly peripheral as non-Americans, and much of our socialising was within the class because we wanted to make the most of an international experience. But I do have a photograph somewhere of Mary trying to master a pair of ice skates.'

Asked to identify the major influence on her outlook some 13 years later, Mary Bourke cited her time in Harvard as being more important than any one person or event. It was a very interesting period in the US – 'the end of the Johnson era, culminating in a large number of Federal programmes in education and for minorities'.

> The Vietnam War forced a lot of young people to re-think. There was a great deal of discussion on socialism, on equality, civil rights, and poverty. Many of the very bright students were turning down large law firm salaries, to get involved in projects and counsel for legal education, which was a totally transformed approach. When I came home, I related all this to Ireland and have continued to do so.[8]

There had been a tendency in Ireland to wait too long: 'Not to be listened to until you had grey hairs.'[9]

As The Byrds and Bob Dylan made their mark on the music charts and young bucks cruised in Oldsmobiles and Fiat 850 Sports Spiders, Hayes Bickford's – the Bick – became *the* night spot in Harvard Square. The Graduate Student Association won its anti-war referendum, calling for the immediate withdrawal of American troops from Vietnam. On 24 February 1968 students demonstrated peacefully in the University Hall – the first ever sit-in in a Harvard administration building. On 15 April, staff took out an advertisement in the *Crimson* supporting students who decided to 'refuse co-operation with Selective Service' – the draft – because they considered the Vietnam War to be unjust and immoral.

At term end, 12 June, it was Mrs Coretta Scott King who delivered her husband's class day speech – an 'emotionally charged' occasion in Sanders Theatre, where she criticised the US President for his response to the wave of assassinations, praised the students and 'blasted' the Vietnam War. Once again, the United States was in turmoil. Robert Kennedy, brother of JFK, had been shot dead just three months after beginning his own presidential campaign when he took on Eugene McCarthy in the primaries. 'The first urban populist' was how Richard E. Neustadt, director of the Institute of Politics at the John F. Kennedy School of Government in Cambridge, Massachusetts, described Bobby at a service in Harvard's Memorial Church. The service was attended by 'a solemn audience sprinkled with the scarlet windbreakers of the class of 1943', according to the *Harvard Crimson*.[10]

It was a highly politicised and much more confident Mary Bourke who returned to Ireland in late 1968. Harvard and other universities really became centres of dissent a year later, but the US experience had, nevertheless, shed new light on a conservative profession. One could practise law *and* have a conscience – the sort of social conscience which her grandfather had applied in his legal practice in Ballina. If she had any lingering doubts then about the direction her legal career would take, they were dispelled during two, often lonely, years out of Dublin as a junior counsel on the judiciary's Western Circuit. 'I saw Ireland quite differently – how we needed change, law reform and that even our parliamentary structures needed opening up,' she said in a newspaper interview in 1977.[11] She felt that her period in the west of Ireland was more beneficial to her than starting off in Dublin, where one needed to be in court only for one's own cases. 'On circuit, there is nothing else to do but stay in court and so you learn a lot more.' Women in court were still something of a novelty, she recalled in that interview, describing how she was once staring intently at the faces of the jurymen during a case – women were not permitted to do jury service at that time. Suddenly, she found herself blushing from head to toe: the foreman of the jury had winked at her. The contrast with what she had left behind in America could not have been greater. Different attitudes to women, different attitudes to youth; being young, there was an automatic assumption that she knew little. And how miserable lodgings could be in the west of Ireland in those days!

'It was in every sense an eye-opening experience,' Fergus Finlay, Labour

Party principal and a key member of her presidential campaign, has observed.[12] 'The clash between the culture she had just come from and relished, which expected young people to get involved and to contribute, and the culture she was now working in, which was hide-bound and traditional, was total.' It was, he says, 'both a relief and a challenge' for her to be appointed Reid Professor of Constitutional and Criminal Law at Trinity College Dublin in 1969. At 25 years of age, she was the youngest incumbent since the chair had been founded in 1888.

While travelling the Western Circuit, Mary Bourke tutored in law at University College Dublin and lectured on Common Market law in TCD at a time of growing student unrest. Not surprisingly, she found the demands made by the 'gentle revolution' justifiable, and 'very heartening'. The UCD students were 'hungry for knowledge and far more attentive than their TCD equivalents', but she was shocked at the lack of contact between senior staff and students.[13] In Northern Ireland, Catholic students in Derry were becoming involved in a civil rights campaign which had been influenced by the US movement. On 1 January 1969, a People's Democracy civil rights march to Derry set out from Belfast. Three days later, three hundred people were injured in a confrontation between the marchers and militant Protestants at Burntollet Bridge, near Claudy, County Derry.

Harvard alumni had been tutored to take on the world, with confidence and style. There should have been little surprise, then, at the final short paragraph in *The Irish Times* report on her appointment by the Board of Trinity College to the Reid Professorship. 'Miss Bourke is a candidate on the Dublin University panel for the Seanad,' it added.

Miss Bourke was now a political animal.

'Seanad distinction for woman barrister – Dublin University's Choice' read *The Irish Times* on 13 August 1969.[14] 'At the age of 25, Miss Mary Bourke, a barrister-at-law from Ballina, County Mayo, becomes the youngest member of the new Seanad, and also the first Catholic senator to be returned by Dublin University [TCD]. The other two Trinity members will be the outgoing senators, Dr Owen Sheehy Skeffington (who headed the poll) and Dr W.J.E. Jessop. Another senator, Dr W.B. Stanford, did not go forward again. Mr John Ross was an unsuccessful candidate.'

Mary Bourke described later that it had all happened by chance. Modelled on the British House of Lords, the Seanad or Upper House of the Oireachtas was formed during the creation of the Irish Free State in 1922 to represent minority interests and those with a specialist knowledge or experience of public service. Under the 1937 Constitution, Seanad Éireann was re-established more firmly under the government's control with 60 members, of whom 43 are elected on a vocational basis, 11 are nominated by the Taoiseach and three seats each were reserved for candidates from the two universities – TCD and UCD.

Chatting to friends about the composition, Mary Bourke argued that 'if there was university representation at all, it should surely be representative of all generations of university graduates – up till then the TCD senators were usually respected and elderly professors or lecturers'. They all agreed. But who should it be? 'And then it rather backfired on me,' she said in an interview that summer. 'And soon these friends were helping to organise my election campaign.'[15]

She did do some groundwork, though. 'I was not at all sure that I would do well. I had three disadvantages: I was young, I was a woman and I was a Catholic.'[16] She consulted a member of the Protestant hierarchy, Canon Luce, back in Mayo – an unusual, if astute, move. He was 'most enthusiastic' and encouraged her. 'He thought it was a great idea to get young people in the Seanad.

'I still remember my father's face when I told him. He was out digging potatoes in the garden in Ballina, and he leaned his elbow on the spade and looked at me for a long time without saying anything.'

'I didn't even know what she was talking about at first,' her father says now. 'At that age, all university senators were around 50 to 55. I suggested we go and see old Canon Luce together.' Her family had every reason to be taken aback. There was no political tradition to follow here, though affiliations were strongly Fine Gael. Though she had served as secretary, her younger brothers Adrian and Henry had been the really active ones on the Student Representative Council at TCD and she had given much more time to the Law Society. She had attended 'a few Maoist meetings', she said later, but had given up 'out of sheer boredom'.

Still, her parents threw all their energies into the campaign, writing to just about every Protestant and TCD graduate in the west of Ireland. All four brothers became involved in letter-writing to draw up a long supporting committee list, and Mr Justice Kingsmill Moore, who had been a senator himself, was an invaluable adviser. 'An excellent indicator of what is required, and has very successful experience in wooing the electorate,' Mary said of him in a letter home to her parents in June 1969.

It was and is still 'fearsomely exciting to glance into that letterbox of time', says Adrian, who did much of the envelope sending and the strategy planning with maps and drawing-pins. Being Catholic, young and female were factors that would have militated against his sister with a largely conservative electorate. The sitting senators were 'dinosaurs', he says. 'And here was this sapling, going to knock over these oaks . . .'[17]

Her election address focused on her views as a young person, a liberal, a lawyer and a woman, in that order. She referred to her 'law and morality' address of two years before. On women's issues, for too long Irish women would complain sporadically about discrimination while also being content to 'relax back into the sphere of influence to which they belonged – the bosom of the family', she wrote. Now they were beginning to play a significant part in the political, economic and social life of the country, she said.

'This concrete achievement is a much more cogent argument than the slogans of an aggressive feminist,' she went on. 'The more we are ready to branch out and fulfil ourselves in the life of the country, the more doors will open in the face of quiet ability and feminine qualities of efficiency and good humour.'

Her mother travelled to Dublin in a gesture of moral support, expecting perhaps to pick up the pieces after her daughter's defeat. Adrian, who with his equally tall older brother, Henry, was to be an ideal tallyman at the election count, remembers how his mother was a 'powerhouse of energy and work'. At one stage, he recalls, his sister was contacted by an English tabloid newspaper. It was curious to know more about this slip of a girl running in this university Seanad election and talking about contraception.

Mary arranged a time to meet, out in College Park. 'Off she went, with no minders, wearing a mini-skirt. When she came back, she mentioned it and talked about the photographer placing her on a bench and kneeling below her. The photograph 'might be on page one or page three', she told us. My mother said little, but dispatched Henry and myself out with fifty pounds each to buy up every copy of that newspaper the minute it hit the streets next morning in Dublin.'

'We made a fairly good fist of it, and helped to preserve the Bourke Catholic-west-of-Ireland-conservative image. But I think we may have drunk most of the money. And, you know, it wasn't such a bad photograph after all . . .'[18]

There were no pieces to pick up, and no political tag – just one delighted independent senator who had entered the record books as the youngest, the first woman and the first Catholic elected on the TCD tally.[19] Her election agent was Trevor West, then a lecturer and assistant junior dean at Trinity, and son of the headmaster of Midleton College, a Protestant secondary school in County Cork.

Adrian rounded up good friends, including Ann Lane, a lively young Cork woman from Millstreet, an insurance company employee who had been involved in Adrian's own campaign for the Student Representative Council and who was to become a major player in the candidate's career later on. She chose to administer the campaign office at 21 Westland Row. Nanny Coyne was staunch in her support, and provided endless trays of tea and biscuits. Afterwards, the candidate said that she thought that her 'old nanny' may have been the only person who had complete faith in her ability to win.

Trevor West was charming, erudite, a good sportsman and keen cricketer, who wielded considerable influence with college graduates. He led an energetic campaign with a punchy, if often cautious, manifesto in which Mary Bourke sold herself as a 'young person', as 'a liberal', as 'a lawyer' and as 'a woman'.

As that young person, she would energetically and vigorously represent the views of a younger generation which was aware of the 'vital part' that TCD played in the country's intellectual life, and she would oppose any moves to merge the two Dublin universities.[20] As a liberal, she would advocate reform of the law in relation to individual liberty. Civil rights being a major issue north of the border in 1969, she made reference to the Second Vatican Council's success in promoting pluralist values, but was critical of 'a tendency to feel self-satisfied south of the border'. As a lawyer, she would 'review extensively the content and scope of legislation before the Seanad'. There was no mention of the fact that women's representation in public life during the de Valera era was abysmal: a mere five women in the Seanad and two in the Dáil, and few opportunities for advancement in the civil service and professional sphere.

Her manifesto was just the sort of gentle jolt that a somnolent elec-torate needed, but most crucial in this, as in any TCD Seanad plebiscite, was her supporters' list. Proposed by Professor C.B. McKenna, Regius Professor of Laws, her seconder was Howard Robinson, influential finan-cier and father of her boyfriend, Nick. The list included several influential members of the Church of Ireland hierarchy – the hand of Canon Luce? – such as the Archbishop of Dublin, Dr George Otto Simms; the Bishop of Tuam, the Rt Revd Arthur Butler, the Dean of Kildare, the Revd A.D. Buchanan; several Trinity academics, such as Professor Brendan Kennelly, the Kerry poet; Jocelyn Otway-Ruthven, professor of medieval history; Professor Theo Moody of the modern history department; Professor Basil Chubb, political scientist; and Eavan Boland, a poet and close friend at college.

David Norris, her fellow undergraduate, was asked to assist and remembers feeling 'very flattered'. This was 'a step into adult politics'. His role was to assist in delivering that element of the old Protestant vote. He was not taken aback at the outcome. 'At that age in life, one expects to succeed. Our own lack of surprise was probably very naïve.'

Though she had sold herself on the youth vote, it was the older alumni who had swung the result – she was elected on the second count, with 1,140 first preferences. There was a practical reason for this. Only a small number of recent graduates had filled in the registration forms for the Trinity electoral roll. Anyone relying on their support would have polled a few hundred votes at most. At the same time, the candidates did have to appeal to the Irish beyond the Republic's borders – those TCD graduates in the North, for example, and those working in Britain and further afield, who were Irish citizens and had claimed their right on the electoral roll at commencements.

It was not something that members of the Dáil or parliament had to think of: emigrants have not been entitled to vote in general elections, in contrast to the situation in most other European countries. Various attempts over the years to lobby for change have begun to yield fruit only in the 1990s with shelved plans for a limited franchise for the Seanad only. But in the late 1960s, the word 'diaspora' was not common currency. The millions of Irish who had gone abroad – most significantly in the aftermath of the Great Famine in the 1840s – were a largely forgotten resource.

Just over two decades later, when she ran once again as a rank outsider in an election, Mary Bourke from Mayo would mark the Irish diaspora on the political map.

'The Youngest Senator' was the focus of press attention in the aftermath of the poll. At the count centre, she said that the Seanad should be used as a forum for 'new and possibly unpopular views'.[21] Perhaps it was considered an off-the-cuff remark, but there was little attempt in the early profiles to define what she meant.

'Mary's first action as a senator will probably be an appeal to all TCD graduates in the North to come together, whatever their religion, and work for peace,' the late Mary McCutchan, women's editor, wrote in the *Irish Independent* just three days after the British government had assumed effective control of Northern Ireland.[22] Ten days before, rioting and a 50-hour siege in the Bogside of Derry during the Apprentice Boys parade had left 112 people injured. The Taoiseach, Jack Lynch, sought British support for an immediate dispatch of a United Nations peacekeeping force to the North and warned that the Irish government 'can no longer stand by'.

'There is a unique liberal bond between Trinity graduates,' the new senator said in an interview in the *Irish Independent*. 'And now that government structures in the North seem rather inadequate, I feel it's up to individuals to help in every way possible.'

Asked about her position as one of only a handful of women in Irish public life, Mary Bourke said that she did not believe in 'suffragette-type activity'. 'I believe that the best way of overcoming prejudice against women is not to emphasise that you are a woman but to show that you can do a job efficiently and well.' It was a remark that could be dismissed as naïve, given the recent history of women in Ireland under the 1937

Constitution. Alternatively, it could be welcomed as an honest admission of her own failure to encounter any discrimination.

As a barrister, it was 'rather the opposite. Everybody seems to be falling over themselves to prove that they are not prejudiced and as a result I have probably found it easier than many of my male colleagues to get work,' she said. She would, however, be 'both consciously and unconsciously' focusing on matters of particular concern to women in the Seanad.

Within two years, her attitude would have changed significantly, even as a nascent Irish Women's Liberation Movement launched forth. She had no truck with US feminist movements because, in her view, 'a hostile approach' to men was no way to attain equality, she told a lunchtime lecture in St Anne's Church in Dublin in April 1970. But by 1971, she was telling a Christus Rex Congress in Bundoran, County Donegal, that the new native movement represented the only radical force in the 'stagnant pool of Irish life', and criticised law-makers for their lack of commitment to social legislation. The political awakening of Irish women might prove to be 'the lever to break open the rigid structures of the present political parties, which had no basis in unity of ideal or viewpoints'.[23]

As a forward-looking lobby, it was 'not impressed by Civil War terminology' and was focused on social injustice, she said. Speaking to *The Irish Press* that year, she noted that the movement might seem to be 'too aggressive and radical for some . . . But I haven't yet met a single woman who doesn't agree that there are many factual inequalities which affect her, and which she would like to see redressed.'

It was when the new Seanad sat for the first time that Mary Bourke's political direction was identified. The independent senator, sporting a beret, promised to be 'the most charming dissenter in the House', the political commentator John Healy wrote in *The Irish Times*.[24] A caption in the newspaper below her photograph outside Leinster House erroneously awarded her an FF (Fianna Fáil) party affiliation. She had 'no objection' to the tag, she wrote in the newpaper's letters page the following day, 'provided this is clearly understood, as I understand it to mean, "friendly face"'.[25]

The proposed Seanad chairman, Michael Butler Yeats, son of the poet, probably did not regard her as a particularly friendly face that first day. Himself a TCD graduate, he was a card-carrying member of Fianna Fáil, and had run for the party in two Dáil elections. Trinity senator Dr Owen Sheehy Skeffington, who had headed the poll, opposed Yeats's nomination as *cathaoirleach* (chairman). Only one other person supported him in the dissenting vote: Senator Bourke.

By the following April, she was already frustrated. She complained to Mary Kenny in *The Irish Press* that she was under-employed.[26] She had approached the job in hand with great enthusiasm and 'a certain naïvety', but found the pace of debate monumentally slow. 'Quite seriously,' she said to Kenny, 'I often feel like walking up and down outside the Seanad with a big placard saying I AM UNDER-EMPLOYED HERE. THIS BODY IS UNDER-USED – AN EXPENSIVE EXERCISE IN A SMALL COUNTRY. I feel a sense of guilt in drawing a salary.'

She was not, perish the thought, advocating the abolition of the upper house. 'I would not criticise its constitutional position at all. What is wrong is that it's under-used. It meets erratically – at the moment, it hasn't met for five weeks; there is a tendency on the part of the government to regard it as a place for loyal supporters who failed to get a Dáil seat.' Discussion was confined to particular issues, and the body merely acted as 'a rubber-stamp'.

Ms Bourke's clear diagnosis of the problem was not matched by a solution, Kenny observed, other than to put pressure on the government to change the Seanad's role. 'Later, crazed with the change of things, who knows but that she may join that large sector of her generation who believes that the only real way to political change is through direct action, on the streets and behind barricades. For the moment she still believes in democracy . . . But then there are the public speeches,' Kenny wrote. The most recent, on civil rights in Ireland, advocated removing the issue of divorce from the Constitution, and repealing the ban on birth control in the 1935 Criminal Law Amendment Act. She was not 'rooting for divorce', the senator told Kenny, but was concerned with the legality of carrying such a prohibition, given that it curtailed the rights of those citizens in a minority who supported it.

'I don't think, either, that to introduce the possibility of divorce would weaken the marriage structure in this country. The strength of the family bond and the whole feeling that divorce is wrong for the majority of the people comes from their religious beliefs and their education, and if these have any meaning, they ought to safeguard the people as before.

'But as it is, the law is being used in the wrong way: if we are a democratic society, then I think that our primary value should be to protect civil rights, and for many people divorce and contraception are part of their civil rights.'

Mary Kenny's assessment was prophetic. 'Miss Bourke is rather pretty,' she wrote in language which now sounds almost embarrassing. 'Slim, quietly elegant, with a round, wide, Irish face and green-hazel eyes. She comes from Ballina, where both her parents are doctors and neither of them is political. One day, when she finds a political ideology that she could embrace in a proper and committed way, perhaps she will stand for the Dáil. Then the sparks will fly.'[27]

CHAPTER 5

Pills and Bills

Women's voices: a summer night, 1970, in a room above Mrs Gaj's restaurant in Baggot Street, Dublin. Everyone seemed to be talking at once. Yet, in spite of that, it struck June Levine that 'one had the sense of being properly heard for the first time ever, just the same'.[1]

It was not the first time she had attended a meeting of the new Irish Women's Liberation Movement (IWLM), but it was a night to remember. 'Consciousness boiled up from the depths of all the female energy in that room . . . It uncovered the everyday wounds which we had experienced as females, experienced in isolation, not understanding that it was not all inevitable, discovering that each one of us was not the oddball, the only one who could not accept the way things were supposed to be. We discovered that most of us had been damaged, enraged, humiliated by similar things, had felt put down by "normality". In pooling our experiences of life we discovered the world as it was for females. It was not the way it need be . . .'

Years later, Levine has written, she was to recognise the 'pre-women's movement state' for what it was – 'emotional and intellectual Purdah'.

The journalist Mary Kenny had invited her to her first such gathering, in the home of a colleague, Mary Maher of *The Irish Times*. Though Levine barely knew her, she was aware that Maher, from Chicago, was breaking 'the stereotype of women's journalism in Ireland'. She was also hosting this gathering at home, because she could not get a babysitter.

Others present that night included Mairín de Burca, then an official with Sinn Féin; Dr Maire Woods, who was involved in left-wing politics; Margaret Gaj, the Scottish owner of the restaurant, which was the haunt of Dublin radicals in the late 1960s and early '70s; Mairín Johnston, a Labour Party activist and trade unionist; Mary Sheerin, recently returned from Paris and working in publishing; Mary McCutchan, women's editor of the *Irish Independent*; Mary Anderson, also of the same newspaper's women's page; Nuala Fennell, then a housewife breaking into freelance journalism who was to become an elected politician; and Nell McCafferty, a journalist from Derry.

The group would develop and split, evolving into a 'marriage of co-operative opposites', Levine wrote. The women's movement in the US was well established by then, with Betty Friedan's National Organisation for Women (NOW) campaigning for equal rights and opportunities. The Boston Women's Health Collective, one of the earliest and best-known women's health information centres in the United States, had been organised the year before, while San Diego State University had established America's first degree programme in women's studies; within 15 years there would be nearly 450 in universities around the world. Women were also now allowed to join the US Secret Service to protect the president.

Italy recognised divorce for the first time in 1970. In France, the women's liberation movement had been formed by many groups with different philosophies, while a new law aimed to give parents equal authority over their children and allowed the wife to retain her property from before or during the marriage. In Britain, the 1970 Matrimonial Proceedings and Property Act, followed by the Matrimonial Causes Act, recognised the principle of matrimonial property – assets held jointly by both spouses. Barbara Castle, former British Labour minister and feminist, had led the successful fight for passage of the 1970 Equal Pay Act, while Margaret Thatcher had been appointed Tory education and science minister in the same year.

'It is interesting that many women do not recognise themselves as discriminated against; no better proof could be found of the totality of their conditioning,' wrote the American feminist, Kate Millett, in *Sexual Politics*, part of a library of feminist writing published in the early 1970s which was to influence two generations.[2] Also in 1970, Germaine Greer published *The Female Eunuch*, which urged women to reject marriage, adopt sexually diverse lifestyles and take individual action to improve their status. In other spheres, women were gaining confidence, and ground, such as the first all-women's climb of Mount McKinley. Diane Crump had become the first woman jockey to ride in the Kentucky Derby. Women's prize money at international tennis tournaments, which had been a fraction of the men's take, had begun to rise, largely through the campaigning efforts of Billie Jean King.

'We in Dublin were all pretty vague about how those equal rights and opportunities could be defined for Irish women,' June Levine wrote in her memoir, *Sisters*. 'There were groups in London since '68 and '69. Still, the strange stirring, the sense of dissatisfaction or yearning described by Friedan in 1963 when I was staggering blindly through my life, hadn't publicly surfaced in Ireland. The women in that room over Gaj's – and I always think of us as the Gaj's group – weren't at all sure of what we wanted. It certainly was not more of the same.'[3]

Eventually, 'feminist socialists', 'socialist feminists' and 'the small number of women who had moved not an inch from their original position' would form a group of 16, with activists like Marie McMahon, one of Dublin's first female printers; Fionnuala O'Connor, a Lisburn schoolteacher who later became the *Irish Times* Northern correspondent; Bernadette Quinn, a pharmacist, and her sister, Rosemary Humphries; journalist Hilary Boyle; and Mary Earls, who was to become a bookshop owner.

A manifesto, entitled *Chains or Change*, was published by the IWLM in 1971. Documenting discrimination against women in Ireland, it carried a series of demands: equal pay, equality before the law, equal education, contraception, justice for deserted wives, unmarried mothers and widows. Some of its details 'shocked even some of those who had contributed to its research', Levine noted. 'Things were even worse for Irish women than we had thought, and we still hadn't had the Report of the Commission on the Status of Women,' she said, referring to the first official document high-lighting the extent of inequity; it was published in late 1972, and circulated in the early months of 1973. The IWLM pamphlet 'contained a brilliant summary' by Mary Maher, entitled 'Five Good Reasons Why it is Better to Live in Sin', which was to serve Levine consistently through the ensuing years as a reminder 'to examine why I should ever take a sub-servient position to any man, in sin or otherwise'.

The summary encapsulated the inferior position of women in Ireland, at a time when when the so-called sexual revolution was sweeping North America and Europe. The first good reason stated was that one could keep one's job; if a woman was working in the public service or for the trade unions or banks in 1970, she was expected to resign on getting married. The second reason – that the Irish tax system discriminated against marriage, by taxing married women more than their single counterparts – was an anomaly in Catholic Ireland which was to be rectified later. The third reason was that marriage obliterated a woman's commercial identity, in requiring a husband's signature for opening bank accounts, taking out insurance and other routine financial transactions. A married woman had about the same rights as an infant in Irish law. The state's children's allow-ance was paid to the husband, and even gynaecological operations in some hospitals required a husband's consent.

The fourth and fifth reasons were unlikely to be taken seriously by any woman about to be married, the pamphlet noted. 'A woman who is only living in sin can remember reason number four: you can leave when things have finally become unbearable, merely by walking out the door. A married woman who leaves her husband is presumed to have deserted him and has no right to his home, furniture or income.' This led on to reason number five: 'If you live in sin, you don't submit to the insult that society offers women who marry – the status of property. An adult and equal relationship is something two people forge together. The institution of marriage is something invented to preserve male superiority and a system of female chattels.'

'How many sinners did this document create?' June Levine wondered .

Some months before, *The Irish Times* carried a two-paragraph, single-column report. Ireland's youngest senator, it said, would be married quietly to 'newspaper cartoonist and artist Mr Nicholas Robinson, of Clare St, Dublin, tomorrow'.[4] Mary Bourke was not one of those women mapping out future plans on hot summer nights in Gaj's. In December 1970, 26-year-old Mary Bourke was to be wed.

But not in Ballina. Not by the babbling Moy. Not even in Trinity College Chapel, looking out on to the cobbled front square. The 'mixed' marriage took place in the rather anonymous church at Dublin Airport, with a few friends and colleagues present. It was a practical choice: there would be an early flight to Paris the next day. They travelled on to Tenerife where they spent their honeymoon in a house owned by Nick's father. None of the Bourke family was there to throw confetti or wave them off.

Over a quarter of a century after that wedding, reports and profiles repeatedly state that the Bourke parents objected to their daughter marrying a Protestant. Those close to the couple are less willing to accept this as the case, and her father denies that this was the reason. He and his sons still regret the decision not to attend. Given the family background, complete with Protestant branches, and the quest for a dispensation so that their children could attend Trinity College, Dublin, it would have been surprising if Mary's parents were unable to accept that mixed marriage was a fact of 1970s' Irish life. Was Tessa Bourke a mite disappointed, perhaps, about her daughter's choice? At the time, it looked as if Nick had few prospects; he was drawing cartoons. It was a painful period, and the only serious disagreement that the family had; but it did not last beyond a few months, and wounds were quickly healed through the discreet intervention of Mother Aquinas, Dr Bourke's aunt.

Even as she set off for Spain, the senator was in the news for trying to cut short her holiday. On 14 December 1970, *The Irish Times* reported that a 'strong protest' would be made by senators when the house resumed the following day over the 'extraordinary long recess' of 137 days!

Quoting a recent letter to the newspaper by Senator Bourke, where she had pointed out that the economy could not afford a Seanad that was 'merely decorative' in this 'time of crisis', the report said that the sixty senators who made up the upper house and were being paid £1,500 a year, were 'seriously embarrassed' by the archaic system of parliamentary procedure, which had left them 'idle' for more than one-third of the year.

'In a democracy,' the young senator had written, 'there are sound reasons for retaining a Second Chamber in the legislature, provided it is allowed to play an active role in legislating and debating matters of public interest.'

As befitted tradition, the senator took her husband's name. Pressed in an interview much later on to defend her decision to marry so young – though in those days, it was not unusual – she said that, for her, marriage had proved to be 'a liberating experience', which had given her the freedom to grow in a happy partnership.[5] Nick, urbane, confident, comfortable at her side, would give an innately shy but ambitious young woman constant support in the social circles she was bound to move in if she was to succeed. It was obviously attractive to have a reliable and stable partner if one was pushing out social boundaries and taking intellectual risks. She would not abuse it. Family life would be kept separate, and very private.

As well it might, for a time, when public life exacted a price. By March 1971 the senator was among Mary Kenny's list in *The Irish Press* of the 25 most influential women in Ireland, along with Dr Thekla Beere, successful civil servant and head of the Taoiseach's new Commission on the Status of Women; Nora Browne, chair of the Irish Housewives Association; Oonagh Corbett, chair of 'the most powerful group of women in this country', the Irish Countrywomen's Association; Mairín de Burca, secretary of Sinn Féin; Sinead de Valera, the 'gentle, legendary' 92-year-old wife of the President; Bernadette Devlin, 'stormy, fiery, fearless' People's Democracy 'maverick', who had, Kenny wrote, 'burst on the Irish scene with the Northern troubles of 1968', becoming the youngest member of the British Parliament since William Pitt the Younger when she was elected in 1969 at the age of 21.

Kenny also singled out Brigid Hogan O'Higgins, Fine Gael TD for Clare South-Galway and shadow education minister; Maeve Kyle, the athlete; Eileen Kane, the Irish-American anthropologist; and Maureen Lynch, the 'utterly charming, utterly disarming' wife of the Taoiseach. There was Maeve Conway, head of education at Radio Telefís Éireann, the national radio station; Frankie Byrne, broadcaster and 'radio sob-sister'; Máire Mhac an tSaoi, poet, daughter of the Fianna Fáil founding father Seán McEntee, and wife of parliamentarian Conor Cruise O'Brien.

Sister Benvenuta McCurtain, the intellectual Dominican nun; the writers Edna O'Brien and Kate O'Brien; Maureen Potter, comedian; Clodagh Kennedy, 'not necessarily the best, but possibly the most influential' of Irish clothes designers; Miriam Woodbyrne, head of the largest model agency; and Professor Eva Philbin, head of the UCD chemistry department, were also on Kenny's list.[6]

LEFT: *Eleanor Dorothy Macaulay, Mary Robinson's grandmother; and Mary's parents and grandmother at Enniscrone, County Sligo, 1951; from left to right: Dr Aubrey Bourke, Granny O'Donnell and Tessa Bourke* (both Private Collection)

Mary Robinson's uncle, Sir Paget Bourke (centre, right), and Mrs Susan Bourke, being presented to Princess Elizabeth and Prince Philip in Nairobi, Kenya, in 1952 (Private Collection)

CLOCKWISE FROM TOP LEFT: *Mary Bourke's First Communion; with Nanny Coyne and Henry at Butlin's Holiday Camp; on a Bourke family outing to Enniscrone beach, County Sligo; with her blue ribbon at secondary school in Mount Anville, Dublin* (all Private Collection)

Senator Mary Robinson after her election to the Seanad in 1969 (Irish Times)

Mary Robinson with her husband Nicholas when she was called to the Inner Bar (Irish Press)

Senator Mary Robinson with her husband and Bride Rosney. Rosney, a school principal, became involved in her political election campaigns and was appointed special adviser to the President in 1990

Canvassing in the Dublin West constituency in 1981 with her newborn son Aubrey (Irish Times)

With Dr Marion Broderick on Inis Mór, Aran Isles, County Galway, during the presidential election campaign (Pat Langan, Irish Times)

Canvassing during the 1990 presidential election campaign on Clare Island, County Mayo

*Kevin Robinson and trusted companion, electioneering for Mary Robinson in
Claremorris, County Mayo, during the 1990 campaign* (Pacemaker)

'Brilliant, articulate member of Seanad Éireann with a string of academic letters after her name,' Kenny wrote of Mary Robinson *née* Bourke. 'Highly trained legal mind, said to have been one of the cleverest girls ever at TCD. In person unassuming but most principled politically; the impression comes over that she is ever on the side of Justice. Married to gifted cartoonist Nick Robinson.'

That same month, Mary Kenny was helping to co-ordinate IWLM participation in a television debate on the popular and sometimes controversial Saturday night *Late Late Show*, hosted by RTE broadcaster Gay Byrne. His researcher, Pan Collins, had attended an IWLM meeting, June Levine recalled.[7] Although she wasn't present herself that night, she knew that all these women would have been a 'ready-made circus' for television.

So 'nothing was left to chance', Levine wrote. 'We planned to present ourselves at our most acceptable, informed, rational, even moderate.' Key members on the panel would talk on particular aspects: Mairín Johnston on discrimination at work; Nell McCafferty on poor allowances for deserted wives, unmarried mothers and widows; Lelia Doolan, television producer, on education and social conditioning; Mary Cullen, historian (though Gay Byrne introduced her as the wife of a psychiatrist!), on working mothers. The group lacked a legal brain, however. Efforts had been made for some time to woo Senator Mary Robinson. She agreed – not to join, but to appear on the panel to point out the legal inequities. Lelia Doolan, Mary Cullen and Mary Robinson had been asked, quite deliberately, to present an educated, middle-class, respectable image. Mairín Johnston and Nell McCafferty would suffice for the rabble-rousing element. 'We were our own handlers!' says one of the group.

The strategy – live on the night of 6 March 1971 – worked well until the audience, which included IWLM members, was asked to participate. Gay Byrne was objective and professional, playing fair with the text of the pamphlet, *Chains or Change*. It was when IWLM member Nuala Fennell asked Senator Robinson how Article 41 of the Constitution could be reconciled with the lack of machinery to safeguard an adequate wife's housekeeping allowance that the temperature began to rise. Fennell made the point that 11 per cent of personal income in Ireland was spent on alcohol.

At this point, a woman in the audience proposed that a local committee could intervene to ensure that the wife of an unemployed man, drinking all his social welfare money, could be provided for directly, without changing the Constitution. Mary Kenny, who had been advised as part of the IWLM strategy to keep a low profile, could not resist an intervention. Was a patriarchal society seriously going to consider this, she asked wryly? Did the men who passed legislation in Dáil Éireann really care at all?

'Mary Robinson went on to point out that the answer to that was the fact that so many Irish citizens and voters were women,' Levine wrote. 'The woman in the audience came in again, asking if there was an Attorney General's office in Ireland where one could go, as in the States, to say you were being discriminated against because you were a woman? Was there a Department of Justice? she asked. "There is a Department of Justice . . ." Senator Robinson began, but laughter from the audience made it impossible for her to continue.'

Gay Byrne quoted from that day's edition of a provincial newspaper, *The Limerick Leader*, on the case of a mother of four who had been appointed senior city corporation architect the previous year in a temporary capacity. When the post had become permanent, she had not even been granted an interview because she was married and had become 'automatically ineligible' for the position.

During the commercial break, the programme's panel found itself enlarged 'in a most unexpected way'. The Fine Gael TD and future party leader Dr Garret FitzGerald had 'dashed from his fireside' and presented himself at the RTE television studios, having been 'roused' by Mary Kenny's remarks about legislators. Those who realised what had happened were furious. 'In the first place,' Levine wrote, 'it was obvious then that such a takeover could happen only on a women's programme, and also that we were to be used in a bandwagon bid for country-wide publicity for the Fine Gael party.'

A 'free-for-all screaming match' between FitzGerald and various women in the audience ensued. The newly formed Women's Progressive Association, initiated by a Dun Laoghaire councillor, Margaret Waugh, to encourage more women to participate in public life, made its voice heard.[8] The audience was 'well laced with socialists, Marxists and Nationalists, who argued back and forth about it all being the fault of capitalism or British imperialism', and FitzGerald was criticised time and again for using the programme to push his party's agenda.

In spite of all the careful planning, the show had been 'chaotic', Levine said. 'Almost everything we had planned to avoid had happened. Mary Kenny had got shrill, the rest of us hadn't exactly kept our cool, the Marxists had taken up valuable time, a man had stolen the limelight . . .'

Yet the Irish public now also knew that a women's liberation movement existed, and the pamphlet was widely reviewed. The group set about organising its first mass meeting, in Dublin's Mansion House, for April 1971.

If spring was in the air, so was constitutional reform – or, more correctly, contraception, if one was to believe *The Belfast Telegraph*. Everyone was talking about it, 'in the homes, in the pubs, on the buses of Dublin', the newspaper said, and at the centre of the controversy was 26-

year-old Mrs Mary Robinson, described as one of three university senators who had just failed to get formal permission to publish a Bill permitting the restricted sale of contraceptives. 'The argument over a possible change in the criminal law banning contraceptives in the Republic looks like developing into the biggest clash between the Catholic Church and the Southern State since the Mother and Child Row of 1951,' the newspaper reported.[9]

Echoes of that old row were still reverberating, and the principal person involved would come to play no small part in Mary Robinson's own political career. The proposed scheme was part of a 1947 Health Act drafted by the Fianna Fáil government which aimed to introduce free and voluntary ante- and post-natal care for mothers, as well as for all children up to 16 years of age, without a means test of income. Initially shelved by the Fianna Fáil leader, Eamon de Valera, when the terms were objected to by the Catholic hierarchy, it was revived two years later under the Republic's first coalition government by the Minister for Health, Dr Noel Browne.

Once again, the bishops objected to it – specifically the lack of a means test and the freedom of choice of doctor – as did the Irish Medical Association, which regarded it as 'socialised medicine'.[10] The Catholic hierarchy made it clear that the family was the final arbiter on sex education, and expressed concern about non-Catholics treating pregnant Catholic women or giving them sex education which might not accord with Catholic social teaching. Dr Browne, who refused all demands to insert a means test, lost the support of the government and his own party, Clann na Poblachta, with his party leader, Seán MacBride, demanding his resignation.

The coalition government fell in June 1951, a new Fianna Fáil administration introduced a public health scheme, means-tested, and Browne continued to hold his Dáil seat as an independent until 1953. Though he regarded the Fianna Fáil act as capitulation to the Catholic hierarchy, he joined it and then founded a National Progressive Democratic Party.[11] In 1963, he joined the Labour Party, holding a Labour seat for four years from 1969. In 1973, he became a senator.

Senator Robinson was, as one newspaper noted, 'upset – and genuinely surprised' at the amount of personal publicity she had been receiving in spring 1971 over the proposed Bill to allow the restricted sale of contraceptives in the Republic for the first time. Two other senators, John Horgan and Trevor West, her old election agent, were also sponsoring it, she pointed out.

Yet, 'The bar-stool conversations and the letters to the papers always refer to "Mary Robinson's Bill",' that report said. Certainly, she had approached West and Horgan, and they had decided against having further sponsors from the main political parties in an attempt to avoid letting it become a political issue. She had also signalled her intentions the previous year, when she told the Medical Union of Ireland that she would try and change the existing legislation – the 1935 Criminal Law Amendment Act – which banned the import and sale of any contraceptive in the Irish Free State, with a fine of fifty pounds and/or six months in jail as the penalty.

The legislation was not specific about personal use, however, and by 1971 an estimated 25,000 Irish women were being prescribed the contraceptive pill by their doctors for so-called medical reasons. The pill could be imported and sold legally as a cycle regulator.

'Recent statements by Premier Jack Lynch and his Foreign Minister Patrick Hillery clearly show that the government is interested in allowing divorce and contraception – partly to make the Republic a more attractive proposition for Northern Protestants,' *The Belfast Telegraph* wrote.[12] The paper was referring to the Fianna Fáil leader's unprecedented statement that contraception was a matter of conscience, rather than for the state; he made the remark at a party conference in 1969, the year that Fianna Fáil also recorded its largest overall majority to date in a general election. 'But after the uncompromising restatement of traditional opposition to birth control from the Archbishop of Dublin, Dr McQuaid, the ruling party is waiting and watching to see which way the wind of public opinion seems to be blowing,' the paper added.

Increasingly, after 1969 and events in the North, the Taoiseach's main objective was the preservation of peace in the Republic.[13] The principal objective of the Archbishop of Dublin was the faith and morals of his flock in the face of what could amount to 'a curse upon our country' – the contraceptive Bill. Contraception was 'a right that cannot even exist' in current Church teaching, he said, issuing a letter to be read at all Masses in the Dublin diocese on 28 March 1971. Other bishops, including the Bishop of Killala, Dr McDonnell, also warned against it. 'Will this measure give us a sort of society that we do not want?' he asked during a sermon in St Muredach's Cathedral, a pebble's throw across the river from the Bourke family home in Ballina.

The condoms through the letter-box and rubber glove fingers in the post marked the first phase of Senator Robinson's attempt to effect real change through legal channels, at a time when other young, educated women in Dublin were trying to lobby for change by other means; she had professed herself to be embarrassed at the 'unsolicited' support of a handful of representatives from the IWLM who had chanted 'we shall not conceive' outside Leinster House, and who had stormed the building through the window of the men's lavatory.[14] Yet, she added, she could not blame 'the only socially conscious pressure group in the country' for trying extra-parliamentary political action, given that she herself had already identified parliament as being increasingly irrelevant and cumbersome.

'Schoolgirlish' was how the leader of the Seanad, Tommy Mullins, had dismissed the presentation of the Contraception Bill. The highly emotional response from the Catholic Church, members of parliament and the public contrasted with her own view of contraception, as elicited back in TCD during that inaugural speech to the Law Society in February 1967. She did not aim to 'make contraceptives freely available', she emphasised. Under the new Bill, distribution would be subject to strict controls. But it was simply unacceptable, in her view, held consistently since TCD, for the state to legislate on a matter of private morality. 'I don't want to become solely identified with this particular issue,' she continued. 'There are lots of more important things that need to be reformed, like the poor housing conditions, or the discrimination against women in pay and employment.'[15] The fact that the Bill had become the subject of controversy before its publication had led to misrepresentation. 'I've had letters from people who thought I was trying to legalise abortion. I'm not.'

It has been suggested since that Jack Lynch's administration might have been looking east, as well as north, when floating the contraception issue. Bound to Britain by an economic umbilical cord, Ireland was now also seeking membership of the Common Market or European Economic Community (EEC). In any event, Fianna Fáil played it safe, leaving the initiative up to the three senators, who failed to have their Bill given a first reading in the houses of the Oireachtas. The bishops held a special meeting in Maynooth College in March, rejecting the argument that the issues of divorce, contraception and abortion were of purely private morality, and stating that civil law should 'respect the wishes of the people'. In spite of liberal-sounding statements from the Taoiseach and the Foreign Minister, the party was under pressure in the constituencies to hold firm, in line with Catholic teaching. The opposition was similarly divided.

The Protestant churches entered the fray, with the Church of Ireland, Presbyterian and Methodist prelates indicating that their congregations had a right to freedom of conscience. And so did the women's movement, fresh from its mass meeting in the Mansion House, Dublin, which over a thousand attended – and over fifty queued, at one point, for access to the microphone.

A delegate group had been formed after the rally. There was a need to do something 'worth while' to keep the momentum up. Two issues were of major concern: contraception; and a piece of legislation known as the Forcible Entry Bill, which proposed that any man squatting illegally would be jailed, along with his wife. The former did not arouse unanimous support; the latter, it was generally agreed, was central to the women's struggle.

June Levine does not remember who proposed it first. But at eight o'clock in the morning on 22 May 1971 some 47 women arrived at Dublin's Amiens Street station to take the train to Belfast. Accompanying them were newspaper journalists and television cameramen. The group had a shopping list – of contraceptives. The aim was to challenge the hypocritical situation where anyone could travel to Belfast, buy such products and bring them back without interference from the customs officers, in spite of the fact that this was in breach of the current legislation – the Criminal Law Amendment Act, which Senator Robinson had been trying to change.

No one was arrested crossing back into the Republic. The women made their point, chanting 'enforce the Constitution now' and 'the law is obsolete' as they arrived back in Dublin to a large crowd of supporters serenading them with 'We Shall Overcome'. Tossing the packets of contraceptives along the platform, the women were ignored by officialdom. They marched across the street to one of the city's main police stations, at Store Street. 'We could see the gardaí through their office windows,' June Levine wrote. 'They didn't even glance out. They pretended we weren't there.'[16]

Senator Robinson was not among the women. On 7 July 1971 she tried, and failed, to win support for the first reading of her Bill. She expressed disappointment at the reaction of the leader of the house, in view of the government's own recent statements on the need to create a pluralist society in the Republic. She did not know if the government had changed its mind, but if it had, this was:

> very regrettable for those who would like, as I think most senators here would like, to see a better relationship with those living in the North of Ireland . . . If we are serious about the North, we must change our attitudes. We must change our legislation and be able to say to the people in the North of Ireland that they can come into the South of Ireland and find the same tolerance of different moral attitudes, the same tolerance of different ideas, the same possibility of informing themselves on important medical and social matters and the possibility in their own privacy of following their own consciences in relation to family planning.[17]

She was not to let the matter rest. '"Speak up," says senator,' read an *Irish Times* report when she alluded to an all-party committee which had been set up to review the Constitution years before.[18] It had drawn attention to the constitutional ban on divorce in the Republic as one obstacle to a united Ireland. Referring to her own Bill to lift the restriction on the availability of contraceptives, Senator Robinson said that there had been 'at least implicit approval' from the Taoiseach and from the Foreign Minister, Dr Hillery. 'However, when the reports from the constituencies came in, the government chose to oppose it.'

Many theologians to whom she had spoken in private would not speak out in public, she claimed. 'It is not that we have people with nothing to say. Our people have things to say, but they do not say them.'

CHAPTER 6

Making an Impact

'I am not a member of Women's Lib. I appeared on the television show because they asked me to talk about the legal and constitutional aspects. But I am not a member. I'm not trying to be "hands-offy" about it. But I'm more in favour of *people's* liberation. I think the Women's Liberation Movement is a too radical fringe which is also imbalanced.'

Late 1971, and Senator Mary Robinson is being interviewed for *The Cross*, a religious journal, by a Catholic priest, Fr Brian D'Arcy. One of the young progressives in the Church, from the border area of Enniskillen, County Fermanagh, Fr D'Arcy was in the early stages of a very successful media and entertainment career. He was trying to probe the reasoning behind the Senator's contraceptive Bill, and her views on Catholic Church teaching.

'I have great difficulty here too,' she replied. 'Almost always when I ask a priest [about] the teaching of *Humanae Vitae*, I get a different interpretation. I certainly accept the right and duty of the Church to teach and guide and I accept *Humanae Vitae*. After that, you are down to hair-splitting, but in summary I am willing to accept the teaching of the Church.'

She would have no option. The contraceptive debate would run for another three years before any sort of legislative reform would be agreed upon, with many twists and turns and other distractions for the senator *en route*. Preparations were under way to join the EEC along with Britain, Denmark and Norway, and she was one of 14 European legal experts nominated to the Vedel Committee to study the extension of powers of the European Parliament. Already a member of the executive committee of the Irish Council of the European Movement, the senator had done considerable work on the EEC as a constitutional lawyer and legislator.

Her views on Europe, Ireland's accession to the EEC and the implications for the Northern conflict were articulated on several occasions in 1971, most notably at a Dublin Rotary Club lunch in December, just over five months before the Irish referendum on accession on 10 May 1972. As a constitutional lawyer, she was very concerned about the effect EEC directives would have on Irish law. Unless anomalies were removed – and this would not be easy – Irish court interpretations of constitutional matters could be appealed to the EEC.

Speaking during one Seanad debate on EEC membership, Mary Robinson had already criticised the government for its public information campaign on accession. Membership would represent a fundamental constitutional change, she warned. An independent commission should be established to study the legal implications of joining the EEC for Ireland. An evolving and expanding Europe might necessitate more legislation and another referendum; such a plebiscite was, in fact, to take place in 1992.

Returning to the subject in November 1971, Mary Robinson said that she was not satisfied that the constitutional and legal dimensions of joining the EEC had been considered properly before holding the membership referendum. Constitutional change to remove inconsistencies would not be easy, and it was not a matter either for an Attorney General's committee. She urged consultation with the legal profession.

On the positive side, there could be significant implications for the Northern conflict, she told the Dublin Rotary lunch. The tragic acceleration of violence there, both legal and illegal, had at once 'simplified and distorted the problem . . . Historical clichés are being resurrected to fortify entrenched positions. We are reverting to an outdated nationalism which was the root cause of wars between the states, culminating in two World Wars.' An examination of the real nature of a European commitment in an Irish context could help to counterbalance this tide of nineteenth-century nationalism. In fact, EEC membership could help bring North and South closer together, she forecast in an article for *This Week* magazine the following year.

Referring to her legal role in Europe, Senator Robinson said that an analysis of the present European Parliament, Council and Commission showed that they were undemocratic and not responsible to the peoples of the regions they represented. The Parliament was not elected directly, the Commission was not chosen by the Parliament, and the Council and Commission had legislative power without democratic control. If Ireland intended to join the EEC, it should do so 'demanding change in this institutional structure . . . We should not accept the present framework beyond the transitional period. The Community must not only enlarge, but evolve.'

Ireland did nothing of the sort. The debate was so focused on economic issues – and on the benefits to be gained by Irish farmers – that policy was never really an issue as the government negotiated entry. With startling tunnel vision, the fact that Ireland was an island with extensive, if largely underexploited, marine resources was almost totally ignored by diplomats: the current difficulties within the Irish fishing industry, which should now be one of the largest in Europe if development had not been thwarted at various stages, bear testament to this.

As for specific proposals on regional and social policy these were completely ignored. Early in 1972, after the Community's Vedel Committee had reported on its findings, Senator Robinson sought the support of Foreign Minister Patrick Hillery for radical reform of the European Parliament to ensure that it had a greater legislative role. Such reform could be carried out under existing treaties before the Community's enlargement. But she was to be disappointed. With only weeks to go before accession, the Irish delegation at an EEC summit in Paris returned home in self-congratulatory mood, praising imaginative decisions and playing up the Irish emphasis on seeking a comprehensive regional policy.

Robinson was not alone in this argument. There was public debate and considerable opposition to joining the EEC on a variety of fronts. Common access to European waters had aroused great anxiety in the fishing sector, which had little political clout. The chairman and chief executive of Bord Iascaigh Mhara (the Irish Sea Fisheries Board), Brendan O'Kelly, is on record as warning the Fianna Fáil government of the consequences attached to accepting the terms then on offer from Brussels. The advantages offered to the underdeveloped Irish fleet in terms of new markets and funding for vessels and research would be outweighed by common access, he argued.

O'Kelly was acting as consultant to the Minister for Foreign Affairs and was asked to 'strengthen' Hillery's hand by echoing some of the industry's very real fears. When he did so, in the pages of a Sunday newspaper, he found himself *persona non grata* on the Irish delegation in Brussels. He was advised to take the first flight home. The terms, as rushed through the Dáil before the end of that year, aroused considerable criticism in the following months. The Labour deputy, Justin Keating, charged that the government had deliberately misled the electorate. Contrasting it with the terms secured by Norway – which did not join, but did negotiate – he said that if there was 'a scrap of honour', there should have been some resignations.[1]

There were no resignations. When the Common Fisheries Policy was agreed in 1983, a coalition government of Fine Gael and Labour – which had been in opposition at the time of accession – was no more enlightened towards the marine sector. It agreed to a system of 'equal access' to Irish waters based on historical performance of Ireland and other member states, rather than geographical proximity – rather like saying that because Irish farmers might be better grape-pickers, they should be allowed to take from French vineyards.

As the Irish delegation continued its accession work, it was slated by Senator Robinson. Addressing a meeting of the Irish Council of the European Movement in October 1972, she asked: 'Is it not astonishing that after the months of preparation, after many visits by the Foreign Minister, Paddy Hillery, to Luxembourg, to Rome, to Brussels, that the Irish delegation at the summit had no specific concrete proposal to make, but just general wishes?'

This had not helped Ireland's image as a small country joining Europe, she said. 'We allowed other countries, particularly Britain and Italy, to fight the battle for a specific regional policy and then we came home as if the trophy were truly ours. It would have been very much in Ireland's interest to urge the creation of a real democratic framework at the European level. This would have gained us real friends in the Community and also with countries like Norway who have remained outside.' (In a referendum dominated by the implications of accession for its fishing industry, Norway had decided to stay out of Europe – and would do so again in November 1994.)

'Why should the Taoiseach have *carte blanche* to decide Ireland's point of view and to take these decisions at the European level?' Mary Robinson asked. 'How weak are our internal democratic institutions that there was no democratic debate and that there was no participation in that particular decision-making?' These were pertinent questions. Decisions must be democratically debated and democratically controlled at European level, she said. 'It is vital not to see this institutional development in Europe as a diminution of national sovereignty. What is happening at the moment is that we are giving up large areas of national sovereignty without any democratic control.'[2]

She identified the challenge in an article for *The Irish Times* in January 1973, as Ireland's ten European parliamentarians took their seats for the first time in the European assembly in Strasbourg. 'The effect of joining the European Community is that certain subjects, which were previously the concern of both the national government and parliament, are transferred to the jurisdiction of the Council and Commission, the executive bodies which exercise the legislative power in the Communities,' she wrote.

The Oireachtas must determine how to define its role in relation to regulations and directives emanating from the EEC Council and Commission which might have to be translated into Irish law; and how to become aware of, and react to, policy formation and administrative practices within the Communities. Second-guessing legislative proposals in time could influence their content, she suggested. The ideal solution would be to set up a range of specialised subject committees to which proposals in the different fields of EEC activity – agriculture, transport, economic and monetary union – could be referred, similar to the system prevailing in the German Bundestag. The problem was that the Oireachtas was modelled on the Westminster parliament, and did not have any such committee specialisation.[3]

Mary Robinson returned to the subject later that year when she attacked the government for failing to provide sufficient information on draft EEC legislation, and to extend the accountability of Irish ministers on EEC decisions in which they were involved. Addressing the Cork Literary and Scientific Society in November 1973, she said there was an increasing awareness that the Community had evolved without the democratic institutions which would make it responsive to the needs of those living within the Community. It could diminish national sovereignty, she warned.

National parliaments had a vital role to play in this interim stage, as they had a much stronger democratic base in their own countries than the European Parliament had acquired at the EEC level, she went on. Therefore, parliaments would have to ensure that they asserted maximum control and influence over the decision-making at the Council of Ministers, and that they directed their efforts to secure the complementary establishment of democratic institutions and the reinforcement of the European Parliament as a real assembly with legislative power and control over the executive.

Referring to the Oireachtas joint committee on European Community Secondary Legislation, she was critical of the extent of information given on the scope and importance of such EEC laws in an Irish context. Not only would a better flow of information enable deputies and senators to assess the effect of European proposals, but Irish ministers who partici-pated in important decisions at the Council of Ministers should also be prepared to make a short statement in the Dáil, following the relevant meeting, so that there could be 'an accountability'.[4]

Mary Robinson's views not only showed remarkable foresight, but also revealed how ill-prepared Ireland still was to take its place within the EEC – a point made by the anti-EEC lobby before the membership referendum. It would not be long before she would be proved right.

The young senator faced tumultuous change, even as she took on both Europe and de Valera's Constitution publicly. She had become pregnant with her first child. Her private life, such as it was, would now take on a new dimension. She had never been one for socialising without a specific purpose. There was never much 'time out', and her husband even advised her on her wardrobe of smart, sober suits and dresses. The pregnancy and birth also helped to heal rifts with her own family after the wedding.

Speaking at a public meeting in Dublin in April 1972, she called for the removal of some offensive phrases in the 1937 Constitution, such as 'in the name of the Most Holy Trinity', and the reference in Article 6 to all powers of government, legislative, executive and judicial, deriving from the people 'under God'. An oath taken by public representatives swore to hold office 'in the presence of Almighty God', which effectively excluded some citizens. A secular constitution would be a unifying influence, she claimed.

This unifying influence, the effect on North-South relations and EEC membership came up again in two letters to *The Irish Times* that September, written with the Dublin lawyer, John Temple Lang. In the first, published on 1 September, the two lawyers supported the recent call by the North's Social Democratic and Labour Party (SDLP) for a non-denominational constitution and laws: 'The Dublin government has so far failed to show the statesmanship and leadership that the country has urgently demanded for the last three years,' the correspondents said.

> This failure to take any effective action in helping to solve the problem of Northern Ireland is in striking contrast to the vigorous campaign which was pursued in favour of the Republic's entry into the EEC. The Northern question is far more important for the economic, social, cultural and political well-being of the whole country than is the EEC.
>
> The widespread feeling that there is little that can be done in the Republic to help the Northern situation is wholly wrong, as all shades of Northern opinion agree. We can all help by insisting on an immediate referendum which will give the people of the Republic a chance to vote overwhelmingly, as we believe they would, in favour of legal changes creating a non-denominational state.

They invited everyone who was concerned about the Northern situation, and those in particular who saw the need to take an active part in the discussion about EEC entry, to join in insisting on this. On 5 September, the two lawyers welcomed the news that the government was considering arranging a referendum to remove the 'special position' of the Catholic Church from the Constitution. 'It would, however, be a major blunder if the same referendum did not also deal at least with the clause on divorce.' The purpose of removing the 'special position' clause was to prove to the North that the people of the Republic wished to have a non-denominational state, they argued.

> There is no need to draw up a whole new Constitution before making this contribution to the Northern situation. A genuine

wish for a non-denominational state will not be shown by removing a clause which has no practical effect of any kind, while retaining the divorce clause, which is of considerable practical importance. Indeed, failure to give the people a chance to remove the divorce clause will not only confirm the Dublin government's reputation for ineffectiveness, but make the Northern people suspect that future moves towards a non-denominational state would also be confined to meaningless gestures. Nothing more inclined to irritate a practical and hard-headed people could be imagined.

The same referendum could make an even greater contribution to peace and reunification if it gave people a chance to vote for a statement that they wished to see Ireland reunited only by peaceful means. 'This would be supported by an overwhelming majority of the people of the Republic, and would enormously strengthen the hand of moderates everywhere against extremists on both sides.'

It would also make 'crystal clear' that a vote to remove the divorce clause in the Constitution was not a vote in favour of divorce, the two lawyers said; further legislation would be required for that in any case. It would be a vote in favour of peace and reconciliation between Irishmen, and 'a gesture of friendship to our Northern Protestant fellow countrymen. The Irish people might not wish to vote for divorce, as such; they would certainly vote for an end to violence.'

An announcement to the effect that the autumn referendum would deal with the divorce and 'special position' clauses in the Constitution would, if made before the Northern conference, be 'the most important step towards reunification ever taken by any Irish government' and 'the greatest advance towards a solution of the troubles of the North yet made by any interested party', they said. It would go far to 'redeem the inactivity of the Dublin government over the last three years'.[5]

Perhaps it would have; once again, as with Europe, Mary Robinson was ahead of her time. Referenda to amend two articles of the Constitution – one being to lower the minimum voting age from 21 to 18, and the other (Article 44) to remove the reference to the special position of the Catholic Church and to recognise other religious denominations – were carried out on 7 December 1972. The divorce clause was not included. The turn-out of 50.7 per cent was the lowest in any referendum since the adoption of the 1937 Constitution, and the North continued its slow downward spiral into violence and despair.

On 2 October 1972 Mary gave birth to her first child – Lucy Therese – called Tessa, after her grandmother, for short. No publicity: Senator Robinson's private life was to be a private matter.

Adoption was another dimension to the senator's campaign for constitutional reform and greater civil liberty – a broad platform which would also include such issues as the rights of illegitimate children, marital breakdown, equal pay, free legal aid, and other issues relating to equality. She had become president of a single parents' organisation, Cherish, which was founded in 1972. Under the 1952 Adoption Act, couples in a marriage of mixed religions could not adopt a child. Senator Robinson, supported by Labour and Independent senators Evelyn Owens and John Horgan, proposed to change the relevant section, 12, and did manage to secure a second reading for the Bill. The government committed itself to introducing its own amending legislation, if possible before Christmas.

However, not for the first time in Senator Robinson's political career, events in the North were to intervene. In November 1972 the Fianna Fáil government introduced the Offences against the State (Amendment) Act in a drive to clamp down on IRA activity. The opposition parties had decided to fight the Bill, which provided for evidence of IRA membership on the word of a garda superintendent. During its second reading, two bombs exploded in Dublin, killing two men and injuring 127 people. The Bill was pushed through by an overwhelming 69 votes to 22 at 4 a.m. on 2 December, with most Fine Gael deputies joining their party leader, Liam Cosgrave, in abstaining.

In the Seanad later that day, Senator Robinson attempted to amend the new legislation. If deemed as emergency legislation under the Constitution, it would have to be renewed after 90 days, which would give more time for proper debate. She failed. The following month, her obvious frustration earned her another *Irish Times* headline, when she described the debate on 2 and 3 December as 'the saddest moment of the year'. It was now clear that the panic had been engineered, she told the Seanad. It was also clear less than 24 hours later that this legislation was 'not needed imminently to preserve the security of the state'.

The bulk of legislation brought before the Seanad during the past year had consisted of piecemeal measures, she said. She noted the failure of the government to amend the law on contraception, referred to government promises on the Adoption Bill; and criticised the Prisons Bill, permitting transfer of prisoners to military custody, which had been presented as 'temporary' when there was no such guarantee.

For good measure she added that the government should consider an equivalent of Britain's Equal Pay Act, and called for a survey of the many state-sponsored bodies in the country. Referring to the Seanad's relatively light workload, she lobbed a missile. 'Make no mistake about it. This House is not in the mainstream of Irish life at the moment. It is not fulfilling a role leading it to exercise democratic control over government activity or participation in the legislative process.'

Just two and a half weeks earlier, Ireland had joined the European Economic Community along with Denmark and Britain, without much ceremony. Dr Patrick Hillery was rewarded with an appointment as Commissioner for Social Affairs. On 20 January there was another brutal reminder south of the border of the Northern conflict when a car bomb exploded in Sackville Place in central Dublin, killing a 25-year-old bus conductor and injuring 13 other people.

On 5 February the 19th Dáil was dissolved and an election called for 28 February – some five weeks before the 140,000 new voters, aged between 18 and 21, were entitled to vote. The plebiscite was to return the first new government for 16 years, when Fianna Fáil, with 69 seats, lost power to a coalition of Fine Gael (54 seats) and Labour (19 seats).

The Irish Times women's page nominated Mary Robinson as Taoiseach before either the Dáil or Seanad election had taken place. Identifying the job as 'to lead' and 'not merely to respond eventually to sufficient pressure by making changes, but to introduce ideas on their own merit, to listen to arguments, to direct without dominating the programmes and policies of a progressive nation', the writer outlined why:

> Because more than any other Irish woman in public life today, she has made her mark as an intelligent, independent, courageous and determined politician. Not quite four years ago, Mary Bourke was an unknown barrister from Ballina, a pretty young thing with a first-class degree from Trinity College, Dublin, and a brilliant academic record from Trinity through Harvard University. Her election to the Seanad surprised everyone, including herself. She could easily have settled in for a pleasant four years in the Leinster House debating club, at a comfortable bonus of £1,500 a year in salary.
>
> But Ireland's youngest senator has instead stirred up a steady whirlwind. In 1970 she led the protest against the Seanad's long holidays during a period of national crisis; six months after her election she said she was disappointed with the Seanad, that parliament was becoming irrelevant. In 1971 she demanded to know why the recommendation on divorce of the Dáil constitutional committee hadn't been acted upon, and introduced a Private Members' Bill to legalise the sale of contraceptives. In 1972 she virtually forced the government to agreeing to amend the present inadequate adoption laws, by putting forward her own Bill once again.
>
> She was perhaps the most concise and constructive critic of Ireland's negotiations with the EEC after her appointment to the Community's Legal Committee, and fought steadily and skilfully

against the Prisons Bill, the Forcible Entry Bill, and the Offences against the State Amendment Bill. Last month in the Seanad, she once again criticised the Seanad itself for not accomplishing enough work to justify its existence, saying 'the Oireachtas is fast rendering itself redundant, and we have now reached the stage where the policy-making and thinking is taking place elsewhere'.

In a little over three years, she had made more impact on Irish life than virtually anyone in Dáil Eireann . . .[6]

She wouldn't be taoiseach. For that, she would have to be elected to the Dáil. However, in the Seanad elections of May, she topped the Dublin University poll against stiff enough competition from nine other candidates, and was elected on the first count, with 1,472 first-preference votes. Second to her in terms of first preferences was Dr Noel Browne, the former Labour deputy and minister, who was also elected on a Dublin University ticket, while her old election agent, Dr Trevor West, regained the third seat in the TCD constituency. Dr Browne had decided not to contest the Dáil election after he had declined to follow the other members of the parliamentary Labour Party into signing a coalition government's pre-election statement of intent.

Sadly, Tessa Bourke had died suddenly while on a visit to Dublin following the birth of another grandchild. She had a history of thyroid trouble before her final collapse.

Very quickly, the new and apparently more socially liberal administration would find itself in the midst of a continuing contraception debate – continuing as a result of a 'new mood of questioning' which marked the early 1970s in the Republic, according to the historian Professor J.J. Lee. On the one hand, the 'stormy petrel' of the new administration, the former writer and diplomat-turned-Labour Minister for Posts and Telegraphs, Dr Conor Cruise O'Brien, was denouncing nationalist 'self-delusion' about a united Ireland in the face of events in the North. He introduced legislation designed to curb IRA access to state television and radio. On the other hand, largely through the influence of Senator Robinson and supporters, the Constitution itself was under scrutiny.

This new attitude marked 'the biggest single change in the nationalist response to the Ulster question in the 1970s', Professor Lee has judged.[7] 'Nationalist Ireland had steadfastly refused to contemplate the implications for Protestants of a Catholic parliament for a Catholic people. Some were now prepared to begin seriously considering the question.'

The Fine Gael Taoiseach, Liam Cosgrave, was not within these ranks, however, as the contraception issue would prove in July 1974, when he voted against his own administration's Bill as a matter of conscience. In the meantime, Senator Robinson was called to the Inner Bar of the Middle Temple in London in July 1973, while her brother Henry, who had started off his married life in the basement flat of 'Wilde House', the family's Dublin home in 21 Westland Row, was also called to the bar of the Middle Temple. In October the political correspondent of *The Irish Times*, Dick Walsh, reported that Mary Robinson was preparing another attempt to change the Republic's anti-contraception laws. The proposed Bill was designed to facilitate family planning by legalising contraceptives dispensed under regulations to be set out by the Minister for Health. The Minister would retain control of the advertising of contraceptive methods, and contraceptives would become available in chemists' shops and in hospitals, while certain others would be available on prescription only.

The government appeared to have four choices now, Walsh declared. 'It could oppose it, which would produce an unpopular reaction from increasingly powerful pressure groups and the Labour Party's vocal left wing; or it could delay discussion until the result of a Supreme Court hearing on the constitutionality of the present law is known; it could support Mrs Robinson's proposal, therefore making its passage a certainty in a strict party vote; or it could ask her to withdraw in favour of a government-sponsored measure, of which there have been some hints at least.'

The government's reaction was too early to call, Walsh noted, but support had been canvassed. 'In view of current conciliatory attitudes to Northern Ireland, outright rejection of the measure would be an embarrassment.' However, the Bill's appeal was to the Republic's citizens, rather than to Northern Protestant opinion.

'Mrs Robinson's attack on this occasion seems to differ significantly from other efforts to change the anti-contraception laws,' Dick Walsh observed. 'Her proposals imply that responsibility for change rests with the Minister for Health rather than the Minister for Justice. She believes that contraception should not have been allowed to remain so long in the area of criminal law.'

Specifically, this Bill would amend two laws: section 17 of the 1935 Criminal Law (Amendment) Act which she had sought to change before, and also the Censorship Provisions of 1939 and 1946, which governed the advertising of contraceptive methods. The last attempt to change both had been made in 1971, Walsh recalled – not just by Mrs Robinson in the Seanad, but also by Dr Noel Browne and Dr John O'Connell in the Dáil. Both Houses had refused to grant a reading, but 'Mrs Robinson hopes that official reaction, as well as public opinion, have changed since then.'[8]

Public opinion was one element in the equation. The Catholic hierarchy was another. In spite of her optimism that the hierarchy would not oppose the new contraceptive Bill drafted by her in 1973, the senator was confronted with a bishops' statement in November reiterating the moral wrongs of contraception. The statement did concede that the law was a matter for the legislature, a significant step forward for the time.

It was a concession which the senator seized upon. Stressing that the debate on the proposed changes in the law should not be regarded as an issue involving a Church-State confrontation, she issued a statement on 27 November which endorsed the bishops' view that the full legislative responsibility lay with members of the Oireachtas.

Her five-point statement also agreed that there was a moral duty on legislators to weigh all the relevant factors conscientiously and impartially for the common good, and agreed that the basic issue was quality of life in the Republic. However, there should be the guarantee that the laws of the state would not impinge unnecessarily on the liberty of the individual to exercise freedom of conscience and make private moral choices. It was the duty of legislators to ensure that there were proper safeguards and controls to prevent abuse and exploitation, she said, but she noted that Ireland was the only EEC member state to use its criminal law to prohibit the availability of contraceptives.

> It is not a question of 'the actual degree of inconvenience which the present law and practice causes to people of other religious persuasions', but rather a question of whether it is tolerable, in terms of life in the Republic, that the laws of the state should taint with criminality, and describe as criminal offences, matters which a minority of citizens – not necessarily a religious minority – regard as morally justified and their own personal concern.

And 'we should be slow to condemn standards of morality' in other EEC member states, she added. 'Indeed, the jurisdiction to which we can look with most relevance is Northern Ireland, where there has been no suggestion of the breakdown of family life or the disintegration of public morality.'[9]

Not so in the view of Cardinal Conway, Archbishop of Armagh and Primate of All Ireland. In an interview on RTE Radio, he underlined the Catholic Church's view on the Bill, and offered Northern Ireland as an example of a state in which the quality of life had been changed for the worse by the free availability of contraceptive devices.

The cardinal's view was not shared by the leader of the North's SDLP, representing middle-class Catholic opinion. The SDLP leader, Gerry Fitt, who took part in the same radio programme, insisted that in a united Ireland the conscience of the Protestant people, who did not accept the dogmatic Catholic view of contraception, should be taken into account.

Reporting on the debate before the second stage of the Bill was due to be taken in the new year in the Seanad, Dick Walsh noted that the campaign against Mrs Robinson's family-planning Bill was gaining momentum, having been fired up by the statement from the Catholic hierarchy. Deputies and senators had received hundreds of letters that week, he said, insisting that they did not have a mandate to vote in favour of changing the law. Significantly, the coalition government had decided that there should be a free vote without a party whip, but Fianna Fáil had yet to choose its formal stance as main opposition party.

Mrs Robinson, heavily pregnant with her second child, had received a considerable volume of correspondence herself. She had told Walsh that she was receiving hundreds of notices of support in a proportion of 'five to one'. The supporting letters, she said, had come mostly from women who were married, almost all of whom had signed their names and said that they did not object to their opinions being quoted. In contrast, opponents – she suspected most of them were men – signed their letters with pseudonyms.[10]

In fact, the bishops' statement was to have less impact on Senator Robinson than on the government as a whole, coming at a crucial time in Northern Irish politics. It would also prove difficult for her family in Ballina; her deeply religious parents attended Mass regularly across the river.

'I wasn't happy. Anything but happy,' her father said, 25 years later. 'But it didn't make any difference. Not an inch, she went her own way. Not that we wouldn't have a good row about it when it went beyond the beyond – the condoms train, for instance. It was difficult. We were pillars of the church here! But my sister Ivy, who was in India for all this, came back and said that Mary was absolutely right. Like my father, she had a wonderful mind and had worked with mixed religions. She had grown up, faced the world, and approved of what Mary was doing 100 per cent. You see, we were never anti-Protestant; our whole family on both sides was studded with mixed marriages. There was very little sectarianism here in this area.'[11]

In December 1973 the Sunningdale Conference between the British and Irish governments and the three main political parties in the North agreed to set up a power-sharing executive. Significantly, the initiative would also write in an 'Irish dimension' to the Northern conflict. What-ever the bishops' position on contraception, a statement like this, coming at such a moment, would do nothing in the eyes of Northern Protestants to improve the Dublin government's image as an arm of the Catholic Church.

In the event, the proposed formal conference to ratify the Sunningdale declaration was never held. In May 1974 the existing Northern Ireland

Executive collapsed in the face of an Ulster Workers' Council loyalist strike.[12] However, on 19 December 1973, the Irish government's decision on contraception was effectively forced by a ruling from the Supreme Court in favour of a County Dublin mother-of-four, Mrs Mary McGee. Having been fitted with a diaphragm on medical advice, Mrs McGee had ordered spermicidal jelly when her own supply ran out. The delivery was stopped by Customs, under the contentious section 17 of the 1935 Criminal Law (Amendment) Act. The Supreme Court ruling declared the ban on importation of contraceptives under the 1935 Act to be unconstitutional on the grounds of privacy of the family and marriage.

On 13 February 1974 the government announced that it had decided to introduce a contraception Bill, based on the Supreme Court decision, and intended to allow a free vote. It was 24 hours after what *The Irish Times* described as a 'day of confusion and some bitterness' during which a motion to debate the second stage of Senator Robinson's Bill was defeated in the Seanad by 43 votes to 5.

The government had given Mrs Robinson a guarantee that a Bill would be introduced in the current session of parliament before the Seanad sitting of 13 February. Though her Bill had been tabled for a second reading, it was not called in the Order of Business by the leader of the Seanad, Michael O'Higgins. In the confusion, James Downey, another *Irish Times* political correspondent, noted considerable failures of communication, with O'Higgins referring to 'the recent announcement' on the government's proposals (there had been none) and anticipation of an announcement in the Seanad.

Senator Robinson earned the Labour Party's support for what its secretary and senator, Brendan Halligan, described as her 'reasonable request' that there be an early second reading debate, perhaps to be adjourned without a vote. She said she did not propose to move an amendment to the Order of Business, following the government's decision. However, a motion to have the Bill debated was moved by Noel Browne.

In a speech during which he was reported as clashing several times with the chair, Dr Browne quoted the poet W.B. Yeats – 'You have disgraced yourselves again' – and referred to 'poltroons'. The government's attitude was 'confirming Northern Ireland loyalists in their "justified beliefs" in Rome rule,' Dr Browne said.

Mrs Robinson, with 'apparent reluctance', seconded Dr Browne's motion. Three other independent senators, John Horgan, Trevor West and Dr Augustine Martin of the National University of Ireland joined the pair in the division lobby. After the vote, the newspaper reported, Dr Browne called out: 'Belfast papers, please copy.'

The affair was followed by what Downey described as 'widespread angry feelings – in several directions'. There were visible signs of strain between the two coalition parties, and between the government and the Seanad leader: 'Some Labour senators were incensed at being obliged to vote against holding a debate – and therefore against their own convictions.' Some of the government's anger was directed at that *enfant terrible*, the outspoken Noel Browne, whose action in forcing a vote, and whose references to Northern Ireland, were considered by ministers to be 'untimely in a high degree'. However, supporters of the Robinson Bill said that the government had only itself to blame, by delaying a decision for too long, and by allowing confusion to grow about its intentions, according to Downey.

The guarantee given to Robinson was of little value, in their view, since it involved a Bill the terms of which were unknown, and a free vote with the result extremely uncertain. The supporters warned that they would press very firmly the demand for discussion of the Bill on the next sitting day, and were prepared to obstruct government business in the Seanad.

It appeared that no official discussions had been held with Fianna Fáil with a view to facilitating the passage of the government's legislation. 'Ministers, justifying the possibility of restrictive provisions in the Bill, say that the defeat of a Bill to legalise contraception would be disastrous for North-South relations,' Downey wrote. 'But supporters of the Robinson Bill retort that the kind of restrictions which seem to be contemplated may turn out to be unenforceable and indeed unconstitutional.'[13]

The debate on the second stage of Mrs Robinson's Bill was resumed in late March, amid criticism from the opposition leader in the Seanad, Brian Lenihan, who described the step as 'nonsensical'. There was speculation that it was calculated to 'clear the decks' for the government's own legislation, which seemed unlikely to have a second reading in the Dáil before Easter.

Amid continuing in-party and inter-party divisions, *The Irish Times* noted that the opposition's position was complex. A number of members of the Fianna Fáil front bench were strongly in favour of legalising the sale of contraceptives, and took the view that any mooted government restrictions on sale would be 'insane', while recognising that many of their colleagues, particularly the rural deputies, were opposed to contraception in principle, or because they had been frightened by an 'intense anti-contraception letter-writing campaign'. Inevitably, the newspaper reported, 'a temptation exists for any opposition which smells an issue which could bring down a government . . .'[14]

On 27 March, the Seanad finally refused a second reading of the Robinson Bill. On 16 July the Taoiseach, Liam Cosgrave, led six of his Fine

Gael deputies into the opposition lobby and so helped to defeat his own government's Bill for the Control of the Importation, Sale and Manufacture of Contraceptives, by 75 votes to 61. Cosgrave had given no prior warning to his cabinet. His move was to be a 'nine-day wonder', according to Professor J.J. Lee. 'But it did emphatically underline' his 'personal distaste for the type of legislation that would appear to be necessary if a united Ireland were to emerge by agreement in the foreseeable future', Lee has said.[15]

Two months earlier, on 13 May, another dent had been knocked in the Catholic Church's hold on the Constitution when a young Dublin couple succeeded in their High Court action to have declared unconstitutional a section of the Adoption Act of 1952. The section had prohibited them from adopting the wife's illegitimate son because his religion differed from that of his mother.

Somehow in the middle of all this activity, Senator Mary Robinson had her second child, William. It seemed like a ten-month pregnancy, because she hadn't been sure when he was due. Legal cases were taken selectively, to ease the triple burden of a Seanad career, lecturing in Trinity College and travelling to Europe, and her legal practice.

Ann Lane, ever loyal and now her secretary, was the linchpin in the office, regularly staying up till the early hours of the morning to catch a disappearing deadline. Often she was also the babysitter at home in Wellington Place. Nanny Coyne would be wooed back from England (where she had gone to work after the Bourkes had finished college) to help with domestic duties.

CHAPTER 7

It Will Be Hard to Stop Her

The report was brief and to the point. Mrs Mary Robinson – 'an independent senator who has at times severely criticised the Government and who yesterday voted against the state of emergency' – had joined the Labour Party, *The Irish Times* recorded on 2 September 1976. So began a tumultuous career in party politics which was to run for a decade, with repercussions extending into the presidency.

But then the mid-1970s were convulsive years. Picture this Ireland: an island looking to Europe through its recent affiliation to the EEC; an island of young people fed up with jaded civil war politics, and with the suffocating influence of the Catholic Church on social legislation. Women, in particular, were emerging out of the darkness. In January 1976, women were summoned for their first jury service in the state's history. The location was a circuit court in Trim, a small town in County Meath. Though the cases before the court that morning did not require a jury, they were told by the judge that they had, indeed, made history.

Ireland had joined the EEC for economic reasons, but its membership was to have a profound impact on social legislation. In March 1976 the Community rejected the Irish government's application to be excused from introducing equal pay. The application was also vigorously opposed by women's groups and by the trade unions. And the battle lines had been drawn between the Catholic Church and those groups seeking social change over the right to contraception – the charge beginning with the women on the so-called 'contraceptive train' from Dublin to Belfast and back in May 1971.

A protracted public inquiry in May 1976 over the siting of an oil refinery in Dublin Bay was the first hint of a new environmental movement, as was the frequency with which conservation issues cropped up on the letters page of *The Irish Times* – a fairly accurate barometer of liberal middle-class concern.

Then there was the issue of Northern Ireland, which in August 1969 had exploded onto the pages of newspapers and television screens around the world in a way few commentators had imagined possible. In March 1976 Liam Cosgrave went to Washington and made an appeal to both houses of the US Congress, in which he asked Americans not to give financial aid to the Provisional Irish Republican Army. The following month the names of innocent victims of the Northern conflict were read out during a peace vigil in St Anne's Cathedral, Belfast. There were 1,289 names on the list, and the reading took four hours.

The bombings and shootings continued in the six Northern counties and from time to time the conflict touched the South. On 21 July the British ambassador to Ireland, Christopher Ewart-Biggs, and Judith Cooke, a senior British civil servant in the Northern Ireland Office, were killed when a bomb exploded under their embassy car near the official residence in Sandyford, County Dublin. The massive explosion left a huge crater in the road. The ambassador had been formally presented to the President of the Republic, Cearbhall Ó Dálaigh, just two weeks before.

As a new popular peace movement in Belfast began to gain international attention, the response in the Republic was to declare a state of emergency. This move was to pose a dilemma for the aspiring public representative, Mary Robinson. At the time, the government still comprised a coalition, formed after the 1973 general election, between the Fine Gael and Labour parties.

Like other western European countries, Ireland's political system reflects a rainbow of political views. Fianna Fáil and Fine Gael, the two largest parties, reflect centre-right opinion and differ only in detail (one of the most important being which side their supporters fought on during the 1922–23 civil war over the independence treaty signed with the British government). Labour, the junior partner in the 1973–77 coalition, had shed many skins since its foundation by two leading socialists and trade unionists, James Larkin and James Connolly, in 1912. Connolly's legacy was an especially emotive one, since his was the senior voice in the 1916 Rising against British rule. Sitting in a chair as a result of gunshot wounds he had sustained in that short and fervent battle, Connolly was executed in 1916 along with 14 compatriots by a British firing squad.

Labour served as the main opposition party in the early years of the state and helped Fianna Fáil into power in 1932. The two parties were perceived by some as natural allies, partly due to Fianna Fáil's populist appeal and partly because of Labour's dual, and somewhat confused, identity. There were complex historical reasons for this. In the years immediately after the 1916 Rising, an expanding Irish Transport and General Workers' Union was channelling industrial unrest into support for the nationalist cause. But, by 1921, members of the pro-independence party, Sinn Féin, felt that 'the cause of Labour was threatening . . . to displace that of the Republic'.[1]

Labour's electoral strength tended to rise and fall with the vicissitudes of the economy. In 1943, when the economic effects of the Second World War were being fully felt, it had seemed set to become a major party again. In what some describe as typical Irish fashion – although it is, of course, universal – the party rose to the challenge by 'tearing itself apart in an internecine struggle' and continued to be riven by splits for the next twenty years.[2]

By the 1970s, the uneasy amalgam of ardent socialists and doughty old trade union activists was coming under the influence of a new generation of trade union leaders who had graduated from student politics, and who demanded a more professional approach to party activity. One of this new breed was the party's general secretary, Brendan Halligan, a Dubliner who went to university comparatively late, obtaining a first-class degree in economics from UCD. He was on the look-out for 'names' to attract new voters.

Mary Robinson's was one of those that came up. Halligan is credited with introducing the young independent senator to senior party figures in 1976. She had struck him as a natural recruit because of her identification with civil liberties in the Seanad.[3] Her name was already synonymous with issues of social justice. There were her attempts in the Seanad to legalise contraception. Further Bills on family planning, on adoption, on illegitimate children were to follow. In April 1974 she questioned the continuing willingness to allow Victorian statutes to be the basic framework of the Irish criminal code. Why did the country still uphold an 'antiquated and anomalous' classification of crimes into felonies and misdemeanours, which had been abolished in other common-law jurisdictions years ago, she asked at a Publicity Club of Ireland lunch in Dublin.

'Who is to blame – the lawyers? The successive Ministers for Justice?' she asked, when she called for the establishment of a commission on law reform. 'The members of the Oireachtas down the years? Or the ordinary citizens of this country, for not having insisted on just and equitable laws which promote and foster social justice?'[4]

In May 1974, during a penetrating analysis of the civil libertarian aspect (or lack of it) associated with the Republic's response to the Northern troubles, she criticised the erosion of the right to trial by jury in the Special Criminal Court, and called for an independent inquiry into allegations that the court had tried people who had no connection with any unlawful organisation or subversive group. She was also sharply critical of that section of the Offences against the State Act which dealt with forfeiture and disqualifications on certain convictions by the Special

Court, and referred to a blacklist compiled by the Department of Justice of names, addresses and occupations of persons, and their date of conviction in the Special Criminal Court.

There had been no denial by the Minister for Justice of the existence of such a list – dated 11 January 1974 and leaked – but rather there had been an attempt to justify it. As had been pointed out in the influential current affairs magazine, *Hibernia*, the name of one person, with his address and employment, described him as having been convicted on 21 May 1973, although he was in fact acquitted. Mary Robinson was convinced that the list contained further inaccuracies.[5] Over two decades later, a legal challenge to this court's existence was dismissed in both the High Court and Supreme Court. The challenge by a man charged with the kidnapping of a banker was based on the government's proclamation in May 1972 that the Special Criminal Court should deal with subversive offences arising out of the Northern Ireland crisis, and was never intended to deal with 'ordinary crime'. Only the government could take the decision to abolish it now, or force it to confine itself to subversive offences, the judge ruled; its continued existence, in spite of protests by civil liberties groups, was a political matter.

She was rarely out of headlines in 1974 – on civil liberties, on the need for overall legal reform and on Northern Ireland. Addressing the Royal Institute of International Affairs in London on 2 July 1974, she reflected on the fall of the Sunningdale agreement on power-sharing in the North. It had not catered sufficiently for the Protestant majority, while giving the Republic most of what it wanted; now that it had collapsed, Dublin could take no initiative. There was a danger that the Northern majority would do so – unless Britain intervened.

In her view, two issues required immediate attention. The military, political and economic consequences in the event of a military, political and economic withdrawal from the North by Britain had to be examined frankly. Secondly, the people of Northern Ireland must be afforded the dignity of life without fear. Too many politicians tended to spend too much time with speeches unrelated to the private lives of the people.

It was a theme to which she would return time and again over two decades. Referring to a debate in the Dáil the week before, she said that it was evident that there was the ability to place the problem in an economic or political context broader than just the North or South. By creating a Protestant enclave, those people who were displaced were exported. There was no tradition of them moving south of the border.[6]

Answering questions after the address to the Royal Institute, the senator took issue with legal advice to the government that there could be no extradition from the Republic to Northern Ireland in relation to charges of paramilitary activity. She believed that it was possible in Irish constitutional terms to extradite for terrorist offences and not for political offences.

'A confused and confusing alliance between militarist Republicans and a certain kind of Irish liberal.' This was how the Labour Minister for Posts and Telegraphs, Dr Conor Cruise O'Brien, who had supported her in her Seanad election campaigns, described her public stance, and her condemnation of the introduction of internment without trial as a method of curbing paramilitary activity in the North. 'Hibernia liberals' was a term used by the minister, who was responsible for applying the controversial section 31 of the 1960 Broadcasting Act – designed to ban access to the airwaves by spokespersons of certain organisations. Mrs Robinson had been critical of the section, which was not actually invoked until October 1971 by Fianna Fáil minister Gerry Collins, and had announced her intention in late 1974 to put down a motion on it in the Seanad.

Interviewed on RTE radio's This Week programme on 27 October 1974, she expressed resentment at these attempts at censorship. She had voiced her views as an independent senator and professor of law, she said. Asked about Dr O'Brien's suggestion that Irish liberals could, without realising it, be helping the IRA, she said that in 'a particular time of difficulty in a country . . . there will be an attempt to censor views which do not correspond in every particular with a ministerial view . . . I am not saying that Dr O'Brien is not entitled to criticise – he is particularly entitled to criticise me because he is a constituent of Dublin University – but he was using the weight of his office, the guaranteed publicity, speaking as a minister, to smear the liberal voice as having been in deliberate alliance with activists.' There was a great danger in this, she said. 'We need a strong, liberal voice and more parliamentary control in the true sense over the activities of Irish life.'

Dr O'Brien had even accused her of not condemning the killing of judges in the North. 'That is a very slanted point of view,' she replied on radio. 'Does he really think that I condone the killing of those judges? He said I had attacked the integrity of judges. In fact, I condemned the collective silence of the legal profession, including the judiciary, at the operation of internment. They operate side by side with a system which undermines the legal process and is a fatal flaw in bringing up a society, creating confidence and building in an alienated minority truth and faith in the system.'[7]

Dr O'Brien had not been present at the meeting condemning internment the previous week. However, he was critical of Senator Robinson's presence on the Mansion House platform, and had read all the reports, he said. Speaking three days later in Dublin, he said that there was a need for 'liberals who really know what liberalism is all about'. There was considerable confusion in the Republic about what attitude liberals should take to a situation in which the democratic state was 'challenged by an armed military conspiracy', he said. 'There are those, claiming to be liberals, who greet with angry protests every response of the state to the conspiracy and who refuse to recognise the existence of such a conspiracy as a genuine threat to democracy and freedom. That is a travesty of liberalism,' Dr O'Brien's script said. 'That is dancing to the tune of the IRA.'

He was referring to Senator Robinson, a 'lady of considerable ability and style who has fought with courage and effect for at least one important and genuinely liberal cause'. The Mansion House proceedings were in his view, however, so 'profoundly illiberal' as to cast scorn, not on any given political party or on government, but on the 'central institution of democracy, parliament itself', he said.[8]

The Irish Times came to the senator's defence. An editorial noted that Dr O'Brien's misinterpretation of her role at the anti-internment meeting and his 'generalised smears' contributed to creating 'just the climate of confusion' which the minister had said he abhorred. 'Reading Dr O'Brien's weekend speech attentively, it is not hard to see in it tendencies which, given the right mood of hysteria, could lead to the introduction of more far-reaching restrictions on individual liberties than are necessary to restrain violence – or indeed, than are capable of holding violence in check. Because, whether Dr O'Brien likes it or not, there comes a point at which public opinion will not accept that the remedy is appropriate, but finds itself swayed, not towards a more democratic government, but towards sympathy with the disrupters. One does not need to be a "fake liberal", to use Dr O'Brien's strangely reminiscent terminology, to question legislative proposals,' the newspaper continued. 'Has Dr O'Brien got a word to say, when he attacks the media and Senator Robinson, about politicians whose contribution to the debate on the murder campaign is silence? There are ministers who have not spoken out; there are back-benchers of every political party who have kept their counsel. If the climate is one of confusion, it is because there has been a lack of moral leadership from the source from which the people have every right to expect a lead – the members of the Dáil and Seanad. Does Dr O'Brien speak for the government? He can hardly expect anyone to take his speech seriously if it does not represent government policy and does not set out details of the sort of legislation which he considers necessary. Without such precision, he is only introducing new elements of division into the situation.'[9]

The minister and senator would be given further opportunity to define their views of liberalism in a fascinating and often heated half-hour broadcast on RTE's *Here and Now* radio programme on 29 October. Dr O'Brien drew on the example of New York, where, he said, the freedom of the individual was much less threatened by central government than it was by the Mafia. Senator Robinson said that she would place much less emphasis on reassuring the establishment, and more on reassuring the independent voice. Liberalism was the voice of dissent, especially when that entailed essential human rights. The US president, Woodrow Wilson, had noted back in 1912 that liberty never came from the government, but always originated with the subjects of it, she commented. He had said that the history of liberty was the history of resistance.

Senator Robinson was 'singularly unfortunate' in choosing Woodrow Wilson as a champion of liberalism, O'Brien countered. 'Woodrow Wilson was a man who defended the peculiar institutions of the American South, including total disenfranchisement of black and coloured people,' he said. 'I don't accept him as even a liberal, let alone the liberal voice.'

He accused his opponent of fomenting 'establishment baiting', a charge which she rejected. Nor was she proclaiming herself as a fan of Woodrow Wilson, but that single, small quotation did confirm that liberty did not come from government but from a 'constant monitoring, a constant argument for restraints of government control'. She had performed a role as a liberal in studying the Special Criminal Court and in pointing out the encroachments on liberty there.

'Your school of liberalism is very vigilant to threats coming from parliament,' Dr O'Brien responded. 'You are so vigilant in that quarter that you don't notice other things creeping up behind from other quarters.' He described a meeting with two delegates from border areas at the recent Labour Party conference in Galway. They had told him that they would like to support his tabled amendment, condemning the IRA, but both feared reprisals against their homes and families. 'Their freedom of speech was quietly snuffed out by a threat,' he said.

Sure, those sorts of threats existed, the senator said. She could never be accused of a flirtation with the Republican movement, and emphasised that there had to be a 'liberal oversight' in times of crisis. However, no government should be allowed to cut corners.

All right: the senator's form of liberalism was 'useful', the minister acknowledged, but was too narrowly focused in one direction. She had 'made some mistakes' in carrying her form of liberalism into the Mansion House meeting, he claimed. 'I think she was discussing internment without trial before an audience which included considerable numbers who were in favour of the IRA. She should have identified that campaign as a threat to freedom. She doesn't appear to have done that, but she can correct me if I am wrong,' he conceded. He referred to the intimidation of juries and the recent murders of the judge and resident magistrate in Belfast. 'By omitting these things – I am not saying her views are radically different from my own – she showed the weakness that is inherent in her single-centred anti-establishment version of liberals.'

Senator Robinson replied that she had spoken early on in the Mansion House meeting, and had been introduced as a lawyer. Not enough lawyers had spoken out against internment, she said. She had made it very clear that she saw difficulties in the jury system. Things were also said from the platform from which she had no difficulty in dissociating herself. One taunt in particular about parliament being a 'British establishment' was a 'hoary old chestnut', she said. 'The danger is that from now on I will have to exercise a self-censorship,' she said. 'Am I going to have to watch myself? I accept that a liberal can be a dupe. The freedom to choose the platforms on which I speak is something I will have to watch carefully.' But in her view Dr O'Brien was in danger of abusing the weight of his ministerial office. And she could sense in herself 'a feeling of having been censored and rapped and it will take an extra piece of courage next time'.

'If she feels cramped as a result of my criticisms, it is not because I am a terrifying individual as Minister for Posts and Telegraphs,' Dr O'Brien responded. 'It is because she internally recognises that there is a certain amount of force in my argument.'[10]

Equality, the EEC and the potential of law as an instrument for social change were constant themes in Mary Robinson's speeches throughout 1974 and 1975. Yet in December 1974 *The Irish Times* reported that her voice had been added to the growing number of women's organisations objecting to the composition and terms of reference of the government's proposed new Women's Representative Committee. It had confused two quite separate issues, in her view – an equal pay review committee and the broader area covered by recommendations in the Report on the Status of Women.[11]

'I think the Women's Lib movement is a too radical fringe,' she qualified in the religious magazine, *The Word*, which described her as 'Ireland's best-known woman politician'.[12] 'I don't believe in suffragette-type activity,' she was quoted as saying.

Since first elected as a senator for Dublin University, she had introduced five separate private members' Bills on adoption, illegitimate children and family planning; but, the magazine noted, she accepted the right and duty of the Catholic Church to teach and guide – a view reflecting, perhaps, the steadying influence of her fellow Mayo traveller in the area of civil liberties, the Maynooth University moral theologian, Professor Enda McDonagh.

At the same time, *The Belfast Telegraph* was noting that she was 'very much aware' of the discrimination suffered by women, both in Ireland and elsewhere. On a visit to Tokyo in June 1975, she had discovered that

International Women's Year did not seem to have hit Japan. Though it might have a role in raising awareness, the year was also 'one of the greatest bores of all time', she told journalist Betty Lowry, when she was interviewed before an annual dinner of the Women Graduates' Association of Queen's University, Belfast. 'Speaking as a woman in politics, the sooner the year is over the better,' she said. 'I've been trapped into speaking only on what are wrongly designated as women's topics. I think the mistake of the International Women's Year is to reflect the awareness of women in such a narrow way.' The greatest family problem was the economic dependence of women, she judged. 'All family problems spring from that root.'

The interview noted that she had been in Tokyo for a meeting of a little-known body called the Trilateral Commission, on whose executive committee she represented Ireland. The commission, comprising politicians, academics, journalists, businessmen and trade unionists from North America, Europe and Japan, was a 'right-wing' think-tank, whose influence varied depending on whom one talked to at the time.[13]

Mary Robinson had been 'recruited' on the international conference circuit. It seemed an exciting prospect: she was still revelling in the influence of Harvard and the Kennedy 'Camelot' era. Among the fifty-odd commissioners of the body, formed in 1973 by 'concerned citizens in western Europe, Japan and North America to foster closer co-operation and public understanding on common problems in these regions' were top executives from Coca-Cola, the Wells Fargo Bank, the Bendix Corporation, Harvard, Yale, *Time*, the Caterpillar Tractor Company, Hewlett–Packard, the Chase Manhattan Bank, the Bank of America, the Georgetown Centre for Strategic Studies, Rolls-Royce, Courtaulds, Dunlop Holdings, General Electric, Rio Tinto Zinc, Barclays Bank and British Steel. There were voices from the US House of Representatives and the Senate, the British House of Commons and House of Lords, strategists like former US Secretary of State Henry Kissinger and former NATO chief Lord Carrington, as well as business magnates like David Rockefeller.

Senator Robinson was instrumental in setting up an Irish branch and recruiting members of all political affiliations, such as the future Fine Gael leader, Dr Garret FitzGerald, the Mayo Fine Gael senator, Myles Staunton, Labour deputy Barry Desmond, Fianna Fáil deputies Michael O'Kennedy and Dr Michael Woods, senior civil servant and economist Dr T.K. Whitaker, university lecturer Dr Freddie Boland, civil service union representative Dan Murphy, and the managing director of the Industrial Development Authority, Michael Killeen. It was no masons' secret society. The assistant general secretary of the Irish Congress of Trade Unions, Donal Nevin, was invited to join but declined. Editors of daily newspapers and the radical periodical, *Hibernia*, were invited to lunch in Dublin's

The 'new look' Mary Robinson for the 1990 presidential election campaign. Aisling Eyre was the make-up artist

OPPOSITE: *Sweet victory: Robinson acknowledges applause at the RDS count centre, Dublin, November 1990, when she was declared president-elect. Behind her are Labour Party leader Dick Spring, Taoiseach and Fianna Fáil leader Charles Haughey, Wicklow TD Liam Kavanagh, and defeated Fianna Fáil presidential candidate and former Defence Minister Brian Lenihan* (Irish Times); INSET: *with Spring and Haughey;* ABOVE: *A victorious Mary Robinson is congratulated by Brian Lenihan after the election count*

The president-elect is welcomed home to Ballina, County Mayo, in November 1990 (Eric Luke, Irish Times)

The Bourke and Robinson clans celebrate victory in Mayo in 1990. (Back row) Elizabeth Bourke, Tessa Robinson, Fiona Kerins, Mark Bourke, James Bourke. (Middle row) Frank Kerins, Pamela Kerins, Catherine Bourke, Nicholas Robinson, Aubrey Robinson, Mary Robinson, Dr Aubrey Bourke, Ruth Bourke, Adrian Bourke. (Front row) Charles Bourke, Rebecca Bourke, Richard Bourke, Jane Bourke, Simon Bourke, Robert Bourke (Private Collection)

Two faithful supporters: Ruairí Quinn (LEFT) directed Mary Robinson's presidential campaign and went on to become Minister of Finance in the 1994–97 coalition government; and Ann Lane, Mary Robinson's secretary for 28 years, with the President and Nicholas Robinson in her home town of Millstreet, County Cork, in December 1995 (Denis Minihane, The Examiner)

With her father, Dr Aubrey Bourke (Irish Times)

Presidential inauguration day, O'Connell Street, Dublin, December 1990 (Irish Times)

Hibernian Hotel on 1 October 1974 for a briefing. One was later to describe the organisation as a 'shadowy think-tank'.

Financial support was sought from the banks, with the senator writing personally in many cases. At one point, in 1975, she was informed by the Commission that its letterhead should not be used for anything like solicitation of funds, under the US law for such institutions. Many of the branch meetings would take place in Senator Robinson's legal practice, 27 Merrion Square. Various studies produced by the Commission were sent to other politicians, both in and out of government, including Labour members of the 1973–77 Fine Gael-Labour coalition. The Irish Council of the European Movement agreed to an 'informal' link. The senator's participation at this stage was to haunt her later on.

Haunting the Irish government, meanwhile, was the fall-out from the legal challenge Senator Robinson had pursued to allow women to sit on juries. Observers had noticed the signs of a new political shrewdness. She proposed that the Seanad establish specialist committees to take fuller advantage of its vocational character; she urged women to make more use of litigation in their campaign for equality, and suggested several instances of discrimination which could, and should in her view, be challenged in the courts.

Delivering a radio lecture in 1975 on women and the new Irish state, she reflected on the 'absurdity' of this very title. Did it not highlight the absence of women as a significant force, their non-participation? Her language was not strident – she didn't want to be labelled an ardent feminist. But she did point out that the specific role of women in the Constitution, and subsequent legislation like the 1955 Factories Act regulating women's working hours had been 'processed through the filter of a completely male-dominated parliament' and 'commented on by a completely male-dominated media'.[14]

In February 1976 she was appointed to the chair of the textiles industry training committee with the state industrial training authority, AnCO. The following month she called for the introduction of divorce, along with an extension of civil annulment in comprehensive legislation, to deal with the growing problem of marital breakdown.

It wasn't her first statement on this issue, and it wouldn't be the last. Professor McDonagh, who was a member of the Irish Theological Commission, had recruited her for a review of the Irish Constitution in an attempt to heal the rifts with Northern Ireland. Among the recommendations of its radical report in 1972 was a reference to divorce and the removal of offending clauses relating to the Republic's territorial claim on the North. In a speech to the Irish Association of Civil Liberties in 1974, the senator said that it was an important principle of private international law that every state recognised the right of another state to permit divorce.

In fact, Ireland had allowed for divorce in the past, before de Valera's 1937 Constitution instituted its ban, she pointed out. The earliest reported Irish Divorce Act had been passed by the Irish parliament in 1729. On the establishment of the new Republic, jurisdiction passed to the Free State parliament and three private divorce Bills had been presented. But the government of the day had reacted strongly, and in 1925 had carried a motion requiring amendment of standing orders, to block introduction of the Bills. The stance inspired the famous speech by W.B. Yeats in the Seanad when he warned of the impact on Northern Ireland and the 'wedge' placed 'in the midst of this nation'.[15]

The dramatic increase in the number of Catholic Church annulments had made a change in civil law imperative, she said in 1976. A failure to evolve proper, humane civil remedies for the sharply increasing evidence of marriage breakdown had resulted in 'legal instability, hardship and injustice', she told a symposium on divorce at University College, Galway.

She called repeatedly for a new, integrated and comprehensive approach to family law, and for legislation on contraception. Her immediate aim seemed to be a seat in Dáil Éireann. Some colleagues suspected that a representative role within the EEC was her long-term objective. A recent redrawing of constituencies in Dublin had opened up new ground for Labour candidates. Unfortunately for her, her application for membership of the parliamentary Labour Party in 1976 coincided with the coalition government's renewal of a State of Emergency in reaction to the Northern troubles.

Mary Robinson opposed the move: the consequent legislation and additional powers afforded to the judiciary and police force in the Republic would represent an infringement of individual constitutional rights. This was a dilemma that was to recur during her political career: trying to marry steadfast principles on civil rights with efforts to achieve an acceptable political solution to the Northern conflict.

Loath to risk confrontation within the Labour Party, she withdrew her application temporarily. As *Hibernia* put it, 'this manoeuvre naturally incurred the wrath of the party leaders, notably her old sparring partner, Conor Cruise O'Brien, and she received a chilly reception from the platform when she took the rostrum at the Labour Conference a few weeks later'.

Her principled civil liberties campaign earned her praise from the tabloid *Sunday World* in September 1976. 'But she has to be a little careful for her eyes are on the £20,000 Eurodeputy job and she dare not offend Fine Gael or Labour too much,' it noted. On her membership of the Labour Party, the paper added 'her blueshirt [Fine Gael] background' would have caused her trouble within Fianna Fáil – in spite of her civil liberties stand which appealed to that party, as it opposed any moves perceived to repress the national cause. Fine Gael would have seemed to be her 'natural nest', and people like its future leader, Garret FitzGerald, would have welcomed her some years earlier, but for her 'radical' public pronouncements on various issues. Observing that she had opted for Labour, the newspaper said that her views on the party were 'somewhat of a secret', but she did see it as a 'vehicle for Europe'. The speculation was that she would like to try for a European seat under the Labour flag.

'Conor Cruise O'Brien is not an admirer of hers,' *The Sunday World* concluded. It was not impossible that he himself would fancy a 'Euroseat', instead of a job in a British university which appeared to be his other option. 'But watch Mary Robinson. She is a good lawyer, a fine-looking woman, a determined politician and a lady out to better herself. In short, she is the most ambitious woman ever to arrive here. It will be hard to stop her.'[16]

The decision to postpone Labour Party membership was to have its consequences, however. The 1977 general election came too early for her. She had set her sights on the constituency of Dublin Rathmines West, a middle-class residential area in the south of the city. A group within the Labour Party had plans to secure it this time round. The 'Left Liaison', as the radical grouping was known, was determined to try to steer Labour back to the path of straightforward socialist principles and saw Mary Robinson as precisely the kind of liberal they would prefer to shun – considering her an opportunist to boot, about to sidestep the hard slog of party work and cash in on a high-profile Seanad career. A couple of years before, Left Liaison had earmarked four Dublin constituencies where it intended to run candidates. The likely candidate in one of these, Rathmines West, one of the four, was a Dublin dentist named David Neligan. He was an ardent radical and a loyal supporter of Dr Noel Browne, the independent senator who was constantly impatient with the pace of social change. Browne had previously sought Mary Robinson's support for a Bill to legalise homosexuality. She did not oblige – perhaps the first recorded instance where some observers felt that she had displayed the more pragmatic, ambitious side of her character. In her own drive to provide contraception legislation, she had put some distance between herself and the old campaigner, revered by many as the conscience of the nation.

Neligan received an invitation from Mary Robinson to visit her in her book-lined legal office in Dublin's Merrion Square. He arrived on his bicycle and promptly found himself being 'interviewed'. Mrs Robinson wanted him to let her run in his stead. Neligan was not happy about this, although he was reluctant to stand himself. He had always been a theoretician, and had little taste for the back-slapping, baby-kissing demands of an election campaign. Party rules intervened, however. Mrs Robinson was not eligible, it seemed, because she had to be a member for a full six months before she could stand as a candidate.

At this stage, Brendan Halligan stepped in, pulling one of those adroit political strokes that would eventually kill party solidarity and split the membership in that constituency. His interpretation of the rule, supported by the party's administrative council, was that the qualification to run as an electoral candidate rested on six lunar, rather than six calendar, months! Thus, Mary Robinson was allowed to seek nomination at a constituency selection convention.

In the event, she lost the vote to Neligan and his running mate, local councillor Michael Collins. That night, party headquarters summoned its highest body, the administrative council, to an emergency session. The meeting agreed to impose her candidacy.

Neligan was incensed, but with the party organisation rather than with Robinson personally. When he stood aside, he took the front page of that week's *Sunday Press* with him, making the lead story of the day. The film *The Graduate* had been running in Dublin cinemas, giving the newspaper's subeditors great scope for the story's headline. Also with him – though a little reluctantly – went many party activists, who simply did not want to work with the 'lunar' candidate.

'It was a blunder Senator Mary Robinson admits to as "a political lesson" to keep her troops home from the selection conference in Dublin (Rathmines West),' *The Irish Times* observed on 4 June 1977. 'The senator assumed that the local Labour members would see things her way and nominate three rather than two candidates, thus avoiding any nasty confrontation with supporters of Dr David Neligan.' Yet, the columnist observed, confrontation was inevitable in this, as in other constituencies, where members of the Left Liaison of the party were seeking nominations. Much of the blame for Labour's 'current embarrassment' lay with the party's head office, the newspaper said, for what it called 'the ham-fisted methods' for dealing with dissidents. 'In Rathmines, bitterness had been brewing for 18 months over the tussle with the administrative council as to whether or not Rathmines would be allowed even to hold its own selection conference.'

The administrative council's strategy had been to allow the Left Liaison people to stand only where their votes would ensure that a stronger Labour candidate might get elected, the columnist went on. Rathmines was 'particularly awkward' because the local branches were inclined to resent the 'rather indecent haste' with which Senator Robinson had sought nomination simultaneously with joining the party. That the constituency council also firmly refused to ratify the two branches she had formed, by a vote of 25 to one, also suggested that they had been put together with similar 'indecent haste'.

Referring to the lunar calendar controversy, *The Irish Times* said that Senator Robinson had been 'saved by moonstroke', allowing her just enough soldiers to put her on an equal footing with Dr Neligan. 'Her own fear of being seen as opportunistic persuaded her not to send them marching.' Regarding her as 'undoubtedly ambitious', the paper remarked that there may have been a touch of complacency about her actions. 'All the same, it's a pity that she should be pitted against the "Left" in this instance, because few members of the parliamentary party have her track record on progressive issues, and she supported them when they were neither profitable nor popular. Hopefully, joining the team won't impede her courage on the controversial matters she's taken up . . .'[17]

The election went badly for Labour. Fianna Fáil swept to victory with 84 seats, Fine Gael taking 43 and Labour 17. The following month, Dr Garret FitzGerald would be elected leader of Fine Gael, while Frank Cluskey became the Labour leader narrowly defeating rival candidate Michael O'Leary. Life continued. For Mrs Josie Airey, it meant acceptance by the European Commission of her case that the Irish government had violated an article of the 1950 Convention on Human Rights guaranteeing citizens the right to civil legal aid. This entitled her to initiate proceedings leading to a full judicial separation from her husband.[18]

Labour had been counting on building its electoral strength in Dublin, but it did not win a single seat on the north side of the city. Mary Robinson was one of the casualties on the south side, but only by 406 votes – not the 'disaster' that *Hibernia* later described it as. Yet her campaigning style was said to be weak. Her association with the issue of contraception in particular gave plenty of ammunition to critics on the right, the magazine judged.

A letter she sent to *The Irish Times*, published on 2 July 1977, exposed some of the wounds of a bitter campaign:

> Dr David Thornley could hardly regard his dentist, Dr David Neligan, as an impartial and objective source when commenting on my political career and he might have had the courtesy to cross-check before launching forth. I could have saved him embarrassment by pointing out the following – that David Neligan was not a declared candidate when I informed him in early August last of my intention to seek a nomination for Labour in Rathmines West,

so there was no question of asking him to 'move over' or elsewhere. He subsequently announced his candidature in September.

She had decided to stand for the Seanad again as a Labour Party member, she confirmed. 'I regret being obliged to correct the inaccuracies of my party . . . through the medium of a national newspaper,' she added.

Candidates who fail to be elected to the Dáil can run in elections for Seanad, but for Mary Robinson disaster struck again; she lost 40 per cent of her previous total in the subsequent Seanad poll, though she was returned. Conor Cruise O'Brien topped the poll. She had already written in 1976 to her university electorate to explain her reasons for joining Labour, and to assure them that she would continue to represent their interests, but some of her supporters had expressed regret at what they perceived to be the abandonment of an independent position.

In one letter sent to her by a graduate in Malawi, dated 18 July 1977, she was chastised for appearing on television with Fr Denis Faul and 'IRA worthies'. In fact, Fr Faul, a civil libertarian and teacher in Dungannon, County Tyrone, had been strongly critical of the British Army and the police, but had also repeatedly condemned IRA violence. 'The contrast with your uncle Paget is striking,' the writer said of her relative, representing the British Crown in the colonies.

Mary Robinson was undeterred, and moved into local politics to work on building up a powerbase. In the Seanad, she revived her contraception Bill as a Labour Party proposal, and ventured into new territory, the conservation of Ireland's heritage. This new movement was a reaction to the 1960s' building boom under the Fianna Fáil government, which took little account then of the country's rich archaeological and architectural inheritance. At that time the 'builders' party', as some knew Fianna Fáil, represented everything that was anathema to the liberal middle-class constituency with which Mary Robinson was identifying.

In 1979 she delivered a rousing speech at a protest against a building development on Dublin's Wood Quay. The city corporation's plan to build civic offices on what was part of old Viking Dublin on the banks of the River Liffey had aroused much public opposition, galvanised the year before by a mendicant friar and professor of medieval history at UCD, Fr F.X. Martin. Over three thousand Viking artefacts had been discovered on the site ten years earlier, and there was still much archaeological work to be done if funding was to be forthcoming.

When a High Court judgment in favour of preserving the site was overturned, Fr Martin and his supporters struck. On 1 June 1979 a group of them, including poets, politicians and trade union activists, occupied the site under the Black Raven flag of the Vikings. Mary Robinson's recipe for 'Black Raven Brownies', published much later in a cookery collection to raise funds for St Patrick's Cathedral, is a souvenir of those days on Wood Quay. Her contribution to the collection was based on that 'rather decadent cookie' she was introduced to during her student days in Harvard. The recipe was christened by Fr Martin.

But the protest itself left a bitter taste for all involved. Despite the marches, appeals from international archaeologists, and the compromise formulated by the Labour Party and presented by Senator Robinson, the first phase of the construction eventually went ahead.

Within the Labour Party, internal problems still festered. There were those in the ranks who felt with some justification that Mary Robinson was not a 'team player', citing as an example her use of the media to communicate – on the fall-out from Rathmines West, for example. There would be other such instances later on in her career. Yet the media were often only carrying messages, like that which she delivered at the first conference of the Equal Opportunities Commission for Northern Ireland in September 1977. In her contribution, she said that the Irish and British governments appeared to be prepared to tolerate and condone a 'flagrant' evasion of the law of the land regarding equal pay. Women workers, particularly in the private sector, had cause for bitterness, given that equal pay had been a legal right since 1 January 1976, she told the conference, which was also attended by the British Secretary of State, Shirley Williams.

In the same week, Mary Robinson also called for the establishment of an independent body to investigate all complaints against the Garda Síochána. She sought vigilance in relation to the activities of the Special Criminal Court, and urged a greater degree of involvement by senior members of the Bar in the operation of that court. In this, she was supporting a demand by the human rights monitoring group, Amnesty International, which had called for an independent investigation into recorded cases of police brutality. At the time, the government was considering whether or not it should extend the Emergency Powers Act for another year. An *Irish Times* editorial supported the senator: 'An effective body could do much to help the gardaí maintain their good name, as it could to prevent the abuse of power in an unusually hectic period,' it said.[19]

Ireland had accepted the emergency legislation too readily and too lightly, she warned in an interview with Ed Mulhall in the TCD student newspaper, *Trinity News*, in November 1977. Asked to justify her membership of the Labour Party and her position as a university senator with a tradition of independence, she said that the decision to 'go forward' had not been a happy one, but it was a choice that she had made reluctantly because she valued this tradition of independence. The advantage of party membership was that she was very keen to work within a party structure, Mulhall wrote, 'and not merely contribute on an ad hoc basis'.

On the extent of her commitment to socialism, she said: 'I am committed to the view that socialism is the only possible way in which Ireland can achieve the equality, the social justice and the opportunities for all citizens that are needed.' She had found it 'unique and disturbing' that, given its history and its social, economic and demographic reality, Ireland did not have a strong and vibrant socialist party.

'She considers it vital that we should have one,' Mulhall wrote, 'and helping towards its development is her major preoccupation and major interest.' On her own political future, she would like to see the Labour Party broadening its base to become 'relevant to the west of Ireland' and to fishermen, he said.[20]

It was in an *Irish Times* newspaper interview in July 1979 that she had challenged her colleagues to redefine socialism in Irish terms.[21] So far, she maintained, the party had failed to put forward socialist proposals which pertained to Ireland. It had 'borrowed a language that is more suitable to an urban society like Britain'. It had conjured up images of an 'anonymous' and intrusive 'state arm', and thus it had 'put people off'.

In her view, the emphasis should be on the devolution of power, rather than on its centralisation. This should translate into the provision of co-operative housing, co-operative land acquisition and free legal aid. 'After more than fifty years as a Republic, we haven't established our real values,' she said. She also maintained that her outlook had changed since she had moved into 'active' politics: 'I am now more inclined to relate anything I do to the overall economic and social context. I have become so much more aware of the inaccessibility of legal services to people, and the intimidation and lack of preventative help that they have.' In her mind, access to legal aid was as much a citizen's right as access to medical services.

The sentiments expressed may have simply reflected Mary Robinson's growing disenchantment with the party, but it also reflected her radicalisation – on which she was to backtrack publicly, if not privately, a dozen years later. She was still pushing for a comprehensive system of such aid and for legal reform which would tackle the issue of marital breakdown. However, she now realised that there were other basic issues that could not be overlooked. The housing crisis was one such. She cited cases of families living in dank, dark, Dublin basements. Even if certified as unfit for human habitation, housing in such conditions did not necessarily guarantee that a local authority would be able to accommodate a family elsewhere because of the dearth of public housing.

Perhaps it was this shift in consciousness, or perhaps it was for more pragmatic 'image' reasons: in 1980 she resigned from the Trilateral Commission. She was still an executive member in the CV attached to her Seanad election address for 1977. In 1976 she had expressed reservations about the 'big-business' element, but felt that affiliation could be used to 'educate and, if necessary, challenge the viewpoints being put forward'.

A naïve approach? In 1977 *The Irish Press* published a letter from a County Cork reader, Mrs P.J. Fehily of Dunmanway, who expressed 'grave concern' that Senator Robinson and the Minister for External Affairs, Michael O'Kennedy, were members of 'a private consortium of giant multinational corporations drawn from western Europe, North America and Japan'. This consortium was connected to the 'Bilderbergers, set up by Prince Bernhardt of the Netherlands in the days before his impeachment for receiving bribes' and associated with the EEC, she wrote. Its first objective was to 'integrate the economies of these wealthy nations'. The Commission's second objective appeared to be 'One World Government, with the reins in the right hands of course!' [22]

Questions were also being asked in other fora, notably the European Commission. Several members had participated in a meeting of the Trilateral Commission's European section in Brussels on 26 May 1977 – a body with 'political pretensions', formed to strengthen ties between the principal countries of the 'free' or 'capitalist' world, it was noted in a written question a few weeks later. Was this participation an endorsement of this particular political strategy, and was there not a risk that it could harm the EEC's specific policy towards Third World countries?

North-South relations were addressed by Senator Robinson in a submission to European members of the Trilateral Commission in October 1978. She recommended that there should be at least one briefing on this issue at each meeting; that co-operation with the Brandt Commission on development issues should be explored; that a special study of development policy be commissioned; and that liaison be established with Third World agencies to discuss such issues as the re-negotiation of the Lomé Convention.[23] She received a positive response. In a letter dated 4 January 1980 to fellow executive members, however, she tendered her resignation and expressed deep disillusionment over the lack of real commitment to 'leadership and creativity' in examining North-South issues. She also expressed her regret at the 'increasing personal influence' exerted by Dr Henry Kissinger, and said that she had found that her own attitude towards the Commission had become 'increasingly cynical'. She said that she would convene a meeting of the Irish branch to choose a replacement for her.

A Norwegian member, Otto Grieg Tidemand, wrote to her from Oslo expressing regret, and observed that: 'Neither your nor my membership . . .

matters much to the people of the world. On the other hand, I think it is against the basic thinking of all democratic people to leave an organisation although one disagrees on some aspects of it . . . In a time when the communists are trying to blatantly exercise world hegemony, I feel it is our duty to maintain international organisations of the trilateral form more than ever.'

Back at national political level, an opportunity arose for her again in 1981 when, suddenly and unexpectedly, another general election was called. Garret FitzGerald's coalition government had fallen unexpectedly when he tried to impose value added tax on children's shoes, explaining that if it was left off then women with small feet might take advantage of the exemption. For a brief period, Fianna Fáil returned to office, now led by Charles Haughey, who had been elected party leader in 1979, and who had been described by FitzGerald as having a 'flawed pedigree'. Fitz-Gerald's vicious attack was designed to revive memories of Haughey's dismissal from office in 1970 over an alleged conspiracy to import arms destined for the North.

By now, Mary Robinson was regarded as one of the best-known female public representatives in the country, having won the ground-breaking case in the European Court of Human Rights when she represented Mrs Josie Airey, who had challenged the lack of provision for free legal aid for those seeking access to the courts on family matters. The government promised to look into a system of civil legal aid, which had, so far, been provided on a voluntary basis by the tireless Free Legal Advice Centres run by energetic, committed young lawyers.

Her name was also in the news in April 1981 when she was suspended from the Seanad after the chair refused a debate on the future of an usher who had been given a job by the Department of Labour on transfer from the staff of the Oireachtas. Come the election, she was caught on the hop with a brand new baby – Aubrey, named after her father and older brother. By now, she had moved her legal practice into shared offices with her husband in Fitzwilliam Street.

The Labour Party leader, Frank Cluskey, who was said to have had a 'good, but not warm' relationship with the senator and who had been invited to Trilateral Commission Irish branch meetings, had his own ideas about her constituency of Rathmines, as it was now renamed.[24] She was forced to move to another area, Dublin West. Once green fields, it was now a suburban sprawl of housing estates built in the 1960s.

The lower-middle- and working-class voters of areas such as Ballyfermot and Walkinstown did not relate easily to the rather remote barrister and academic who seemed concerned only with middle-class, liberal issues, such as the rights of the travelling community. 'If you want a knacker for a neighbour, vote Labour,' one rival said, 'knackers' being the popular racist term for the travellers, whose peripatetic lifestyle resembled that of gypsies in continental Europe.

Finally, the Northern troubles rose again to hit electoral politics in the South in a way they never had before, or have since. In October 1980 Republican prisoners in the H-block wing of the Maze prison had gone on hunger strike with a list of demands relating to their status; it ended in some confusion in December with one IRA prisoner close to death. In March 1981 the strike was resumed by Bobby Sands, the 26-year-old newly elected leader of the IRA prisoners. He died in May that year. By that time he had also been elected an abstentionist member of the British parliament in a by-election the previous month.

As six other IRA and three Irish National Liberation Army (INLA) prisoners died, the British government under Margaret Thatcher resolutely refused any concessions. In sympathy with their cause, independent 'H-Block' candidates stood in a number of constituencies in the Republic's election, including Dublin West. Most of them polled only a few hundred first-preference votes. Mary Robinson was never an ardent nationalist, but it was a stark measure of her failure to make inroads in Dublin West that she came ninth in the list of first preferences, behind the local 'H-block' candidate. One story from her campaign illustrates why. A woman sought her advice about housing. The senator told her what she was entitled to. The woman did not vote for her, however: at least one rival had told the voter he would 'look after her'. No prizes for telling people their rights, if they preferred to believe that the key of the house is a 'gift'.

It looked as if Mary Robinson's dreams of a political career were shattered. Ironically, one of the 15 candidates for five seats was Brian Lenihan, whom she was to meet again on the campaign beat 13 years later.

CHAPTER 8

Bruising Battles

In 1981 Gro Harlem Brundtland, a medical doctor, became Norway's first female prime minister at the age of 41. In the United States, President Reagan appointed Sandra Day O'Connor as the first female Supreme Court judge. Italy rescinded legal protection for a man's 'crime of passion'.

British women established a peace camp at the gates of the US air base at Greenham Common. And in Ireland, the year of the IRA hunger strikes, Senator Mary Robinson's political career appeared to be on the floor.

Over the 18 months preceding the 1981 general election, she had been rarely seen at local authority meetings, a newspaper columnist noted.[1] In truth, some said, she was not cut out for the tedium of constituency work. She was, however, an eloquent and able representative of the party in a new initiative on Northern Ireland, the New Ireland Forum. Observers at the time admired the way she challenged the view propounded by Catholic bishops represented on the forum, which produced its report in 1984.

'In retrospect, I think I failed to see, and to reconcile, differences within the party,' she was to observe later, commenting on her experience of political cut and thrust. 'Partly my own inexperience and clumsiness and there wasn't time to prepare.' If disappointed, she was not as devastated as she had been the first time round in 1977, when the contest had been so close.

Commenting on the fact that she had been breastfeeding her youngest child at the time of the campaign, she said, 'If you look at it, it doesn't seem very clever of me.' It was, if anything, a 'learning experience'.[2] In an *Irish Times* interview with Mary Maher, she explained why she had been attracted to Labour, and confirmed that she had turned down offers from both Fianna Fáil and Fine Gael. 'I am a socialist,' she said. 'I wasn't interested in participating in any political party which reflected these almost tribalist attitudes to the past. From my perspective, Labour was the only option open, because it was the only party which aspired to genuine change in Irish society.

'I began to see that I needed a social and political framework for my commitment. I was less content to approach problems as a liberal, and I needed to abandon the purity and comparative comfort of making independent contributions for the less comfortable – and inevitably more compromised but more serious – position of working within the party.'[3]

Throughout, she had steadfastly refused to make much of her ability to run a home, hold down a legal career and still engage in politics. Back in 1977 she had described marriage as 'extremely liberating', filling her with a sense of confidence, stability and belonging.[4] She had always wanted to have children, and publicly acknowledged the benefit of having a husband who was not so imbued with her driving ambition, and of being able to afford to pay a daily home help. But time and again, the barrister with the deep voice, cold demeanour, warm smile and stiff, almost awkward manner had refused requests from journalists to interview her on her family life, despite the fact that this could have been used to her advantage in political terms. Her shyness, her inability to engage in trivial conversation – though she had a sense of humour – was reflected in the movement of her hands, friends said.

Close friends were aware that she was the main breadwinner, that Nanny Coyne had been wooed back from England to help with the children before the third baby was born. And that when Nan died of cancer, there was a succession of childminders, including some who were considered to be far too strict. The senator was not an advocate of discipline. Young minds could be reasoned with.

Mary Robinson's secretary, Ann Lane, took on Nan's mantle. Ann, who had initially been hired by Adrian Bourke to help in the first Seanad elections, had become a part of the family since Mary had employed her as a secretary in her practice in Merrion Square. Trained in computers, the young woman from Millstreet, County Cork, had gladly left her job in insurance to rise to the challenge. Over an eight-year period, during the height of the contraception campaign and vilifying letters and abusive calls, the two women had forged a close bond.

David Norris, TCD contemporary and colleague in the Seanad, was also receiving hate mail owing to his campaign for the legalisation of homosexuality. 'I never took it seriously,' he said later. 'In fact it gave me a terrific sense of security, made me feel normal. Very little of that ever got through to me except in the sense that there were these lonely, maladjusted people out there. But I can't say if that was Mary Robinson's attitude to it all.'[5]

Local politics could be every bit as stressful as national politics, when people could phone at a whim to complain about the lack of enamelling on a bath or a broken window pane in their council house. When Mary and Ann moved office up the road to Fitzwilliam Street in August 1981, it was because Nick wanted to share the rent of his rooms. He had been appointed executive director of the Heritage Trust on a five-year contract. He was also still very involved with the Irish Architectural Archive, which he had co-founded in the mid-1970s. Previously, the two women had shared one room. The Fitzwilliam Street premises were a rabbit warren; there was less of the constant banter.

Mary Robinson turned back to the Seanad again. The 1982 election had attracted stiff competition, with more interest being shown by the political parties. A right-wing Dublin stockbroker, Shane Ross, whose father Mary Robinson had defeated in her first Seanad bid in 1969, pulled in more first-preference votes than she did from Dublin University alumni, in spite of her high profile.

She was returned, but now appeared to throw more of her abundant energy into academia and her very active legal career as a senior counsel, while remaining a member of the Labour Party. She had been called to the Inner Bar in 1980, having already handled many difficult legal cases. Among them – on the recommendation of her friend, Professor Enda McDonagh, who was then on the council of the Irish Federation of University Teachers – was the case of two academics in St Patrick's College, Maynooth. The academics were both former branch secretaries of IFUT; Professor P.J. McGrath had been given notice of dismissal because of his writings, while Malachy O'Rourke, a French lecturer, had received a similar notice, mainly because he was a laicised priest. Their case was won in the High Court but lost in the Supreme Court. IFUT regarded the dismissals as a 'gross violation of academic freedom'.

In January 1983, Mary Robinson resigned from local politics. The news raised few eyebrows.

The 1981 government had lasted only a few months. So had its successor, elected in February 1982, which briefly returned to power the opposition Fianna Fáil party under the leadership of Charles Haughey. Economic issues, the North and abortion contributed to an 18-month period of instability with three changes of administration, each lasting less than nine months, each a minority government. Labour was now led by Michael O'Leary, who was elected after Frank Cluskey had lost his seat in June 1981. O'Leary served as Tánaiste or deputy prime minister in a coalition with Fine Gael, under Garret FitzGerald. But in October 1982 he stood down when his proposal – that prior notification should be given to the electorate of the party's attitude to the formation of an alternative government – was defeated at the Labour annual conference.

'I would not stay on as a scarecrow leader,' were O'Leary's words. He was to join Fine Gael within days, leaving Labour to elect as leader another lawyer, the 32-year-old Kerryman Dick Spring, just three days before the November 1982 election, which spawned another Fine Gael-Labour coalition. Significantly, the question of the North dominated the latter half of this campaign in a manner not witnessed in the two previous elections. Fianna Fáil took an anti-British stance, accusing Garret FitzGerald of aiding and abetting British proposals for devolution. Fine Gael in turn concentrated on the credibility and trustworthiness of the Fianna Fáil leader who was facing down his own internal party problems, and who had been damaged by a series of extraordinary events that summer when a murder suspect was found in the south Dublin apartment of the Attorney General. 'Grotesque, unprecedented, bizarre and unbelievable' was how Charles Haughey described the situation – giving commentators like Conor Cruise O'Brien licence to nickname that administration the 'GUBU government', thus adding an enduring phrase to Ireland's political vocabulary.

Son of a veteran party member and former public representative from North Kerry, Spring had a similar social background to Mary Robinson's. A Trinity College graduate in law, he was a practising barrister who had played rugby for Ireland. He lacked Robinson's legal mind, however, and appeared to hold no apparent political principle, but was to surprise many – not the least the independent Trinity College senator, David Norris, who has remarked on his political skills and his Machiavellian mind. Once in office, Spring appointed a college friend, John Rogers, to the post of Attorney General. This move caused something of a sensation: the betting had been on Mary Robinson getting the job. Even though well out of the political limelight, she had no legal match on the liberal left; indeed, no legal match at all. Rogers, an unknown quantity, was still a junior counsel.

Critics say that Mary Robinson never forgave Dick Spring, and that this was the real reason for her resignation from the party – ostensibly over her opposition to the Anglo-Irish agreement on the North – three years later in 1985. Rogers's appointment as Attorney General was 'an astonishing decision', one party member has observed. 'Mary Robinson undoubtedly had the talent.'

The abortion issue was the first challenge to the new coalition government, and one on which Senator Robinson took a public stance. Three days before the November 1982 election, the government had issued proposed wording for a constitutional referendum on the issue. The two largest parties were tied in to the issue, following successful pressure from a right-wing Catholic lobby group, the Pro-Life Amendment Campaign (PLAC), formed in 1980 to seek a constitutional guarantee to protect the life of the 'unborn'. Labour was noncommittal, but in the joint programme of the coalition, it was stated that legislation would be in place by the end of March 1983 to adopt the pro-life amendment, supported by the two largest parties in the Dáil. The parliamentary Labour Party reserved the right to a free vote on this, the programme stated.

Senator Robinson's stance was clear. In an address the previous September to Cherish, the organisation for single-parent families, of which she had been president since 1973, she said that the real 'pro-life' issue of the day was the plight of the 4 per cent of Irish children who suffered legal disability because they had been born out of wedlock.[6] 'It is strange, indeed, that this real and urgent "pro-life" issue, which would have immediate practical significance and provide encouragement for prospective mothers concerned, has never received anything like the public, political and media attention being devoted to an as yet undrafted proposal for an amendment of the Constitution, which even the proposers admit would be largely theoretical.'

Citing the commitment given in 1981 by the coalition government to abolish the concept of illegitimacy, supported by the Catholic bishops, she observed that it was time Ireland 'came down from the heady heights of moral abstraction to tackle immediately this basic injustice', which, she said, represented 'a blight' on the legal system.

It would be three years before the illegitimacy issue was tackled. In the meantime, the abortion referendum threatened to split parties down the middle. With the Protestant Churches comparing the campaign to the controversy over the Mother and Child Scheme, and the Attorney General casting doubts on the efficacy of the wording, the debate opened in the Seanad in May 1983, with members of the coalition parties arguing against their own government. In what *The Irish Times* described as a 'remarkable performance', Senator Robinson held forth for almost two and a half hours. To bolster her case against the abortion amendment, Mary Robinson cited the Attorney General and Director of Public Prosecutions, the Protestant Churches, views of the European Commission on Human Rights, and a statement from the dean of the Protestant St Patrick's Cathedral in Dublin, the Revd Victor Griffin, among others.

Ireland could be in breach of the European Convention on Human Rights if the constitutional amendment was passed, she said three months later at a press conference hosted by the Labour Party's women's national council to express its united opposition. The text of the amendment was in conflict with a ruling from Strasbourg, which recognised the right to life of the mother as superior to the right to life of the unborn child. By equating both rights to life, the Irish Constitution could be judged to be in breach of the Convention, to which Ireland was a signatory, she pointed out.[7] In such a case, the country might have to dissociate itself from the

Convention. This would be a difficult step since it had brought Britain before the European Court on human rights issues relating to Northern Ireland, she claimed, adding a dose of reality to a largely emotional debate.

The chair of the Labour women's national council rejected claims that it was 'pro-abortion'. The council had never been an advocate of abortion, nor did it intend to be. However, the amendment was no solution to the question. Senator Robinson said that she had been surprised to hear that Seán MacBride, senior counsel and human rights activist, had revealed his intention to support the amendment.

Significantly, Senator Brendan Halligan, now a member of the European Parliament, urged Labour Party members who had been silent on the issue to state their position publicly. There had been a 'disturbing amount of moral cowardice', he said, where people privately opposed to the referendum were not prepared to say so out loud.[8]

The skilled pro-amendment campaign lawyer William Binchy attempted to turn the European Court argument on its head by suggesting that it would try to force Ireland to legalise abortion. There was no question of this, Senator Robinson responded: 'This is the latest attempt to find some bogeyman to justify this unnecessary and divisive referendum.'[9]

On 22 August, the Catholic hierarchy issued its anticipated statement in support of the amendment. Essentially ignoring the legal opinion of the Attorney General, the Church expressed satisfaction that the wording would safeguard the life of both mother and unborn child. 'While some conscientiously hold a different opinion, we are convinced that a clear majority in favour of the amendment will greatly contribute to the continued protection of human life in the laws of our country,' the bishops said. It was a pronouncement which, as the then Taoiseach, Garret Fitz-Gerald, was to note later, seemed at odds with their 1973 statement that 'it is not a matter for bishops to decide whether the law should be changed or not. That is a matter for the legislators.'[10]

Carried by a two-to-one majority in a poll of almost 54 per cent of the electorate, the 1983 referendum left a bitter taste and no victor. The former Taoiseach was to admit later that he should never have accepted the original referendum proposal, however harmless it may have appeared at the time. As he recorded in his biography: 'no one came well out of the affair. The Catholic hierarchy was, at best, weak in the face of extremist pressure. Fianna Fáil for its part was totally opportunist in wooing the "pro-life" lobby. Even the Labour Party, the leaders of which had from the beginning taken up a wiser position than I had on the issue, was at the end of the day as divided as Fine Gael, with over a quarter of its deputies voting with Fianna Fáil, as some of ours also did, for the amendment that had originally been proposed by the Haughey government.'

No tactics of his could have prevented the amendment being forced through by Fianna Fáil in opposition, Dr FitzGerald wrote. 'As long as simplistic attitudes to complex moral issues persist in Ireland, and as long as unscrupulous politicians are prepared to exploit religious feeling, our society will remain vulnerable to the "crawthumpers".'[11]

FitzGerald was the architect of the New Ireland Forum, along with John Hume, the leader of the SDLP. Anglo-Irish relations were at a 'disastrous' stage, in FitzGerald's opinion, by the time the government had changed in late 1982. This was due in part to British reaction to Ireland's stance on the Falklands, following the decision by the Haughey-led Fianna Fáil government on 4 May 1982 to opt out of EEC sanctions against Argentina after a British submarine had torpedoed the Argentinian cruiser, the *General Belgrano*. That opting-out precipitated a domino effect: that July Haughey had, according to FitzGerald, taken a series of negative decisions to avoid discussions with the British government.

Hume had proposed a nationalist council for a new Ireland, while FitzGerald had stated in a speech in Pittsburgh that he envisaged consultations involving all parties in the North and the Republic, in advance of negotiation with Britain. He wanted it to be inclusive – that is, involving the Northern unionists. In the event, initial reaction North and South was negative, and the unionists did not participate.

Senator Robinson was part of the Labour delegation. It was during a hearing with the Catholic bishops that she made her mark, on the divisive ecumenistic issues of divorce, abortion and inter-denominational schooling. 'My palm goes to Senator Mary Robinson,' wrote northern *Irish Times* columnist Sam McAughtry. 'She did something which can only be compared to playing Who's Got the Best Left Hook with Barry McGuigan, when she produced the Code of Canon Law and took on Dr Dermot O'Mahony, Auxiliary Bishop of Dublin, on Church dissolution of marriage.

'Mind you, the lady proved no mug,' McAughtry continued. 'She had a punch up her sleeve. Once, the bishop even said: "That's a very good question." But I'd be openly laying a hundred to eight against a straight answer at this stage of the game, and my money stayed in my pocket.'[12]

The bishops' responses at the New Ireland Forum would prove a useful reference during debates on that other long-running issue: divorce. Back in 1967, a constitutional committee had recommended that the prohibition on divorce be removed to allow for the non-Catholic minorities. The ban represented a 'source of embarrassment', the committee had found, 'to those seeking to bring about better relations between North and South', by fuelling fears among Protestants in the North of a loss of their right to divorce through a united, 'holy Catholic' Ireland.

The Fine Gael-Labour coalition government of 1981 had taken an initiative of sorts through its bid to extend the parliament's committee system. It proposed four such bodies, dealing with women's rights, youth affairs, development co-operation and marriage breakdown. Fianna Fáil, in opposition, refused to co-operate with the last-named body, on the grounds that the Taoiseach, Garret FitzGerald, had pre-empted its work by stating that he wished divorce to be introduced 'in the lifetime of this Dáil'. FitzGerald challenged them to verify that statement – an indication of the sensitivity of the issue. Yet within four years, divorce was to become a national issue.

In May 1985, sentiments expressed in public presaged Senator Robinson's intent. The previous month, she had expressed concern about a proposed government Bill to abolish illegitimacy. The Bill was one of the longest pieces of legislation ever proposed by any Irish government, but it did not go far enough in her view. While guaranteeing equal rights to succession and maintenance of so-called 'illegitimate' children, it did not give natural fathers automatic rights of guardianship.

'If we are delaying too long on seeking to remove discrimination, we're eroding the base we are seeking to deal with,' she said in a statement that could have applied to any of the liberal issues on which she had campaigned. 'The government should not hedge responsibility, but press ahead seeking a consensus within the Oireachtas.'

In late 1985, it appeared as if there was a breakthrough on Northern Ireland, with the signing in London of an Anglo-Irish Agreement. This created a Dublin-London axis, by affording the Republic a greater role in determining the North's political future.

The senator had been looking for a way out. Her legal career had taken off, she was lecturing two mornings a week, losing interest in the Seanad and building a reputation for herself in Europe while also continuing her involvement with the Trilateral Commission. Her continued success in effecting reform through legal channels had included securing the right of women to be assessed for tax separately from their husbands, and the right of women to equality in social welfare payments. A case pursued on behalf of wheelchair-bound socialist and trade union activist, Liam Maguire, on the rights of people with disabilities, did not get to court.

Nevertheless she kept up the pace, taking cases to Europe, such as the right to legal aid in family law. Her belief that Ireland's membership of the European Community would bring about social change was reflected in her 16-year-long involvement in a parliamentary committee on European legislation. Yet, as a report from her own Irish Centre for European Law, which she had founded in TCD, was to observe in 1990, there would be potential for a head-on clash between EEC law and the Irish Constitution at some point, given the judiciary's adherence to a tradition of constitutional supremacy. Ironically, European law was backed up by a constitutional provision.[13]

Nick had convinced his wife in 1982 to move house to Ranelagh, a southside suburb within two miles of the centre of Dublin. She had been very attached to her home in Wellington Place, and had tried to buy the house next door to allow for more space when it came up for auction. Missing out on it was one of the rare occasions when she shed tears. The Ranelagh residence, built in 1829 with a three-storey rear extension added in the 1850s, was purchased by them at auction for £185,000. Semi-detached, it was one of seven houses screened from the main road by a thick belt of trees, and it had a large garden.

She shed few tears for Labour, however, when she tendered her resignation in November 1985 over her doubts about the new Anglo-Irish Agreement. It went too far and would not be supported by any Northern unionists, she forecast. 'In neither part of this island can we afford a long-drawn-out bruising battle on this issue which could distract from, and potentially worsen, the serious economic and social problems in both jurisdictions,' she said in her statement of 18 November.

Was this really so consistent with the views she had expressed – and her warning about unionists taking the initiative unless the British government filled the vacuum – after the collapse of Sunningdale in 1974? Senator David Norris disagreed with her and felt she was making the wrong move. The Protestant independent felt that the unionists had been given too much time and sympathy, if anything.

Her party leader accepted her decision with 'considerable sadness' and said in a letter to her that he recognised that there were risks inherent in the government's approach, but there were also risks in doing nothing. He thanked her for her 'significant contribution' to the party, and the 'major role' she had played in preparing the report of the New Ireland Forum.

A party spokesman said that the resignation was 'a bit unusual'.[14] In interviews a few days later, she cast doubts on Labour's commitment to equality and justice and said that she had 'paid a high price' for relinquishing her independent seat in the Seanad in favour of the party. She was adamant, however, that the Anglo-Irish Agreement had been the determining factor. At the same time, she warned that she did not want to 'be seen in the same bed as Fianna Fáil', because she did not share any of the criticisms of the Agreement that the party's leader, Charles Haughey, had advanced.

Her stance was supported by fellow Dublin University constituency senator Shane Ross, who expressed 'very grave reservations' about the

Agreement; but a third senator, Catherine McGuinness, felt that Mrs Robinson was taking 'too extreme a view'. 'I cannot oppose something which is fundamental to the government and still remain within the Labour Party,' Senator Robinson rejoined. Her political future was 'absolutely secondary' to all this, she told reporters at the time. It had been 'one of the most difficult and painful decisions' she had made in over 16 years as a senator. But the agreement represented, she said, 'the most serious moment in political development on this island since we gained independence'.[15]

Senator Robinson went a little further a few days after in an extended newspaper interview.[16] Asked later if her decision to speak out on the Northern unionist position was motivated by a desire to strengthen her vote among some of her Protestant Trinity College electorate, she said that it had been 'totally outside my whole consideration'.

'I spent a week reflecting and that never formed part of the agonising. I have made no decision about my political future. I might not even stand at the next Seanad election.' The experience of coalition government had been a 'very unhappy' one for the Labour Party, she continued. It had not been able to tackle unemployment or reform of the tax system. 'We have not concentrated enough on what a divided society we have become, and by divided I mean those who are in employment and those who are not. We have a grossly inequitable society, made worse by this ever sharper division. We need a New Ireland Forum on that.'

The hint she had dropped wrote the headline: 'I might not stand for the Seanad', it read, beside a photograph of her relaxing on a sofa in her study with the family's golden retriever. Almost four years later, she was in the headlines again: 'Robinson to leave Seanad,' *The Irish Times* read.

CHAPTER 9

President and Purpose

Fine Gael was still trying to make up its mind about its presidential nomination when the Labour Party came up with Mary Robinson's name. It seemed a strange choice, for her relationship with the party was by now quite strained.

It was five years since she had resigned, at a time when Labour was junior partner in a coalition government with Fine Gael. The Anglo-Irish Agreement was her stated reason for quitting the party. Presented with so much fanfare as a basis for solving the problems of Northern Ireland, the Agreement had, indeed, given the Irish government its first real voice in determining the North's future. But five years on, it had still not brought peace. It had evinced an angry response from the North's unionist politicians – a response for which there might not be much sympathy.

Yet Mary Robinson felt it could not be ignored. Some 11 years before, when the Sunningdale agreement on the North had collapsed, she had remarked that it had 'failed to be sufficiently attractive to those to whom it had to appeal'. Similarly, she felt that the Anglo-Irish Agreement was unworkable.

It was a theme to which she returned constantly in speeches from 1986 onwards. In June 1986, for instance, she told a meeting organised in a Dublin hotel by the Glencree Centre for Reconciliation that the Agreement's Article 11 – which provided for an automatic review after three years 'or earlier if requested by either government' – should be invoked. Even the Irish Foreign Minister, Peter Barry, had expressed serious disappointment about the lack of progress in the inter-governmental conference. She also drew attention to another matter of concern – the MacBride Principles, named after Seán MacBride, which required US companies in Northern Ireland to operate positive discriminatory policies in favour of Catholics if they were under-represented, and to provide 'adequate security for the protection of minority employees both at the workplace and while travelling to and from work'. Fine in theory.

The principles – which were formulated by the Irish National Caucus, the umbrella group for most Irish-American organisations in the US – were modelled on the Sullivan principles (a corporate code of conduct for American companies doing business in South Africa). In practice, they could deter investment, Mary Robinson said. Bob Cooper, chairman of the North's Fair Employment Agency, had expressed similar fears. An American company considering establishing itself in Northern Ireland could find itself in a 'Catch-22' situation. If the principles weren't signed, many organisations would refuse to invest in Northern Ireland. If the company did sign, it could leave itself open to many successful and expensive claims of reverse discrimination. Most disadvantaged would be the Catholic population, already suffering the highest level of unemployment.

'In essence, the MacBride Principles must be examined and understood in the context of Irish American politics,' Mrs Robinson said. 'They were the brainchild of the Irish National Caucus, and have the active support of Noraid.[1] Neither of these bodies has an interest in promoting investment in Northern Ireland for so long as it remains part of the United Kingdom.'

Though some doubted her motives, her principled stand extended to other familiar issues, about which she spoke consistently until she took the decision to retire from public life altogether in 1989. Issues like the speed of reform of family law in Ireland – still 'one of the most complex systems in the world';[2] divorce, which was to be the subject of a referendum that very year; the Status of Children Bill and succession rights, which were in danger of being ignored, she felt, in the debate on the constitutional amendment on divorce.[3]

On divorce, she took on the Roman Catholic bishops, who opposed any lifting of the constitutional ban, and expressed concern about the Northern dimension if the referendum to remove the ban was defeated. She also took issue with the Minister for Foreign Affairs, who had said that such a defeat would not have any bearing on North-South relations.

'One way or the other, the result of the referendum will reveal what kind of society we are,' she told one of many public meetings hosted by the Divorce Action Group during the 1986 campaign. 'Both sides of the debate are concerned about the protection of marriage and family life in Ireland. The real issue is how we handle a problem on which there is a difference of view and outlook. Do we insist that the minority must be forced to comply with the majority view on the indissolubility of marriage?' she asked. 'Or do we believe in the value of a more open society which protects and respects the rights of minorities?'

The result of the referendum on 26 June would have the most 'profound consequences on Irish society and, indeed, on the attitude of young people towards that society,' she said. 'We must show that we have grasped the significance of the commitment at Vatican II to religious freedom and that Ireland's championing of civil rights in countries of Central America and in South Africa is matched by our willingness to protect civil rights and liberties in Ireland itself.'[4]

The motion to lift the ban was defeated with a resounding 63 per cent against lifting it. The turnout was 62.5 per cent of the population, and the result defied all early expectations. Shortly before the government's campaign was initiated on 9 May, a poll had shown that 57 per cent supported its constitutional amendment and 36 per cent were opposed to it, with 7 per cent holding no opinion. The majority in favour was reflected in all four regions, in both rural and urban areas and in all political parties.[5]

By early June, however, a poll indicated that about a fifth of those who had previously favoured the amendment were now undecided, with no decrease in the proportion against divorce. The anti-divorce campaign gained momentum with support from the Roman Catholic hierarchy. The opposition openly exploited fears about the economic position of divorced women: sufficient protective legislation was simply not in place. There was a recognition that divorce in itself was not an answer to anything. The last poll taken before the vote showed a dramatic turn, reflected in the outcome. Such was the bitterness and frustration felt by those seeking to transform Ireland into a liberal society that some said it would be at least a decade before the issue could be raised again.

Running for the Seanad after the 1987 election – which produced a minority government led by Fianna Fáil – Mary Robinson urged continued efforts towards achieving a 'pluralist and caring society', in spite of the 'constitutional set-backs of the past few years'. Substantial aspects of social legislation needed updating, such as marriage law and laws relating to children. Homelessness, the environment, company law reform and a 'cumbersome, over-centralised and stultifying system of government' had to be tackled, she said in her election address. In short, the Dáil and Seanad must be prepared to sit longer hours and to work at a 'new and vigorous pace'.

She added a rider. The TCD constituency had changed, broadening out of its former conservative and largely Protestant enclave to take in the Dublin Institute of Technology colleges. Three sitting senators were seeking to be returned, as were some strong new candidates, including David Norris. 'I would urge you to discount any suggestion that my seat is safe,' she appealed to her constituents.

This time, she had a new election agent, Bride Rosney from Cahirciveen, County Kerry, who had taken over from Dr Mary Henry. She was a teacher of science and principal of a Dublin northside community school, Rosmini. The two women had met during the Wood Quay campaign to save Dublin's Viking heritage, and had cemented their friendship in court. Rosney was one of a group camped out on the site overlooking the River Liffey, in protest at the construction of the new civic offices. When summonsed, she and the group led by the UCD medieval history professor, Fr F.X. Martin, were defended by the senator and junior counsel, Mary Robinson. Rosney became godmother to Aubrey, the new baby. She was an expert at the tallies during Seanad election counts, predicting outcomes faster than most of those around her. There would be a 'flurry' when this 'busy, capable figure' arrived, according to activists. The experience of dealing with Labour was to influence – indeed to sour – Rosney's view of the party from then on.

So concerned was Mary Robinson about her Seanad seat in 1987 – Northern votes had been garnered by the Dublin stockbroker Shane Ross – that a letter of support from the much respected and highly political dean of St Patrick's Cathedral in Dublin, Victor Griffin, which had been written on her behalf for a previous Seanad election, was reproduced in her election address. It described her as an 'earnest and dedicated champion of liberty' who would have earned the approval of a former St Patrick's dean, Jonathan Swift. In fact, the letter's date had been altered, in a case of apparent electioneering that backfired. Dean Griffin had given his backing this time to David Norris.

Shane Ross topped the poll, while Catherine McGuinness lost her seat. Norris, who was running for the sixth time, was elected on the second count, along with Robinson. The margin between them was a mere 22 votes.

'Lawyers are like actors: they prefer to work on a familiar stage with props that are reliable and well known. Indeed, both professions have a remarkably similar need to feel comfortable in planning their entrances and exits!' These were the words of Senator Robinson later in 1987, addressing a legal seminar in Strasbourg. Was she planning her own exit even then? Certainly, from that year on, she seemed to become increasingly preoccupied with her first profession. On 22 May 1989 she released a press statement on Seanad-headed notepaper:

> I have decided not to seek re-election to the Seanad at the next general election, and I am writing to my constituents to explain the reasons and to thank them for their wonderful support over the last twenty years. My activities as a public representative have increasingly focussed on the need for Ireland to meet the challenge of the Single European Market programme of 1992, which is both

an opportunity and a threat of historic proportions. In my capacity as chairman of the Legal Affairs Sub-committee of the Oireachtas Joint Committee on European Community legislation, and as director of the recently formed Irish Centre for European Law based in Trinity College, Dublin, I have concentrated more and more on examining in depth the legal implications involved. Essentially, the demands placed on me by this programme make it difficult to continue to give a full commitment to the day-to-day business of the Seanad. Having had an active and enjoyable twenty years representing the Dublin University constituency, I would prefer, therefore, whenever an election is called, to make way for other candidates of high quality and commitment to carry on the tradition of the university seat.

On 24 May she received a letter from Adrian P. Bourke & Company, Victoria House, Ballina, County Mayo. It was her younger brother and first campaign manager, expressing the 'deepest of regret' at her decision to 'expire from exciting senatorial duties', crediting her with breaking the mould of Irish political thinking – a tone set by her TCD Law Society paper on law and morality back in 1967 – and wishing her a belated happy birthday the previous Sunday.

By 1990 the former senator was throwing all her energies into her legal career. Believing that the solution to Ireland's problems could lie within membership of the European Community, she had established the Irish Centre for European Law in TCD in July 1989 which she was to run with her husband Nick.

As a constitutional lawyer, Mrs Robinson was now heavily involved in the application of EEC – by then abbreviated by Brussels to EC – statutes, particularly in the field of social reform. A major case involving freedom to access of information on abortion for Irish women was before the European courts. In 1988 she joined Senator David Norris in making history when the European Court of Human Rights ruled that new or amending legislation should be brought in to decriminalise homosexuality on the grounds that the existing laws were in breach of the European Convention on Human Rights. The 1861 legislation had allowed a life sentence to be passed for committing certain homosexual acts.

Senator Norris's case was the result of an 11-year-long legal battle, which had already come through the High Court and the Supreme Court. It would be another five years before the judgment was legislated for by the Irish government. Nevertheless, it would give the university lecturer great pleasure to know that the person who signed it into law then, in 1993, was also the 'brilliant' barrister who had applied her 'superb intellect and training' to the case.

Her three children were doing well at their schools, her husband was involved in conservation issues, and her life seemed complete. Primary education for the children was at nearby Sandford Parish, within walking distance of home. William attended Sandford Park secondary school, while Tessa and Aubrey were bound for High School in the neighbouring southside suburb of Rathgar.

And then a colleague turned up on her doorstep, literally, on St Valentine's Day, 14 February 1990. It was John Rogers, the barrister who had been appointed Attorney General under the coalition government in 1984 – the job everyone had expected her to get – and who was a confidant of the Labour Party leader, Dick Spring. He wasn't bearing chocolates or red roses. He said he wanted to have a chat with her, to draw on her constitutional expertise about some ideas he had for a new type of Irish presidency. Within half an hour, she realised why he was there. He was about to ask her if she would 'run'.

The brainwave had been that of a namesake, and no relation, Denise Rogers. The secretary to the Labour Party's deputy leader, Ruairí Quinn, Denise Rogers had been listening to chat about the proposed party candidate for the presidency a few weeks previously. Dick Spring had said in a radio interview that he was determined to ensure that there was an election and that if necessary he would put himself forward. It was a remark that caused some consternation, both within and without the party. It had its desired effect. A number of names were suggested, including that of Dr Noel Browne. Spring believed that his party should be first in with its nomination for the presidency. One morning, Denise Rogers suggested to Ruairí Quinn that Mary Robinson was the obvious choice as 'someone who could make a difference'. She would not be the first woman to be considered as president of Ireland, but would certainly be the first woman to run if nominated. In 1974, when Erskine Childers had died after 17 months in office, his wife Rita had offered herself to the political parties as a potential replacement. Though nothing came of it, she still spent the next few years picking up her husband's work – addressing the Irish Countrywomen's Association in many counties, and becoming involved in community activities on teenage drinking and alcoholism.

Robinson was pale and quiet during John Rogers's visit. She gave no immediate commitment. So strained and tense did she appear the next day that Ann Lane sensed that something was up. This was familiar behaviour. Her boss wanted to say something. 'You're not pregnant again, are you?' Lane inquired.

*

Four months later on a spectacular June morning, she was bouncing along narrow twisty roads on her way to Allihies, west Cork. The road hugged the coast; in the distance, a fishing vessel was steaming into the nearby port of Castletownbere. The Atlantic rolled lazily off the rocks below. Above the road was a blanket bog, banks of fuchsia and the occasional deserted stone cottage. Beyond, the end of the Beara peninsula and the sweep of Bally-donegan Bay.

As the car turned the last hairpin bend into the valley and the village, she caught her breath. What a magnificent contrast to where she had been only the day before, in smug, 'sophisticated' Brussels, the capital of Europe. Within minutes, hands were outstretched to greet her. There were offers of tea. Someone wanted to show her around. Representatives from fishing, farming and community co-operatives in neighbouring Kerry and distant Galway had come to hear her. There were a few inquisitive fishing skippers and fish farmers from nearby Castletownbere. And there were so many journalists that they almost outnumbered the villagers. A bemused young man from the BBC had driven all the way from Belfast through the night: 'It took me the best part of ten hours!'

With her were her husband Nicholas and John Rogers. By now Rogers was at the helm of her presidential campaign. She had needed little persuading once the proposal was put to her, and subsequent meetings to discuss it were formalities. The hard left in the Labour Party had been disappointed initially that Noel Browne was not considered, especially since Mary Robinson had resigned from the Labour Party five years before.

Dr Browne had long retired from politics and was living with his wife, Phyllis, in Connemara on the west coast. Even after his retirement, he had generated controversy with his autobiography, *Against the Tide*, which charted his political career, the death of several members of his family from tuberculosis, his campaign to eradicate the disease, his plans to provide free medical care for mothers and children to the age of 16 – against the wishes of the Catholic hierarchy and the medical profession, which feared that it would reduce drastically the number of private patients. Fearless, he had made the case for contraception when others hung back; was one of a group attacked by dogs used by gardaí during a protest over the US invasion of Cuba outside the US Embassy in Dublin in the 1960s; warned against dealing with multinational corporations; and took on the Catholic Church decades before anyone else dared. It had been agreed to approach Browne informally to sound him out.

Two aspects had attracted her: the idea that she would be the first woman to run for the highest office in the Republic, and the notion that, even if she didn't win, the campaign platform would give her the opportunity to speak her mind on vital issues. The Labour Party's job description sought 'a voice for the voiceless', and she was not long in identifying her constituency as one that stretched beyond the comfortable Dublin drawing-rooms of her liberal, legal friends. Communities like Allihies were separated from the rest of the country by physical distance; within weeks, she would also be seeking the support of women in deprived city suburbs, who had suffered a far greater degree of alienation from the so-called 'centre'.

That evening she was on her way northwards, bound for Tralee, the Kerry county town and home of the Labour Party leader. She was a little apprehensive. Spring wanted to introduce her to a meeting of party members that night to gauge their reaction to her candidature. She need not have worried. A good hour after the meeting ended they were still queueing up to shake her hand.

Though there was a bigger press corps in Allihies, it was in the city of Limerick that her campaign was officially 'launched'; and indeed there were to be several other official launchings from then on. The smaller left-wing political grouping, the Workers' Party, which had six deputies in the Dáil, had supported her nomination in April 1990, as had the Green Party. The 29 signatures on the formal nomination papers had included two independent senators. But to the surprise and delight of Labour Party members in Limerick, Jim Kemmy, a prominent left-wing politician with no party affiliations at the time, rounded up representatives of women's, community and youth groups in support.

Meeting the press was a foretaste of the rough and tumble to come. The single photograph that was published the following Monday showed her holding a mirror as she powdered her nose before the press conference began. The handlers or managers who were to play such an influential role were to remember that photograph. It was candid, and so much more appealing than 'the usual boring shots taken at such events', the Labour Party's press officer, Fergus Finlay, later recalled. That first weekend was a learning experience, he noted in his published account of the seven-month campaign. 'Everywhere she went, she had been introduced as "the next president of Ireland", but it was easy to tell that the announcement was made almost as a little joke, and certainly more in hope than in expectation.'

Finlay had the ear of the Labour Party leader, but in the Robinson campaign he was one of a group. Initially, there was no committee, but the party's deputy leader, Ruairí Quinn, had been appointed director of the presidential election campaign. During these early days, the well-known political activist and television producer, Eoghan Harris, had been so attracted by the idea of Mary Robinson's candidacy that he drafted a ten-page memo outlining some useful 'techniques' which he submitted to the Robinsons. It dealt with both style and substance, according to Finlay, who recalls that one of the most influential paragraphs addressed the psychology of the approach. 'Ordinary people are full of pity, but they are not whiners,' Harris advised. 'Don't run a poverty campaign. Run a caring campaign.'

The Robinsons read the Harris memo avidly, but they were reluctant to identify the author – a controversial figure – to the rest of the campaign team. Instead, a document incorporating some of Harris's suggestions was drawn up by Nicholas and two trusted colleagues who were on the campaign committee, Bride Rosney and Peter MacMenamin, a fellow teacher and senior union official, whom the Robinsons barely knew. It was a move that reflected a degree of distrust between the presidential candidate and her nominating party, given their past relationship. The final campaign committee, chaired by Ruairí Quinn, included the Robinsons, Rosney, MacMenamin, John Rogers, Finlay and Ray Kavanagh, the Labour Party general secretary. Ann Lane was appointed as an observer to counter the presence of a Labour Party observer, Ita McAuliffe. 'The mix was often explosive – but in the end it was both dynamic and creative,' Fergus Finlay wrote. Much of the credit for this was due to the chairman, Ruairí Quinn, but he noted that the most strong-willed member was Bride Rosney.

Not included was the well-known feminist, Anne O'Donnell of the Rape Crisis Centre, who had been proposed initially as campaign co-ordinator and press officer. Articulate on women's rights and subjects such as divorce during the previous referendum, she might have been regarded as an asset. The strategy committee felt that she could be a liability, however, and her name was dropped. Robinson had to relay the news awkwardly to O'Donnell herself just a day after she had secured her agreement to take the job and when she had already begun to arrange leave of absence from work.

Political correspondents regarded Mary Robinson as a rank outsider, but someone who would add a bit of a sparkle to an otherwise lacklustre election. One newspaper said that, frankly, the woman hadn't a chance at all. It was at this point that two other women who would leave their mark joined Robinson's team. In June a senior public relations executive, Brenda O'Hanlon, established a communications strategy committee of activists with relevant experience to pool ideas. One of her first suggestions was to recruit a senior advertising agency copywriter, Catherine Donnelly. Donnelly proved to be indispensable as author of a plethora of campaign slogans including: 'Mary Robinson. If you're old enough to vote, and young enough to care' and 'Politicians debate issues. Presidents address them.' The catch-all cry was 'A president with a purpose'.

Brenda O'Hanlon had no political experience, but she had done work for David Norris, who was elected with Mary Robinson on the second count in the Trinity College constituency in 1987. She was invited to lunch with the candidate in one of Dublin's top restaurants. She suggested that this might be a little too public, and called instead at the Robinsons' home in Ranelagh.

The lunch ran late, and O'Hanlon flew back to work. It was not just the intellect, the confidence and the ability that struck O'Hanlon, who had never met Mary Robinson before: 'It was the total commitment, on the part of herself and Nick, and the amount of thought and attention to detail that had already been given to [the campaign] at this stage. She was prepared to give it whatever it took.'

Her record on liberal issues would be a factor that could play against her with a conservative electorate. Initially, the national press and broadcasting service did not rate the candidate sufficiently for any clashes to arise. This was largely due to the fact that the campaign began outside Dublin, during a good summer when lobby groups appeared to be in slumber. Much use was made of local radio, which was to prove enormously significant – this was a tactic adopted by political parties during the following general election. When the opposition did try to cash in on her liberal record, it was far too late. The foundation had already been laid.

Initially, O'Hanlon worked on a voluntary basis in the evenings after work. By July, however, she knew she wanted to give the campaign her full commitment. Some opportunities only strike once in a lifetime, and she did not want to miss out on this one. She threw her energies into organising the campaign office – a dingy, ill-lit basement in Merrion Square, donated by a trade union. Support came from all quarters; not just from Labour Party activists like Joan Burton, former minister Justin Keating, and Eamon Gilmore of the Workers' Party (now the Democratic Left), but from individuals of various political affiliations or none at all.

Selling an image was not a painless task. Mary Robinson had never been a 'clothes horse' or a fashion plate, and she was not the sort of politician who wanted to be packaged. The truth was, she had not attracted sufficient popular support to become an elected politician in the first place. Nevertheless, the candidate had to accept a change to her academic, blue-stocking image; it was something that she had suggested herself early on. Catherine Donnelly is credited with enlisting Cecily MacMenamin of the city centre fashion store Brown Thomas. A new wardrobe was purchased on a tight budget, and it was suggested that the candidate adopt a new hairstyle. She agreed to a soft body wave. 'The experts advised a perm for practical purposes,' one political commentator wrote in *The Irish Times*. 'Suddenly, here was this chic, tastefully turned-out woman who looked just right for the job.' And the new image was being given 'the thumbs-up from the country's leading fashion lights who felt she was a somewhat old-fashioned relic of eighties power-dressing,' *The Irish Press* noted.[6]

With strategists pitching the cost of the campaign at more than £250,000, Robinson's team also had a finance committee including Niall Greene, a businessman who combined Labour Party politics with work for Guinness Peat Aviation, then a highly successful Irish aircraft leasing company; Kieran Corrigan, described in the media as an 'accountant to the glitterati'; and Greg Sparks, another influential Dublin accountant and Labour Party member. Working closely with both committees were Fergus Finlay, Ann Lane and activists Ita McAuliffe and Ann Byrne, while Mary's close friend, Barbara Fitzgerald, was a constant and vital provider of moral support. A 'Fund to Elect Mary Robinson' was established, with Niall Greene, Donal Nevin and Greg Sparks named as trustees.

An appeal was sent to the managing directors of the country's top thousand businesses to help raise funds for the campaign. It yielded few enough results, given that most businesses generally prefer to give donations to political parties, rather than to apolitical heads of state. However, supermarket magnate Ben Dunne did give a cheque to the campaign director, Ruairí Quinn, when he met him in a pub where a fundraising function was being held.

Seven years later, the candidate was to deny any knowledge of Dunne's largesse, even though it had been agreed at a campaign committee meeting in July that all donations should be acknowledged and that she should be furnished with a list of the donors on a weekly basis so that she could write personal letters of thanks. There are conflicting accounts among those involved in her campaign as to whether Dunne's name appeared on any list that she saw – or even that of Heinz Corporation head and newspaper magnate Tony O'Reilly, who was asked to contribute more than a token 'deposit'.[7]

A personal profile was also drawn up, which reminded voters that this was the first presidential election in 17 years (in other words, no one under the age of 35 had ever had a chance to vote in this plebiscite before). The profile emphasised the candidate's active participation in voluntary organisations such as Cherish, the Liam Maguire Trust and the Women's Political Association, of which she had been elected first president. It went on to list the 'achievements of which she is most proud': Mayo Person of the Year in 1989, and her selection as Irish winner of the Woman of Europe Award in 1988.

Ireland's first female President and Supreme Commander of the Defence Forces inspecting the guard of honour drawn from the Second Infantry Battalion, Cathal Brugha Barracks, Dublin, after her inauguration at Dublin Castle in December 1990. President Robinson is accompanied by officer-in-charge Captain Tom Boyce and her aide-de-camp Colonel Patrick McNally (Eric Luke, Irish Times)

President Robinson addressing both houses of Parliament in Dáil Éireann, February 1995 (Eric Luke, Irish Times)

A people's president — greeted during her visit to Ballymun, Dublin, to launch the Ballymun Partnership project for local unemployment in June 1993 (Mick Slevin, Irish Press); *and with Somali children at a feeding centre, October 1992* (Eric Luke, Irish Times)

The Robinsons are greeted by Queen Elizabeth and Prince Andrew at Buckingham Palace on the President's first official visit to Britain in 1996. She had made an unofficial visit to the Queen in 1993 (Eric Luke, Irish Times)

President Robinson with Prince Charles in London, 1996 (Eric Luke, Irish Times)

A world figure: with PLO leader Yasser Arafat at Áras an Uachtaráin, and with the former Pakistani leader Benazir Bhutto (Irish Times)

At home in Sandford Road, Ranelagh, with the family dog, Tiger (Irish Times)

The Robinson family (from left to right): Tessa, Aubrey and William (Irish Times)

President Mary Robinson with her father, Dr Aubrey Bourke, on the River Moy, Ballina,
County Mayo, with St Muredach's Cathedral in the background

Her marriage of twenty years and her three children were mentioned. The profile also recorded her legal achievements, with highlights identified in this order: the de Burca-Anderson case in 1976, which challenged the jury system as discriminating against women; the Reynolds case in 1973 seeking the right for 18-year-olds to be allowed to vote; the Murphy case in 1982, which was effective in changing the way married couples were taxed; the Wood Quay case in 1978, establishing the Dublin archaeological site as a national monument; the Derrynaflan Chalice case in 1987, confirming the state's right to treasure trove; the Hyland case in 1988, ensuring equality of social welfare benefits for married couples; the Kennedy and Arnold case in 1984, which involved illegal tapping of journalists' phones; the Josie Airey case, where Ireland was found to be in breach of the UN Convention on Human Rights for failing to provide civil legal aid; and the Johnston case, which led to changes in the treatment of non-marital children.

> I have very little experience of this mass projection. I'm more than a little scared, I suppose is probably the word. I'm a very shy person. I'm not a natural gladhander. I probably have considerable limitations, it's too early to know. I've always got on well with a range of people, and I think it probably helped to watch my father all my life – as a GP – relating easily and effortlessly with people, and generally talking to them in a very direct way . . .[8]

It was one of the first of many press interviews, and may have caught the candidate at her most candid. Speaking to Jonathan Philbin Bowman for *U* magazine, an Irish women's monthly, Robinson admitted that she did not think she was going to become a backslapper overnight. She stressed some of her qualities: her association with the women's movement, her background in constitutional law which would ensure that she would be guardian of the Constitution if elected, her work on EC law, and her concern about the lack of scrutiny in Ireland of certain European trade regulations which could have a long-term effect on the economy.

She spoke of reform of the Seanad. 'We have a weakness as a country, as a people,' she said, referring to the need for a 'second balance' which the Seanad served to fulfil: 'It's a sort of exaggeration at times. Put some bombs in Dublin and I would be worried about the law we would pass two days later. I would be really worried about the lack of built-in maturity about civil liberties issues. We lack that utterly entrenched maturity that comes from always having had a secure middle class. We didn't in Ireland, historically, have throughout the last couple of centuries a secure middle class that upheld, through thick and thin, those kinds of values, and there is sometimes even a distrust of the law that comes from our historical situation. We have to understand these things and therefore we do need the check and balance of a second chamber, but we need a more effective one.'⁹

Talking of the effect of the campaign, she said she would like to 'shelter [her] children' as much as possible. 'We've reared three shy children, they're not extroverts,' she said, speaking to Philbin Bowman in the study of her Ranelagh house, where the bookshelves were crammed with novels, art books, encyclopaedias, the complete rules of billiards, and music ranging from Mozart to Culture Club. Yet within weeks, in what she later quipped was 'something of a world exclusive', the family would take their first of many photocalls, this time for *The Sunday Press* of 22 July.

Other early interviews would reflect similar, calculated, themes: her commitment to community involvement, a disillusioned electorate that spread far beyond the 15 per cent vote garnered by socialist parties in the previous election, and the inspiration she drew from the Czech 'people's president', the writer, Vaclav Havel.

'In a strange way, Mary Robinson reminded me of Mother Teresa of Calcutta,' May Clinton wrote in the June issue of the *Irish Farmers' Monthly* – an observation that must have delighted her subject. 'The same passionate awareness of injustice and concern for people's dignity. The same selfless commitment to the betterment of humanity. While others talked about the plight of the poor in Calcutta, Mother Teresa did something about it. Mary Robinson is as determined to use her considerable skills in the battle against injustice in this country. The fact that she had been president of Cherish, the Irish association of single parents, since its establishment in 1973, bears this out.'¹⁰

Polls showed that the Fianna Fáil candidate, Brian Lenihan, was still the main choice for president at 24 per cent, while the independent senator and Dublin councillor Carmencita Hederman, who was still hoping for a presidential nomination for the campaign, polled 11 per cent of support. This was 2 per cent higher than Robinson, the only candidate to have been nominated officially at that stage, some five months from the plebiscite. Charles Haughey, Taoiseach, stood at 12 per cent, while the former Taoiseach and former Fine Gael leader, Dr Garret FitzGerald, had attracted 14 per cent.

Robinson's press coverage was generally positive at this stage, apart from the odd dose of sharp cynicism from the satirical *Phoenix* magazine. It noted, for instance, that many members of the Labour Party were none too happy with the independence of the candidate for whom they were raising funds. Her advertisements stating that she was 'the official Labour candidate but not a member of the Labour Party' did nothing to soothe sensitivities. Even independent senator David Norris felt that Noel Browne had been shabbily treated in not being asked to stand.

The early rows and tensions among committee members tended to arise over the press coverage, principally the conflicting ideas conveyed by various party members in newspaper interviews. There was financial pressure; funds promised by Labour did not seem to be forthcoming. Was this, some of the campaign team wondered, a reflection of the party leader's own lack of enthusiasm? Spring's appearance at campaign functions was scarce enough. There was also a fairly heated disagreement between party members and the Robinson camp over the colour of the campaign logo. Nicholas Robinson had commissioned artwork from a freelance designer, while the campaign chairman, Ruairí Quinn, had ordered it from an advertising agency. Both ideas incorporated a rose, but Quinn's was red and Nicholas's terracotta brown.

Designer clothers were not always the most appropriate things to wear outside the Pale,[11] on the exhausting and exhaustive journey many thousands of kilometres up and down twisty, boggy, pot-holed roads, accompanied by a core group of supporters, including her husband. Out came smart Irish hand-knit jumpers.

By the close of the summer, a third candidate had, at long last, been nominated. Fine Gael, the main centre-right opposition party, had tried for various elder statesmen within its ranks, including Garret FitzGerald and former Foreign Affairs minister Peter Barry. With a background in Northern Irish politics, Austin Currie did an honourable job as the eventual nominee. Given the Republic's weariness with the Northern 'problem', however, some felt that Currie's nomination could only give a backhand boost to the Robinson campaign. His late entry, at the behest of his party leader, confirmed him in many observers' eyes as a token candidate.

Mary Robinson, meanwhile, was hopping over drystone walls on the Aran Islands, chatting with meat-plant workers in the midlands, talking to mothers about the need for childcare and the problems of unemployment in County Donegal. Although well into her seventies, Brigid Murphy the former secretary of Ireland's first president, Douglas Hyde, volunteered to work in her campaign headquarters. She was one of hundreds of supporters in pockets around the country, whose contribution was never fully acknowledged in contemporary accounts of the campaign. One family in Letterkenny, County Donegal, for example, were staunch Fianna Fáil supporters. Yet they were so impressed by Mary Robinson that they threw their full weight behind her.

Interviews in the provincial press were more measured, and there was always an attempt to make the most of local links. *The Derry Journal* noted that her mother was an O'Donnell from Bridge Street in Carndonagh, County Donegal.[12] 'Would you call yourself a practising Catholic?' *The Enniscorthy Echo* in Wexford asked. 'I have never known what is meant by a practising Catholic, but I am not a non-practising Catholic,' she replied.[13]

The Clonmel Nationalist in County Tipperary had a question for her. It referred to a Supreme Court order the previous December which directed leaders of three student unions to stop providing information on abortion clinics in Britain, because to do so was unconstitutional – specifically banned in the Constitution – and unlawful. The case had been referred to the European Court, and the barrister who had defended those students, and was now proceeding to Strasbourg, was Mrs Mary Robinson, SC. During her visit to Clonmel, the newspaper's editorial writer continued, the candidate had quoted the presidential oath: 'I dedicate my abilities to the service and welfare of the people of Ireland'. Given that a vote for her would inevitably be interpreted as an endorsement of her stance, she should be asked if 'the people of Ireland also include, in her view, those who have no voice at all, the nation's unborn?'.[14]

In a written reply, Mrs Robinson said that the Constitution guaranteed the right to life of the unborn, 'and I fully support that right as guaranteed by the Constitution'. She had emphasised that the president was guardian of this Constitution, during her travels around the country, and it was a sacred trust. 'I seek a mandate to carry out that sacred trust,' she wrote, emphasising that, 'as a mother of three children', she felt she could do so with 'compassion and dedication'.

There was no contradiction at all in her position, she continued. Indeed, through sponsoring three private members' Bills in the Seanad to legalise family planning, and through her presidency of Cherish, she had, she said, 'probably done more than any other person in public life over the last twenty years to promote the value and life of the unborn and the rights of children'. During her time in the Seanad she had drawn attention to the number of Irish women going to Britain for abortions, and the evidence from official British statistics showed that the injunction prohibiting the provision of information had not reduced this flow. 'This is a serious social issue which we should address with compassion and honesty,' she went on. 'The best way to reduce abortion is to prevent unwanted pregnancies by promoting responsibility in relationships and family planning and, where unwanted pregnancies do occur, by providing the necessary range of supports to the pregnant women concerned to remove the pressure for abortion.'

The newspaper was not satisfied. Replying to her letter, it said: 'Some time ago here, we pointed to the affinity between paramilitary killers and their supporters and those who have abortions and their helpers. Both claim the right to choose to arbitrarily terminate the life of another.' Like the paramilitaries, 'proponents and practitioners of abortion' believed in 'the rightness' of their actions. 'That is what makes it all so terribly chilling . . .'[15]

Mary Robinson was 'touching up' her knowledge of Irish when her campaign began to build a head of steam. The only president to date who had not been able to speak Irish was Erskine Childers, though the incumbent, Dr Hillery, was a hesitant *gaeilgeoir* when he first entered public life, though he had improved on the advice of Eamon de Valera. She was also making efforts to woo Fine Gael support, when a headline in *The Limerick Leader* – 'Mary makes him sick' – blared out on 1 September. It set the tone for a wicked couple of months. The newspaper reported on a 'blistering attack' on the Labour presidential candidate by the Fianna Fáil TD Willie O'Dea, who accused Robinson of 'having a privileged existence all her life' and of posturing to the less well-off. 'She has never seen a poor day and when I see her spouting on about the under-privileged it makes me sick.'

That September the candidate's agenda came in for close scrutiny in a series of newspaper articles on the role of the presidency. Catherine Donnelly had alerted attention to an article published the previous month in *The Sunday Times* by the respected RTE broadcaster and historian John Bowman. Writing about the style of the office, he noted that the first incumbent to begin a debate on the role was Erskine Childers, in spite of his untimely death in 1974. Not only did this election present the Labour Party with an opportunity, for the first time in decades, to win more than its 10 per cent national support, but with 'an exceptionally gifted candidate' it could 'scupper once and for all the perception of the presidency as a perk for old men who have largely completed their careers'.[16]

'Presumably you have this in your files but – just in case!' Donnelly scribbled in a covering fax note. 'The content has obvious implications. Mary shouldn't make too much of the fact that she intends changing the president's role – or rather she should not imply that she thinks she is the first to advance such an idea.'

The issue was taken up in detail the following month, even as the former Labour minister Noel Browne indicated that he would support Fine Gael's Austin Currie for the office. 'Presidents can make a difference' wrote the commentator Bruce Arnold in the *Irish Independent.* 'Most people know of the restrictions on the president. Few understand his [*sic*] powers.' Only one of the six Irish presidents to date had taken action which challenged the government of the day – Childers's successor, Cearbhaill Ó Dálaigh. Mary Robinson was attempting to place an option for change before the electorate, Arnold said. 'No one would pretend that this is an easy option to realise. After sixty years of plodding along, mainly with retired politicians, with inter-party, nod-and-wink agreements over candidates, and with a general policy of starvation, not just about the functions of the office but also about its finances, why change?' There were good reasons, he said, notably the 'sustained dissatisfaction, particularly among young people and minority groups, with the pointlessness of what the President is and does . . .'[17]

Two significant pieces of press coverage – one, the full family treatment from the international *Hello* magazine, emphasising the candidate's wholesome image as she and her spouse sat in their garden with their children; and the second, a controversial interview with the rock journal, *Hot Press* – distracted attention from the debate on the president's role at a crucial time.

On 27 September, in the fourth of a series of features for *The Irish Times*, a UCD post-graduate student, Jim Duffy, referred to an incident that had occurred during the present incumbent's term of office which sought to compromise Dr Hillery. There was no immediate response. It would come, with full force, some weeks later . . .

CHAPTER 10

Rocking that System

Those close to her noticed the transformation, as she shed her shy, almost aloof demeanour and took people's hands. The appeal was to the marginalised – to emigrants with no right to vote, to people with mental and physical handicaps, to homosexuals, to community groups. One of her many functions was the launch of a biography of Liam Maguire, a wheelchair-bound trade unionist and political activist whom she had represented in an attempt to improve the constitutional position of people with disabilities. But she appealed most of all to ordinary liberals everywhere.

It was in early October, just over a month before the vote on 7 November, that the sparks began to fly. Until then, her opponents may not have taken her too seriously. The state broadcasting service certainly didn't: it had no footage of the early stages of her campaign. Even her 'sponsor', the Labour Party, seemed unaware of the momentum that had been gathered around the country.

The row was over a three-letter word, attributed to Mary Robinson in an interview with the popular rock music magazine, *Hot Press*. She was asked if she would open a new stall in a Dublin city centre record store which would sell condoms in breach of Irish law. 'Yes,' she replied. 'This is a very young country and I think it would be helpful to have a president who was in touch with what young people are doing.'

The interview was wide-ranging. She had always 'felt strongly' that homosexuality should be decriminalised and would continue to express such reservations about certain legal constraints in a personal capacity, even if elected as a guardian of the Constitution. She was critical of the influence of the Catholic Church and of the judiciary; so shallow was the pool from which judges were drawn that there was not enough participation by women. And 'the whole patriarchal, male-dominated presence of the Catholic Church' was 'probably the worst aspect of all the establishment forces that have sought to do down women over the years'. She would love to see 'women priests, women bishops and even a woman pope', she continued. 'It's an awful pity that the Catholic Church hasn't grasped the importance of being on the side of equality and opportunity.'

Within two days, she was fending off attacks, and claiming that she had been misinterpreted. Her reply of 'yes' was by force of habit, and did not mean that she would perform the official opening of the controversial condom stall, she countered. The editor of *Hot Press* stood by the interview, and released a tape-recording of parts of it to justify his case.

For a woman who had been a pioneer of social justice, who had campaigned against the constitutional ban on divorce and who had introduced the first bill to legalise contraception in 1970, her reaction did not ring true. Within a week, Fine Gael took advantage of the situation, with an attack on her 'liberal stance'. The party's director of elections, Jim Mitchell, who had run against her in Dublin West in 1981, even went so far as to resurrect a 'red scare'. Mary Robinson represented 'the acceptable face of socialism', he said.

The 'longest suicide note in history' was how one political source described the 'damagingly candid' interview, when asked by Emily O'Reilly, political correspondent of *The Irish Press*. 'The three-page interview featured Ms Robinson kicking at every national Holy Cow,' O'Reilly reported on 5 October. 'An ill-judged attempt to row back on the RTE *News At One* had a defensive Robinson stating that some of her best friends were priests and nuns.'

The largely positive press coverage of the candidate to date in national newspapers was already being challenged elsewhere. 'Mary so exclusive !' shouted a headline in *The Southern Star* of 6 October. Of the three candidates running for president, Mary Robinson was the most intriguing, if for no other reason than her membership of 'the most exclusive club in the world', the Trilateral Commission, it said. 'Critics have accused it as a force for the Americanisation of Europe', the provincial newspaper said, but the commission's approach to developing countries was most controversial, given that it had made a case for the rich getting richer to help the poor. 'Putting the matter crudely,' the opinion column continued, 'the object of the Trilateral Commission is often seen as turning the powerful northern states against the poorer southern ones. If Ms Robinson should become president, it would be interesting to learn what her attitude would be to poverty in South America and Africa.'

The Trilateral Commission was also prominent in a profile in *Phoenix* magazine on 5 October, written before the controversial *Hot Press* interview appeared. Her committee was dominated by men, it said, though this was not true. And her campaign literature displayed signs of 'political paranoia', playing down the Labour Party connection and making no mention of her defence of the right to disseminate information on abortion, or of that 'ugly word, contraception'. Her reticence was 'no accident', the magazine said. After all, she was appealing to a broad base of support, including the Labour and Workers' Party membership, the liberal vote, the non-aligned vote, and the 'plain women of Ireland' vote which, ironically, 'might be most alienated by any whiff of an abortion smear or even propaganda about divorce and contraception'. She had even struck out into the 'wasteland of the hard right', it said, with overtures to members of the Progressive Democrats. 'Law Library barristers and solicitors nationwide have also received a letter from another of Mary's decidedly non-socialist brothers, Adrian, who, while pleading for money to support Mary's campaign, makes it quite clear that he does not support her political record.'

A more interesting constituency was the Protestant vote, given that she had 'suffered more opprobrium for marrying into the "wrong" church than she did for joining the wrong political party', *Phoenix* said, incorrectly. And another 'tiny but influential constituency' was the media, it said, whose 'darling' Mary had become. Among those women writers attending 'think-tank' sessions for her campaign were *Irish Times* journalists, it continued, remarking that the daily had become 'a cheerleader for Mary', though this might have had as much to do with the newspaper's readership as its staff. The *Phoenix* forecast? She would do well to win over 20 per cent of first-preference votes, and 'the real question is not whether she can make it to the Park or not, but why she decided to go for it in the first place'.

Austin Currie had decided to tackle the 'Northern factor' with which he was so closely identified, rather than trying to play it down. His political broadcast for television carried a clip of him being batoned by police during civil rights protests back in 1968. He appealed to his rivals in the campaign to sign a 'peace pledge' stating that a united Ireland would come about only by agreement of a majority of the population in the North.

Brian Lenihan was sceptical. He was 'not going to make a political football' out of Northern Ireland, he said. Mary Robinson, by contrast, sought an incorporation in the Republic's Constitution of the relevant 'unity by consent' article in the Anglo-Irish Agreement. This was the Agreement that she had so vigorously opposed five years before, Lenihan said, implying that she was guilty of a U-turn. This was not quite so.

The former Taoiseach, Dr Garret FitzGerald, joined in the fray. He broke his 'three-year silence on the Anglo-Irish Agreement', *The Irish Times* reported, to warn the public that the election of either Lenihan or Robinson would 'give a wrong impression' in the North and to British opinion. Austin Currie, his own party's candidate, represented the 'mainstream of opinion in this state'.

Lenihan's campaign had been going well. Always charming and witty, with a warm and human touch, he was displaying great energy in spite of a recent liver transplant, and was leading the opinion polls. Then, towards the end of October, with only three weeks to the vote, he tripped up.

The first sign of trouble was a letter to *The Irish Times*, published on 9 October and referring to one of the series of articles written for the newspaper on the presidential campaign by a UCD postgraduate student, Jim Duffy. The letter wished to clear up facts surrounding an attempt by the opposition party, Fianna Fáil, to prevent dissolution of the Fine Gael-Labour coalition government in January 1982. The party's current presidential candidate, Brian Lenihan, had been one of those who had tried to influence the President, Dr Hillery, on this matter.[1]

That Sunday, a newspaper opinion poll recorded Lenihan's support as falling from 46 to 32 per cent. Mary Robinson's support, in contrast, had climbed from 40 to 51 per cent.

Such was the furore – mixed with some curiosity about the newspaper's decision to announce the revelations rather than break a story about this dimension itself (it was perhaps unwilling to appear to be unduly influencing the election result) – that it seemed as if Lenihan's handling of the affair was going to threaten the future of the coalition government. Fianna Fáil's junior partner, the Progressive Democrats, was not happy at all. The genial Deputy Prime Minister rejected any suggestion of his resignation. Gazing right into the television camera in a direct and emotional appeal to the Irish public, Lenihan said that 'on mature recollection' he had not made any phone calls to President Hillery that fateful night.

He had served almost thirty years in politics and had held ministries in nine different administrations. Loyalty to the Taoiseach, Charles Haughey, had been his forte, but he would still be sacked from his cabinet post. Attempted interference with the office of president was one matter. What was perceived by many – and certainly presented as such by his opponents – as a public lie afterwards was another matter entirely. Bruised, battered, but now unbowed, Lenihan was still determined to run for the presidency. Fine Gael indicated that it would be tabling a motion of no confidence in the current administration.

Despite the 'red scare' attacks early on, Fine Gael had agreed on a vote transfer arrangement, under the proportional representation system, with Labour. This would be crucial in determining the outcome on the day of the vote – offering an 'out' to those Fine Gael voters who might not be too happy with their own candidate. It did not stop one Fine Gael TD from sending a letter to his constituents, warning that a vote for Robinson would be a vote for 'Workers' Party policies' which were 'not in the best interests of the country'. Many voters also received literature from the right-wing lay pressure group, Family Solidarity, urging them to vote for either Lenihan or Currie.

The Lenihan sacking was not perceived by his opponents to be an advantage. It 'devastated the Robinson camp', according to Emily O'Reilly in her book on the campaign.[2] Why so? 'The public humiliation of Fianna Fáil's most popular politician would do what Lenihan's own campaign team had failed to do to date,' she pointed out: 'light a fire under the grassroots.'

As O'Reilly noted, Mary Robinson had taken a clever line on the Lenihan affair before his dismissal from the cabinet. She was advised to take the 'moral high ground' and to point out that it should not 'be blown out of all proportion or detract from the decency of Brian Lenihan's record of public service or be allowed to plunge the government into a crisis'. Yet though her campaign was worried about the sympathy-vote factor in Lenihan's favour, it was Fine Gael which was to suffer most.

Two days after the so-called 'Lenihan tapes' had been played, Austin Currie's support had dropped by three points to 17 per cent, according to a private poll conducted by Fianna Fáil. In another poll, the pattern of vote transfers was good news for Robinson. It indicated a significant fall in Lenihan's appeal across party loyalties, while it also showed most of Fine Gael's transfers would pass to her.[3]

Her two younger brothers – who had taken a step back from political work with her when she joined Labour, given the family Fine Gael affiliation – had thrown themselves into the campaign with vigour. Henry remembers that it was very like her first bid for the Seanad: 'There was never any question in her mind, or in Bride Rosney's, about winning. She had a vision, and a plan. It was a master stroke to begin in March/April as by the time the other parties got moving she had more than established herself nationwide.'

It took the Labour Party some time to realise that she had a good chance, he believes. 'John Rogers was going to give the other parties a good run for their money. One or two senior figures didn't think she would pick up significant transfers. I'm particularly proud that Galway, where I live, was the only city/county to put her over the bar without transfers!'

'The number of women who helped right around the country was phenomenal. In that sense, I'm not sure of the full impact of some of the nasty incidents that happened later on,' says Henry. Those running the campaign office in Merrion Square were constantly amazed at the range of companions and acquaintances who turned up to volunteer help. This was mirrored throughout the country, Brenda O'Hanlon recalls: 'It was a roller-coaster. Not quite spontaneous, but very committed.' That the established political parties were not aware of its full extent is largely due, she believes, to the fact that they tend to talk too much to themselves all the time.

Labour was as guilty of this as any party. Henry Bourke recalls the send-off from Ballina in October for the official campaign bus which his brother Adrian organised. It was only the second time that the Labour leader, Dick Spring, had turned up to lend support; the first time was when he accompanied the candidate on a visit to an Irish emigrant centre in London. 'We got on the bus, and they came out to greet us in every town and village we passed through. We went into Mellett's pub in Swinford, County Mayo, we went into bookies' shops. Spring couldn't believe it. He stayed on the bus much longer than planned, I think. It may have been the first time he realised that she might actually make it after all.'[4]

One of Mrs Robinson's final television appearances – with the other candidates and their spouses on the *Late Late Show* on RTE – saw her husband acquitting himself reasonably well, although she was not quite so relaxed. She had turned in what her campaign team regarded as a bad performance on an RTE current affairs programme, *Today Tonight*, some days before. She was quoted a statement made by her in October 1990, in which she had said that 'I am a socialist – the task is to build the socialist movement' and to nationalise banks and control building on land. She laughed and denied the claim, though this was effectively challenged by one daily newspaper the following day. She had, however, made many statements to the contrary which were on public record. She got away with it, though, thanks again to Fianna Fáil.

Desperately trying to recover lost ground, the main government party tripped up again. Lenihan had been making a remarkable recovery, when a cabinet colleague, the Minister for the Environment, Padraig Flynn, was forced to apologise to the Labour candidate for his outburst on a Saturday radio current affairs show on RTE. He had referred to Mrs Robinson's 'new interest in the family' during the campaign. On the same programme Michael McDowell, the chairman of the junior government party, the Progressive Democrats, described Flynn as a 'disgrace', while his comments had an electric effect elsewhere. The radio station was swamped with calls of complaint. Fianna Fáil, it seemed, was out of touch.

A final Fianna Fáil rally in Dublin caught the governing party with its back to the wall. Charles Haughey compared the 'smear campaign' against his old friend, Brian Lenihan, with the attempt to destroy the great nineteenth-century Irish politician, Charles Stewart Parnell. In her final press conference, Mrs Robinson said that she had been bothered by the 'personalised tone and demeanour' of the latest attack on her by Haughey. 'I have the consolation of knowing that they reflect desperation on the part of my attackers and that victory is close,' she said.

The pre-vote editorial in *The Irish Times* attempted to define the real significance of the moment. For the great majority of voters going to the polls on 7 November, it was a choice between Mr Lenihan and Mrs Robinson, it said:

> To choose Mr Lenihan would be to elect a man who is widely liked, vastly experienced and, in the culture of his party and his times, a man who has served his public well. But he has shown himself to be enmeshed in a set of attitudes and values from which this state must escape; a set of attitudes and values which ought to be consigned to history.
>
> To choose Ms Robinson might be to choose a degree of uncertainty, of inconsistency, of challenge. But underneath the multi-layered persona which has been fashioned by her campaign managers there are qualities which have characterised her years in politics, in public life and in the law. She may have shifted ground in the campaign and she may have back-pedalled where she has believed herself in danger of running foul of public opinion. Yet she represents and has committed herself over the years to a vision of a future Ireland which can be open, generous, pluralist and tolerant. This is where the choice lies, where two cultures and two Irelands clash. We shall learn something about ourselves as a people when the votes to be cast tomorrow are counted.[5]

The last newspaper opinion poll showed Robinson and Lenihan neck-and-neck at 43 per cent, with Austin Currie trailing at 14 per cent. It was noted that the last three-cornered contest for the presidency had been in 1945, when Seán T. O'Kelly was elected against opposition from General Seán MacEoin of Fine Gael and Dr Patrick McCartan, an independent republican supported by the Labour Party.

On polling day, Brian Lenihan rose from his bed in Castleknock, and offered breakfast to journalists – now parasites in the eyes of his bruised family – before setting out on his tour of the day. Much of it passed in a bone-chilling grey blur, as the Lenihan route around 25 polling stations in the Dublin West constituency was covered to the somewhat bizarre tune of the latest hit, 'Simply the Best', from US rock star Tina Turner.

The ballot papers still described him as Tánaiste and Minister for Defence, but no one remarked on it. It had been a long, painful week since, in his wife's words, he had 'got the bump' from his old colleague Charles Haughey, and it would be a long time before that could be forgiven.

In Blanchardstown, County Dublin, his wife, Ann, recalled with annoyance that she had forgotten to place a bet. Driving through vast, bleak housing estates where big dogs prowled around while under-nourished, ill-clad children played, the Fianna Fáil candidate remarked on how much his constituency had grown beyond recognition. There was a polite silence: Fianna Fáil councillors had been instrumental in re-zoning much of the agricultural land.

By midday the Lenihans were at Lucan, and by lunchtime in Clon-dalkin – just in time for leek soup in a local hotel. There, the campaign manager, Bertie Ahern, declined an invitation to eat lunch, and chewed his fingernails instead. Ann Lenihan closed her eyes and sighed. Despite the trauma of the past few weeks, nothing could have been worse than her husband's illness and liver transplant, she said.

Austin Currie, who had made a closing appeal for a vote transfer with Mary Robinson, had already booked a holiday for himself and his wife in Spain. The plane would leave before the election count was over. Two other people were away. President Hillery, who was not due to vacate office until 3 December, had left for Japan the day after the poll to represent Ireland at the enthronement of the new emperor. And Mary Robinson's personal secretary, Ann Lane, had been planning a trek to the Himalayas for some years and was booked to leave Ireland for Nepal on 24 October. She had planned to hike to the base camp of Mount Everest, but was afflicted with altitude sickness at 15,000 feet. The only remedy for altitude sickness is immediate descent. Ann spent some days below in a monastery, and then travelled back to rejoin her group in the middle of November in Kathmandu. There she ran into a compatriot, Wicklow trekking guide Anne Marie McKenna, who had just been on the phone to home. Had she heard the news? Anne Marie asked her, not knowing her background.

Back in Dublin the previous week, Mary Robinson had stood up on a small wooden platform in a draughty election count hall at the Royal Dublin Society in Ballsbridge, and had made a most memorable victory speech to a jubilant crowd. Shortly before, Brian Lenihan had walked in, still defiant and blaming a 'rainbow coalition of various disparate elements on the extreme right and extreme left'. Even as he was being interviewed, there was an almighty crash and a bang as someone fell off a chair. There was a snarl from one of Lenihan's Fianna Fáil faithful: 'That's the fall of RTE . . .'

Labour Party deputies talked of a sea-change, as the last of the 1,143 black boxes were emptied and the tally had given an early indication of the result. Senator David Norris burst in. 'The west's awake,' he cried. Who could have believed it, he asked, clasping the hand of Fine Gael TD Monica Barnes. Who would have believed that Mary Robinson had topped the poll in the Aran islands in Galway Bay? 'Can you imagine what's happening out there in Kilronan?' he asked.

In fact, it was Mary Robinson's appeal to the urban voter that was crucial. Analysts noted that she had taken 47.5 per cent of the vote in Dublin city and county, compared to 39 per cent for Lenihan and 13.5 per cent for Currie. She had come out top in eight of Dublin's 11 constituencies. However, Lenihan recorded his highest percentage vote of any constituency when he took 55.3 per cent in Donegal North-East.

Had the Lenihan affair contributed to Robinson's success? Some point out that this is to understimate the level of genuine support for her around the country. Some political analysts say she would have done well anyway, while others point to the level of transfers which would not have been sufficient to cover her on the second count. Ironically, as one analyst, Jim Farrelly, noted, the party to which her family owed close allegiance, the party which she chose not to join way back in her Seanad days, had rallied to her cause.[6] 'Mary Robinson was elected not by the left vote, the women's vote or the "progressive" vote, but by transfers from probably conservative Fine Gael supporters for whom Mary Robinson's chief attraction was that she was not Brian Lenihan and not Fianna Fáil,' he wrote. As had occurred in the 1980s, Fine Gael voters had cast their lot 'almost completely' in favour of a non-Fianna Fáil candidate. 'Less than 10 per cent of Austin Currie's voters failed to record a second preference and almost 77 per cent opted for Mary Robinson with only 14 per cent for Brian Lenihan.'

These were the same voters who may have voted against divorce in 1986, and in favour of the constitutional amendment outlawing abortion three years before that, Emily O'Reilly observed. 'What this surely proves is that either [Eoghan] Harris and others really had reconstructed Robinson to the point of neutralising her former radical liberal image or that a fundamental change had come about in the national psyche since the 1986 divorce referendum. Perhaps an element of both.'[7]

In spite of warnings that a presidential election did not necessarily reflect national trends, political parties did react, O'Reilly said. The Labour Party shifted to the right, as had its counterpart in Britain in embracing 'social democracy'. It was enough to help it into a coalition government. Fianna Fáil said it was undertaking a radical review of its ethos, heralded a white paper on marital breakdown and promised to repeal the legislation outlawing homosexuality. Fine Gael threw out its leader, Alan Dukes, in favour of John Bruton, who quickly indicated that there would be new policies on neutrality and on the Constitution in relation to Northern Ireland. And, as O'Reilly noted, Bruton 'put divorce back on the agenda again'.

'Exactly one year ago today, the Berlin Wall came down. Five months later, at the invitation of the Labour Party, I applied to the people of Ireland for the job of president,' Mary Robinson began her election speech, drafted by Eoghan Harris, and delivered by her in the count centre at the Royal Dublin Society. 'They said: "Don't ring us, we'll ring you." In other words, "show us you are serious".'

The political soothsayers had predicted that the electorate would give her a vote commensurate with the parties supporting her – third place. Undeterred, she had embarked on a campaign that had taken her to places like Limerick, Allihies, the Inishowen peninsula of Donegal and the islands of the western seaboard. 'Now, seven months later, I find that these places did not forget me. The people of Ireland did ring me, and gave me the job.'

She had been elected president with 39 per cent of the vote. Today was a day for 'victory and valediction'. She had been elected by men and women of all parties and none, and by many with great moral courage, who had 'stepped out from the faded flags of the civil war and voted for a new Ireland'. And above all 'by the women of Ireland – *mná na hEireann* – who, instead of rocking the cradle, rocked the system', she said . . . to even wilder cheers.

The night before, she had joined close friends and family in Barnardo's restaurant in Dublin, just around the corner from the old family 'student' home in Westland Row. Her younger brother Henry remembers sitting beside her. 'She had gone into shock. She was unable to communicate.'

Two days later, the flowers were still arriving at the house in Ranelagh. Among the personal messages of congratulation was one from Fianna Fáil's Padraig Flynn. 'We walked down the garden. She turned to me. "Jesus, Henry, I'm going to be President of Ireland," she said.'[8]

CHAPTER 11

Dangerous Nonsense

Rituals. Symbols. Pipes. Guns. But no victories, no defeats. The annual day out for the Protestant Orange Order in the North of Ireland, 12 July, was marked in very different fashion down South in 1996.

Up North, the bowler hats, pipes and lambeg drums were out to celebrate a three hundred-year-old trouncing of a Catholic monarch by a Protestant king. In the South, the salutes were for the Supreme Commander of the Republic's Defence Forces to mark the fiftieth anniversary of the Naval Service.

She wore a red dress, no hat, as she reviewed the fleet on board the naval flagship, LE *Eithne*, under a blistering Cork sun. Among the visiting European and Canadian vessels was the Royal Navy's HMS *Manchester*, named after the city which had been bombed by the IRA some months before. The British crew tossed their caps in the air and cheered. When the last such event had taken place in Cork harbour 99 years before, the courtesy flag had been the Union Jack. The President inspected the guard of honour, presented the official cased 'colour' flag and handed bronze medallions to a dozen veterans. Among those on duty were the Navy's first two female cadets. The formalities ashore took some minutes, and seemed far less spontaneous – in fact, almost tedious – compared to the sail-past at sea. Out in a light southerly breeze in one of the world's finest natural harbours, one could almost forget that this was a military occasion.

Back at base, all three wings of the Defence Forces were well represented. This was not just the Navy's day. Their Supreme Commander planted her elbows on the podium, leaned forward, spoke with her hands. It was as if 'the heavens approved', she said. Why, hadn't Van Morrison, Belfast rock musician, written a song about 'Days Like This'? Jaws stiffened a little. She was far too at ease to sense the response among a section of the attendance. Nothing obvious: as if to say, 'this isn't Woodstock, or a Croke Park rock gig'. As if to say, with a resigned sigh, did she have to adopt that particular tone?

But then, in five and a half years in office, military occasions had not been her forte. From the outset she had placed great emphasis on respect for the Constitution, and for the role of president – vested with supreme command of the Defence Forces by Article 13.4 of the Constitution, but with no executive function. Yet, from the moment that the 'Blue Huzzars'– 36 motorbiking members of the Second Cavalry Squadron, Cathal Brugha Barracks, Dublin – had collected her for her first formal occasion on 3 December 1990, she had never looked very comfortable in the company of arms.

The band of the Curragh Command had played Handel's March from *Scipio* that day to mark her own inauguration in Dublin Castle. She was invited to inspect the guard of honour while the music played. Such was the pace of her step that she looked as if she might break into a skip herself at any moment. One of her staff remembers that it was only when she looked at a newspaper photograph of the occasion the following day that the full impact of the ceremony struck home. For her, it was revolutionary; comparable to the applause which had marked Nelson Mandela's inspection of the troops in Pretoria when he was inaugurated president of the state that had incarcerated him . . .

The unease with pomp and circumstance cut both ways. In the summer of 1991, the hundred-man Presidential Guard from the Fifth Battalion, Collins Barracks, Dublin, had assembled at Dublin Airport, as was the norm, when the President flew out to London. Wearing a canary-yellow outfit, the President had left the airport's VIP terminal to walk across the apron when a ripple of laughter ran through one section of the line-up. She didn't hear what caused the mirth, but perhaps she might have been tempted to smile if she had. Her attire had obviously reminded someone of the children's television show, *Sesame Street*. 'Here comes Big Bird,' was the remark. A soldier's weekly wages were docked by 50 per cent as a reprimand.

No, her forte was dealing with community groups and her relationship with the new 'Mary Robinson constituency'. Immediately after the election result, her home town had greeted her, as tradition befitted, with some five thousand candles, Hallowe'en sparklers, county flags, tricolours and balloons. The outgoing President, Dr Patrick Hillery, had led the tributes from all quarters on her success, while the Taoiseach, Charles Haughey, had appealed to all sides to put 'untoward, hurtful or wounding' remarks made during the campaign behind them, and had assured the president-elect of his total loyalty.

She set the tone for her office during her acceptance speech at the election count, when in subtle language she bid farewell to the parties which had supported her – because she had now taken up a non-political post. The tone was also set during the inauguration, when invitations to the 750-year-old Dublin Castle, once the seat of British rule in Ireland, were so limited that some close relatives, and the spouses of many guests, were not on the guest list. The eighteenth-century former ballroom had housed many such formal occasions, including the conferring of freedom of Dublin on John F. Kennedy in 1963.

The hand of a philosophy lecturer at UCD, Dr Richard Kearney, was reflected in the speech. He was one of several academics and commentators who had pronounced on the historic nature of the election. It marked the beginnings of a 'national psychodrama' between a new Ireland and the old, he declared.

A 'watershed', said leading psychologist Dr Anthony Clare, a view echoed by former Labour politician and commentator Dr Conor Cruise O'Brien and the poet Paul Durcan, among others. Durcan's family was from her home town, Ballina, and his father had been the judge before whom she had pleaded her first legal case. 'Áras an Uachtaráin will today become famous throughout Europe – as famous as the Hradcany Palace in Prague where President [Vaclav] Havel lives,' Durcan wrote. Waxing lyrical, he predicted that the presidential residence, which Mary Robinson had never visited, would no longer be the preserve of the establishment or party faithfuls: 'Instead, it will belong to all the people and the young woman from Galway in wine suede shoes and blue denim suit will walk arm in arm through the Áras with her boyfriend in his Sunday suit, the fishermen of Allihies will sit down under the chandeliers with fishermen from Greece, the Irish in England will be as at home here (and, therefore, there) as the Irish in Munster; and the Orangeman will be as welcome as the British ambassador; the old will sit down with the young.'

It would become the 'forum of all the people', he continued, and its chambers would 'ring out with madrigals to the words of the poet of liberty John Milton – *and who's to still the madrigals that whisper softness in the chambers?*'[1]

The campaign had cost £200,000. The office would cost beween one and two million pounds annually, in an expanded presidential budget to which other political parties had already given a commitment. There would be no change to the form of address, but the new president would have a female army aide-de-camp, it was reported. She intended to expand the role of the little-used Council of State, by choosing seven new members to represent the interests of women, young people and the farming community. Her husband would 'not be a Denis Thatcher', though he would be a 'good cook', the tabloids said. And though the Taoiseach had pledged loyalty, 'Robinson's views may lead to a political clash with government' was the informed forecast.

'Something more than icing on the cake' was the reaction from Mary Maher in *The Irish Times*, who judged that Robinson's election was a first step towards healing the scars inflicted by the divisive abortion and divorce referenda in the 1980s. Recalling how the newspaper's women's page had proposed Mary Robinson as undisputed choice for taoiseach some 18 years before, Maher said that the new president was never part of that women's movement, but was one of those 'rare women who was able to state honestly, in her earnest way, that though she was sympathetic to women, as to other oppressed groups, she had never experienced any discrimination herself'.

It was not her 'feminist fervour' that had won her that nomination then, but her 'sheer suitability for the job'. As a candidate for public office, she was so distinguished that no one came near her. 'It's still true,' Maher wrote. 'Mary Robinson has not so much triumphed over gender discrimination as simply transcended it.'[2]

On the day of her formal inauguration, representatives of the homeless, people with disabilities and those associated with women's rights were on the limited guest list, along with the cream of the establishment. There was a hand across the border, with invitations to Gordon Wilson, who had lost his daughter in the IRA bombing of Enniskillen in 1987, Unionist MP Ken Maginnis, Alliance Party leader Dr John Alderdice, Democratic Unionist Party leader Dr Ian Paisley, Northern Ireland ombudsman Maurice Hayes, and SDLP leader John Hume. Paisley declined his invitation.

Three poets whose work she had drawn from in her victory address the previous month were not forgotten: Seamus Heaney, Eavan Boland and Paul Durcan were on the guest list, although only 50 names were of her own choosing. Durcan's lines, quoted in that speech in November, had struck a particular chord with those many families affected by continued emigration:

> Yet I have no choice but to leave, to leave,
> And yet there is nowhere I more yearn to live
> Than in my own wild countryside,
> Backside to the wind.

There would always be a light on in the president's residence, she pledged, for the exiles and emigrants about whom the poet had so movingly written. Standing on the dais, wearing a purple silk moiré jacket and short black dress, with a striking gold torc and earrings given to her by the Robinson family, she spoke at her inauguration of a fifth province, which she wished to represent. This was 'not anywhere here or there, north or south, east or west,' she said:

It is a place within each one of us – that place that is open to the other, that swinging door which allows us to venture out and others to venture in. Ancient legends divided Ireland into four quarters and a 'middle', although they differed about the location of this middle or fifth province. While Tara was the political centre of Ireland, tradition has it that this Fifth Province acted as a second centre, a necessary balance. If I am a symbol of anything I would like to be a symbol of this reconciling and healing . . .

Her primary role as president would be to represent the Irish state, she said:

But the state is not the only model of community with which Irish people can and do identify. Beyond our State there is a vast community of Irish emigrants extending not only across our neighbouring island – which has provided a home away from home for several Irish generations – but also throughout the continents of North America, Australia and of course Europe itself. There are over 70 million people living on this globe who claim Irish descent. I will be proud to represent them.

Addressing her particular constituency, she said that she had found the extent of local empowerment at work on her travels throughout Ireland during the campaign to be 'one of the most enriching discoveries'. This was 'the face of modern Ireland', she said, breaking into competent Irish which she had been brushing up on during the campaign to pledge that she also intended to embark on another journey – a cultural voyage of discovery of the wealth and beauty of the Irish language. The best way to contribute to a new integrated Europe of the 1990s was to have a confident sense of Irishness, she said:

Here again we must play to our strengths – take full advantage of our vibrant cultural resources in music, art, drama, literature and film; value the role of our educators; promote and preserve our unique environmental and geographical resources of relatively pollution-free lakes, rivers, landscapes and seas; encourage and publicly support local initiative projects in aquaculture, forestry, fishing, alternative energy and small-scale technology.

And there was her international agenda, for which she now sought permission:

Looking outwards from Ireland, I would like on your behalf to contribute to the international protection and promotion of human rights. One of our greatest national resources has always been, and still is, our ability to serve as a moral and political conscience in world affairs. We have a long history of providing spiritual, cultural and social assistance to other countries in need – most notably in Latin America, Africa and other Third World countries. And we can continue to promote these values by taking principled and independent stands on issues of international importance.

As the elected president of this small democratic country, I assume office at a vital moment in Europe's history. Ideological boundaries that have separated east from west are withering away at an astounding pace. Eastern countries are seeking to participate as full partners in a restructured and economically buoyant Europe. The stage is set for a new common European home, based on respect for human rights, pluralism, tolerance and openness to new ideas. The European Convention on Human Rights – one of the main achievements of the Council of Europe – is asserting itself as the natural Constitution for the new Europe. These developments have created one of the major challenges for the 1990s.

If it is time, as Joyce's Stephen Dedalus remarked, that the Irish began to forge in the smithy of our souls 'the uncreated conscience' of our race, might we not also take on the still 'uncreated conscience' of the wider international community? Is it not time that the small started believing again that it is beautiful, that the periphery can rise up and speak out on equal terms with the centre, that the most outlying island community of the European Community really has something 'strange and precious' to contribute to the sea-change presently sweeping through the entire continent of Europe? As a native of Ballina, one of the most western towns in the most western province of the most western nation in Europe, I want to say – 'the west's awake'.

Strong and stirring stuff. And then she turned to another place close to her heart, Northern Ireland:

As the elected choice of the people of this part of our island I want to extend the hand of friendship and of love to both communities in the other part. And I want to do this with no strings attached, no hidden agenda. As the person chosen by you to symbolise this Republic and to project our self-image to others, I will seek to encourage mutual understanding and tolerance between all the different communities sharing this island. In seeking to do this I shall rely to a large extent on symbols. But symbols are what unite and divide people. Symbols give us our identity, our self-image, our way of explaining ourselves to ourselves and to others. Symbols in turn determine the kind of stories we tell; and the stories we tell determine the kind of history we make and remake. I want Áras an Uachtaráin to be a place where people can tell diverse stories – in the knowledge that there is someone there to listen.

She wanted this presidency to promote the telling of these stories of celebration through the arts and of conscience and of social justice. 'As a woman, I want women who have felt themselves outside history to be written back into history, in the words of Eavan Boland, "finding a voice where they found a vision".' She concluded on a high note:

> May God direct me so that my presidency is one of justice, peace and love. May I have the fortune to preside over an Ireland at a time of exciting transformation when we enter a new Europe where old wounds can be healed, a time when, in the words of Seamus Heaney, 'hope and history rhyme'. May it be a presidency where I the President can sing to you, citizens of Ireland, the joyous refrain of the fourteenth-century Irish poet as recalled by W.B. Yeats: 'I am of Ireland . . . come dance with me in Ireland'.
> *Go raibh míle maith agaibh go léir.*[3]

There was an atmosphere of Camelot about the inauguration, although it was a dull, damp December morning with only a small crowd of spectators gathered outside Dublin Castle on Christ Church Hill. Television had 'ruined the gathering of the crowd in Ireland', one bystander, John Gallagher of Dublin's Liberties, told me. He had made a point of attending, because he had witnessed every presidential inauguration since Seán T. O'Kelly in 1945. The gathering then had been far bigger than for Eamon de Valera. One of the biggest cheers at several of the events in the Castle had been for 'the real president', he said – 'President Keely, a Dublin character, who always came up before the Rolls-Royce on his bike.'

Even as ZJ 5000 – the vintage Rolls-Royce Silver Wraith purchased for O'Kelly in 1949 – purred out of the Castle yard, there was a warm reaction to Robinson's speech at home and abroad. An address 'rich in detail – precision pinning down elusive ideas', and one delivered with pride but without a hint of triumphalism, it was recorded.[4]

Iris Robinson, described as one of Northern Ireland's best-known female loyalist politicians, and wife of the deputy leader of the Democratic Unionist Party Peter Robinson, welcomed Mary Robinson's appointment. It would 'strike a significant blow for women politicians throughout Ireland', she said; but while it would 'change the face of Irish politics forever', the Northern electorate was not yet ready to take a similar step, she stated. None of the North's 17 elected members of parliament in Westminster was female.

The inauguration speech had been worked on over the six months of the election campaign, the President told me seven years later. It reflected 'a process of listening' while on the road. 'When you go out and talk to people and listen to what they hope for in a president, it refines the thinking. I was aware of the limits of the office. It's not about policy-making, it's not about power in the traditional sense, so it was particularly important to have time to get a sense of what people would hope might be done . . . and by listening to their views to carve out actual areas where it would be possible to deliver . . . A lot of it was feeling that it should be possible, but not being quite sure how at that stage.'

The themes of the speech were to be her 'guide', she said, and a constant reference point. The 'list' was not exhaustive. 'But I felt that there was a genuine idea there.' The fifth province was the inspiration of the philosopher Dr Richard Kearney, who had written about it some years before in the periodical, *The Crane Bag*, she said. 'An imaginative idea that captured the inner sense of Irishness that could be open, generous and inclusive and I've learned both at that time, but even more since, about the power of symbols.'[5]

The Times of London judged that this was a politician who was 'serious about understanding unionist fears' in Northern Ireland, and who would make reconciliation a practical priority. The Republic's two leading figures – Robinson and Haughey – now illustrated the contrast between past and future, it said. 'Mr Haughey is a veteran exponent of a traditional nationalism, long on rhetorical appeals to "Irish values" and short on specific ways to achieve the unification of North and South. Mrs Robinson, by contrast, breaks almost every rule in Ireland's book. She is a working mother, an ex-member of the tiny Labour Party, in favour of contraception and publicly available information on abortion and openly sympathetic to Ulster unionism. Little wonder that Mr Haughey muttered "dangerous nonsense" on hearing that she favoured an activist presidency.'

That her office held little power did not diminish the significance of her win, *The Times* said. 'Here is a victory of probity against the pork barrel, of individual merit against the cosy intimacy of a political élite which is divided into two major parties founded in a civil war seventy years ago. She has given hope that Ireland is ready for change.'[6]

Foreign media also expressed favour. While still president-elect, Mary Robinson was chosen as 'person of the week' by North America's top television news programme, broadcast coast to coast by ABC. In Moscow, *Pravda* proclaimed: 'Bravo Mrs Robinson' on a front-page headline. Two US newspapers drew an analogy with the departure of British leader Margaret Thatcher from the 'world stage'. Determined to describe her as 'Ireland's first radical feminist president,' *The Chicago Tribune* noted that Mary Robinson had had her first taste of political activism at Harvard, and quoted an unnamed British diplomat as stating that 'the most conservative country in Europe' had just elected 'one of its most liberal politicians as president'.[7]

The Dallas Times Herald also referred to the departure of the Pakistani leader, Benazir Bhutto. 'But a bright star was born in Ireland when Mary Robinson, a human rights lawyer, became the first female president in that nation's history,' it said. 'While Mrs Thatcher had an august aura about her and Ms Bhutto seemed imbued with tragedy, Mrs Robinson stands before the world as a champion of human rights. She could not have come at a better time.'[8] 'A little bit of Havel, a little bit of Hepburn,' the US magazine *Vanity Fair* said.[9]

The few critical voices were lost on the wind.

'Did you see yer man making a show of himself at the inauguration?' journalist Gene Kerrigan of *The Sunday Tribune* wrote in his television review of the occasion: 'There they all were, the best and brightest (along with some of the worst and dimmest), lined up to welcome President Mary Poppins at Dublin Castle. In she walks, down the aisle. Each side lined with people, staring respectfully ahead as she walked past. And one of them (and, fella, you know who you are) waited until she was just past him and he looked her up and down, from her neck to her ankles. Like a cornerboy appraising the local talent as he finishes his bag of chips before heading off into the back fields with his flagon of Scrumpy Jack.'[10]

The 'relentless cheerfulness' of 'President Poppins' could be hard to take, Kerrigan continued. 'Her win has been shamelessly hyped as signifying wholesale social and political change, when it does nothing of the sort.'

Kerrigan's colleague and editor, Vincent Browne, had a piece of advice for the new incumbent in the same edition of the Sunday newspaper. He referred to her emphasis on symbols in her presidential address, which defined and shaped Irish values. The symbols of the inauguration – the 21-gun salute, the inspection of the guard of honour, and the aide-de-camp – reflected a 'veneration for armies, for guns and for war,' he wrote. 'The new president would be sending a powerful symbol by refusing to have anything to do any more with army personnel tramping the earth in front of her and emitting military exhortations, even if they are in Irish, standing with rifles cocked in line for her to inspect with approval, being accompanied by an imposing military gentleman walking at a respectful two feet behind her. She should have nothing more to do with this dangerous codology, which conveys to people that the ethos of the military is something to be admired – we may have to have armies but we don't have to exult in it.'[11]

Browne also hit out at the wigs and gowns of the legal profession, of which she had been such a part. Such 'garb' was not only 'laughable', but reflected a disdain for clients and the populace at large, he said. 'She should give these boyos short shrift when the occasion arises.'

She didn't, but this did not make the slightest indent on her popularity. Promises made on appointment were to be kept. The welcoming 'candle in the window' or low-watt bulb was one of the first, in the big house up in the Phoenix Park. Teething problems, like the dismissal of former staff at the residence or tensions with her security personnel, received scant attention in the news. The wax-and-flame image reflected a cult which grew up around her at a time of cynicism about elected representatives who did have access to power.

Only in the North, a province so short on trust, would the honeymoon be short-lived. Ironically, it was there that she attended one of her first functions, when the Roman Catholic primate, the Archbishop of Armagh, Dr Cahal Daly, was installed on 16 December – an installation which also signalled a shift towards a more tolerant, 'post-sectarian' Ireland, according to Dr Richard Kearney.[12] Unionists might regard her as a friend, particularly because of her opposition to the Anglo-Irish Agreement. Yet four days after her inauguration, a unionist invitation to a civic reception at Belfast City Hall was expected to cause a 'furious political row' among supporters of the more extreme loyalist Democratic Unionist Party who had been critical of Unionist MP Ken Maginnis's attendance at Dublin Castle. And nationalists, it was reported, would regard her with suspicion because of the growing mood in favour of neutralising the Republic's controversial constitutional Articles Two and Three over the territorial claim to the North. In January, Belfast City Council voted narrowly against inviting her to Belfast.

Even four years later, the media 'mid-term review' would be a panegyric. A series of financial scandals with political overtones inadvertently helped to show her in a very favourable light, as disillusionment with politicians grew; it was a trend right across Europe. In May 1991, her first year in office, a statutory tribunal of inquiry into irregularities in the beef industry had been established, and did not report until July 1994. In September 1991, two semi-state companies came under scrutiny, and in May 1994 there were revelations about 'passports for sale' to businesspeople who would guarantee a minimum investment in the state.

Charles Haughey resigned as leader of Fianna Fáil in 1992 over phone-tapping allegations made by a party colleague, having survived a series of attempts to depose him during his 12-year tenure. Though there was always rumour and innuendo, the Irish public had accepted 'The Boss', as he became known, in the knowledge that he could not have sustained his lifestyle – an island, a yacht, horses, a large mansion in north Dublin – on a parliamentary salary alone. Indeed, Haughey's dependence on contributions from big business towards his personal expenses was to be revealed in July 1997 in the Dunnes Payments Tribunal, an inquiry into payments to politicians. He was succeeded by his former Finance Minister Albert Reynolds, who had made his fortune in ballrooms and petfood. One of Reynolds's first moves as Fianna Fáil leader was to permit a photographer from the glossy magazine, *Hello*, to come to his home for a photo session.

Political scandals of a major and minor nature would run and run, right through Mary Robinson's term of office, in tandem with the revelations about child sex abuse involving members of the Catholic Church. In November 1994, the two combined to bring down a Fianna Fáil-Labour coalition government. The mood was akin to a very public confessional, after decades of darkness. Mary Robinson was to find herself filling a moral vacuum, whether she had intended to or not. Most significantly, her old Labour Party was to form successive coalition governments from 1993, riding on the crest of a wave that dated back to her own election in 1990.

One person was crucial to nurturing her favourable image: Bride Rosney was appointed as the President's special adviser. The 'ultimate backroom worker' was how one commentator described the 41-year-old Kerrywoman, with a quote from an unnamed source to the effect that she was 'sooner my friend than my enemy'.[13]

Bright, meticulous, witty, an individualist, Rosney's politics were left of centre, but it was clear that there was no love lost between her and the Labour Party. For someone who preferred influence to power, she had built up a relatively high profile as chairwoman of the Dublin Arts Festival Committee, an executive member of the environmental organisation An Taisce, and of the powerful Teachers' Union of Ireland. The principal of Rosmini community school in north Dublin took ten seconds to accept, but arranged only 18 months' leave of absence when initially offered the job in the Phoenix Park. In August 1992 she resigned from her teaching job, knowing that she was going to stay. She never wanted to be a 'press handler' in the style of P.J. Mara, legendary voice for Charles Haughey in power, but she did want to serve as the President's eyes and ears. During the campaign, she had fought hard to keep an appropriate distance between Mary Robinson and the Labour Party, while her attention to detail was legendary. As no Irish president had had a special adviser before, Rosney could write her own script. Her task was to co-ordinate programmes, work in liaison with civil servants, come up with ideas and deal with the press. She began as she intended to continue, providing a link between the election campaign and the promise of an actual office and making it clear to civil servants that the incumbent intended to live up to that.

The programme would reflect the agenda drawn up in the inaugural speech: women, emigration, community empowerment, the Irish language, Irish identity, arts and culture, the North, and Ireland's record abroad in Third World development and human rights. In an office without political power, symbolism would take on a new dimension. First, though, the territory had to be defined.

Significantly, the 'fifth province', the focus of the President's introductory remarks at her inauguration, was where early battles were to be fought. Or were they merely forays? As women's voices made the most of the attention in the immediate aftermath ('What do yiz want?' was the cry from politicians, according to *Irish Times* columnist Nuala Ó'Faoláin), there were Cassandra-like warnings of trouble ahead. Already, the government had influenced the President's guest list at the inauguration: the head of the Muslim community in Ireland had not been on the government's list because, a spokesman said, it was not one of the denominations mentioned in Article 44 of the Constitution, an article deleted in 1972. Instead, a representative was on the President's personal list.

Mary Robinson had made it clear that she would not be seeking additional powers, commentators said. Her two independent functions were unlikely to give her difficulty. The first was the power to refer legislation to the Supreme Court for a test of constitutionality before signing it into law; the second was the absolute discretion not to dissolve parliament on the advice of the taoiseach of the day. As a constitutional lawyer, it was anticipated that Mrs Robinson would exercise more caution with the first. Indeed, in an interview during the campaign, she had indicated a preference for challenging legislation in the courts on a set of established facts, after enactment. However, she had questioned the constitutional foundation for the practice that precluded presidents from speaking out on relevant issues of the day without government approval. Would she have a clash, similar to that experienced by two predecessors, Erskine Childers and Cearbhall Ó Dálaigh? Would she exercise her right to address both houses of parliament and the people? Two predecessors had done so – Eamon de Valera on the Dáil's fiftieth anniversary in 1969, and Erskine Childers in a broadcast to the nation on RTE on St Patrick's Day 1974, about the futility of violence in relation to the North.

'If Ms Robinson is to be seen to be active on the ground, she will have to pursue a prudent course if she doesn't want to appear to be a frenzied social worker or running the country,' *The Irish Times* noted.[14] There was the potential for clashes. Her claim of freedom from constitutional restraint for what she did outside 'official functions' had led her to the assertion in her *Hot Press* interview during the election campaign that she would be able to 'look Charlie Haughey in the eye and tell him to back off if necessary' because she had been 'directly elected by the people as a whole and he hasn't'. Unless the government and Mrs Robinson could agree on what was deemed 'official', there would be a good deal of scope for confrontation, the newspaper forecast in another article. But she did have the advantage of being a constitutional lawyer.[15]

Phoenix magazine, never a Robinson fan, was less concerned with trouble ahead. In its 1990 annual it bestowed on her the Eoghan Harris Media Manipulator of the Year Award, for having 'started the year as an obscure, political has-been, rejected by the voters of Ireland and even her more natural constituency of Trinity College, Dublin' and ending it by 'cleaning up in the presidential election, destroying Fine Gael leader Alan Dukes in the process, and perhaps even undermining Squire Hockey himself' – this being a *Phoenix* nickname for Charles Haughey also called 'Charlemagne'.

Under a caption to a photo of the President, described as 'Little Red Robinson', it noted: 'Unfortunately, there are still some people prattling on about how daringly radical Mary's presidency is going to be. These people appear to have taken her and her handlers seriously and expect Mary to overthrow Squire Hockey with a red rose in one hand and a copy of *Hello* magazine in the other.'[16]

But such cynicism was rare at this stage. 'Why are we whispering?' asked her younger son Aubrey, when the family moved up to the presidential residence in the Phoenix Park. It had its 'ghosts': Queen Victoria had stayed there when she visited Ireland, and Winston Churchill had played there as a small boy. She threw open its doors, and threw herself into the job – one of her first functions being the opening of a conference on the homeless.

The row over laying off staff at the residence before Christmas was resolved, though there were admissions that it had been handled badly. The incident provided food for the satirical RTE radio programme *Scrap Saturday*, which was generally good-humoured in its regular send-ups and dubbed her 'Lady Robinson'. Undaunted, the new President committed herself to between 25 and 30 engagements a week, amid comments that she would never keep up the pace. In March, during a BBC Radio Ulster interview, she said that she would 'dearly love' to visit Northern Ireland,

and had been overwhelmed by the response of people there to her desire
to promote reconciliation.

The early tensions were made much of, given the body language
between the Taoiseach, Charles Haughey, and herself. The most publicised
clash then concerned the government's refusal, revealed in June 1991, to
allow the President to accept an invitation from the BBC in London to
deliver the station's annual Dimbleby lecture. Held in honour of the late
broadcaster, Richard Dimbleby, Dr Garret FitzGerald had been the first
Irish speaker, in 1982.

The government defended its decision, in the teeth of criticism from
the opposition. It would be 'without precedent' for a head of state in office
to undertake such an engagement, a spokesman said. Official sources
pointed out that the content of the lecture had 'always been political and
always delivered by leading political figures' such as former West German
chancellor Dr Helmut Schmidt and former EU Commission president
and Labour Party minister Roy Jenkins.

The BBC said that it had not asked the Irish President to talk about any
constitutional matters. She had been asked to deliver the lecture on the
role of women in public life, given her experience as a human rights lawyer,
it said. *The Irish Times* took the government to task. There *had* been a precedent, it said in an editorial. In December 1988 Mrs Robinson's
predecessor, Dr Patrick Hillery, had delivered the Jean Monnet lecture in
Florence at the invitation of the European University Institute.[17]

There were to be other altercations, but many potential conflicts
appeared to have been averted through the good offices of the President
and the Taoiseach's protocol department. Officially, the President only
needed to seek permission from the cabinet for foreign trips. In spite of
intense lobbying by the Chinese embassy in Dublin, she met the Dalai
Lama, winner of the 1989 Nobel Peace Prize, as did two government
ministers, Bertie Ahern and Mary O'Rourke. Though Ireland had championed Tibet's cause at the United Nations after Chinese occupation in
1959, official government policy now was to accept Chinese rule. A
government spokesman said that the President and the two ministers had
met the Tibetan spiritual leader in a private capacity, when he was in
Dublin to open a Buddhist art exhibition.

There was a question-mark over an early trip to London, when it was
confirmed that she would meet British Prime Minister John Major during
a function to mark the opening of the World Bank. There were intimations
that the head of government, rather than head of state, should attend; her
office pointed out that she was already a member of the international jury
which had chosen the bank's new logo, and wished to travel.

Other reported rows only emerged in September, after nine months in office, when *The Guardian* newspaper claimed that the president's high profile had 'got up the nose' of Charles Haughey, at a time when his own fortunes were waning. 'For a man who has projected himself as embodying, literally, the spirit of the nation, his gigantic ego has been severely bruised by Robinson's easy dominance of the limelight,' an article by Peter Murtagh said.

The Taoiseach had been trying to clip the President's wings, Murtagh claimed, citing two examples. In the spring, Bord Fáilte, the Irish tourist board, had asked her to videotape a message for Irish-Americans at St Patrick's Day dinners across the United States. She had obliged with a 'harmless greeting', but Haughey 'blew a gasket'. In April he had sent her a letter, accompanied by the constitutional opinions of two former attorneys general, dealing with the President's powers and referring to Article 13, section 7, of the Constitution. The opinions referred to the President's power to address a message to the nation only after it had been approved by government. As far as Haughey was concerned, Murtagh wrote, this covered interviews – of which she had given many without consultation.

Murtagh quoted unnamed Irish diplomats in the United States as saying that Haughey had decided 'not to let Robinson out of the country', when they expressed surprise that a nine-day presidential tour of the US was to go ahead that autumn.[18]

Her first state visit was to Portugal in June 1991, when she signalled that she hoped to undertake more foreign travel. Interviewed in Lisbon by Renagh Holohan of *The Irish Times* on her first six months in office, she admitted that certain adjustments had had to be made to her life: 'I miss the cases that I was involved with as a lawyer and the easy contact with colleagues and the contact with friends; and being able to walk into shops, a book shop in particular, or to walk down a street. There has been an adjustment to a certain loneliness of being president and of being cut off in that way. There has been, too, a great deal of learning over the last six months and adjusting to the potential of the position . . .'[19]

It was not all hardship. There were waiting staff in attendance, including her former domestic help at home, Laura Donegan, who came to the Áras as personal housekeeper for the duration of the presidency. The television would be installed in the bedroom of the private apartments; it was in this room that the Robinsons always lived during time off. The adjustment would not prove to be so difficult. In July the family's nineteenth-century house in Ranelagh, which they had bought for £185,000 in November 1982, was sold by private treaty for more than £400,000.

The first official presidential visit which she had to host involved someone who had sent one of the first messages of congratulation. President Vigdis Finnbogadottir of Iceland, the world's first democratically elected female head of state, had been in Copenhagen, *en route* east for the enthronement of the Japanese emperor, when she was contacted by *The Irish Times*. 'Absolutely splendid' was the reaction of the 60-year-old leader, by then serving her third term of office, and proud of a possible blood link to an Irish princess, Melkorka, who had been kidnapped and brought north centuries before. 'We are kinsmen, you Irish and we Icelanders,' she said, and it was 'marvellous' to have 'a female colleague so close'. Not only did she wish to congratulate Mary Robinson, but also 'the Irish people who had made the choice'.[20]

As a 'non-political' figurehead, Mrs Finnbogadottir held a similar post to that of the incumbent in the Phoenix Park. She was expected to serve as a cultural ambassador, while also signing in new legislation passed by the Althing or parliament. Once she had come close to refusing, when Icelandic women held a national strike in 1985. The Althing took action to prevent air hostesses with the national airline from joining. President Vigdis refused to sanction the emergency Bill. Though 'persuaded' to change her mind, her point was not lost. The air hostesses went on strike for one day anyway. Independence was always a hallmark of Icelandic women – they keep their maiden names after marriage – but the former French lecturer, broadcaster and director of the Reykjavik Theatre Company was a role model in more ways than one. Divorced, she made legal history when she became a 41-year-old single parent of an adopted daughter, Astridur. It was obvious how much more at ease she was in her job than her Irish counterpart, when she arrived at Dublin airport in October 1991. Yet, the hostess stole the best line, in the Icelander's view, by addressing her as 'my sister President'.

There would be another shared function – a women's conference in Dublin in 1992; but it was not until towards the end of Mary Robinson's term in office that they would meet again. They did so twice within a month. Early in May 1996, both leaders were among a panel of participants at a conference in Stockholm, sponsored by two US-based bodies, the Centre for Strategic and International Studies and the International Women's Leadership Forum. The theme was to determine 'whether women in power did make a difference'.

The meeting would be 'historic and unique' in several ways, it was promised. In fact, it was neither – some described it as disastrous.

CHAPTER 12

Celtic Tiger

'They told me I'd received a seven-year sentence. That there would be no remission for good behaviour, and, that if I do the job at all well, chances are they will double the sentence.'[1]

It was a little joke, and it always raised a laugh among guests to the Park. It usually came some time during the guided tour of the eighteenth-century mansion – perhaps when tea and scones were being served, or during the traditional glass of Guinness. This was how lawyer friends had ribbed her on her election, the President would recall.

'Why is this woman laughing?' the US weekly, *Newsweek*, asked in 1991. With divorce and abortion still illegal then in Ireland, wasn't this champion of liberal causes a captive after all? Little more than a 'thinking person's Princess Di', to quote one observer, in the highest but most ineffectual office in the land?

Yet six years later, the first divorce case had been heard in an Irish court, Charles Haughey was no longer leader of Fianna Fáil, or even in government; and, most significantly, the Labour Party had been in successive coalition administrations from 1993. The country had been thrown into turmoil over abortion and forced to re-examine its own attitudes to the issue, and the prosecution of priests for child sexual abuse had contributed to the waning influence of the Roman Catholic Church.

Emigration had all but dried up due to a dramatic turnaround in the Irish economy, and the Republic was now dubbed the 'Celtic tiger', though reduced dependence on the British economy had been countered by an invasion of franchised British retail chains. The '90s were being dubbed a 'golden age' for Irish language, music, art and film, with Irish actors and directors lionised in Hollywood, and the hosting of a six-month showcase of 'things Irish' in Europe's cultural capital, Paris. An Irish head of state was being tipped to take a top post in the United Nations and, for once, the British press was not lampooning the idea or treating it as some sort of Kerry quip. In fact, editorials in British broadsheet dailies were largely supportive. The US President, Bill Clinton, had put Ireland near the top of his international agenda. Tragically, only Northern Ireland continued to be the sore that would not heal.

'Only' Northern Ireland. Yet never had so much been risked for what appeared to be so little return. In February 1992, President Robinson undertook the first official visit by an Irish head of state to the North, having already been up briefly in December 1990 to attend the installation of the Archbishop of Armagh. She was not welcomed by the Belfast Lord Mayor, Nigel Dodds, a member of the Democratic Unionist Party; and, by a grotesque coincidence, three lives were lost in an attack on Sinn Féin headquarters that day. In May, during a visit to Derry, both the Democratic Unionist Party and Ulster Unionist councillors refused to meet her in protest at the Republic's constitutional claim to the North.

Ironically, before her election she had built up credits with the unionist majority in the North, by acknowledging what she termed their 'genuine fears' and articulating her views on the negative effect of Articles 2 and 3 of the Republic's Constitution. The 'imposed' solution represented by the Anglo-Irish Agreement, and the lack of consultation with those who still wanted to maintain the constitutional link with Britain, had led to her resignation from the Labour Party in 1985. However, in the early 1970s she had also expressed strong opposition to the emergency powers being adopted by the Republic's government in response to the threat from the IRA.

In September, again in Derry, the mayor sent his deputy, Councillor Annie Courtney, to receive Mary Robinson when she arrived to deliver a keynote speech at an international conference on conflict resolution. Still, the constituency she was reaching out to reciprocated warmly – although relatives and friends of the 14 civilians killed on Bloody Sunday in Derry in 1972 criticised her for refusing to support or meet them. A statement from Áras an Uachtaráin said that this was because their campaign 'clearly involves matters of policy'.

The welcomes came in particular from women; among them, activists like Mary Clark-Glass, one of the founders of the Northern women's movement, who was to run as Alliance Party candidate in the 1994 European elections, and Inez McCormack, trade union official, feminist and member of the executive council of the Irish Congress of Trade Unions – a little unusual for a Northern Protestant. The part-time women workers that McCormack represented came from some of the toughest areas in the North.

Married to a founder member of the Derry Labour Party, and active in the civil rights movement, McCormack was on the restricted guest list for the President's inauguration – and had asked why she was being invited before accepting. Though she was acquainted with the President through previous campaigns, she knew she was the only woman from the North on the list. She was also aware that her views were not particularly popular with the Republic's government. She had been a major critic of British Tory policy which, she felt, had contributed to widening inequalities in the province.

Both very private people, the two women had much in common. Like President Robinson, McCormack knew how to handle public life, and how to leave for home rather than for the pub after a meeting. They had been in contact over European equality directives, had met during rallies opposing South Africa's apartheid régime, and had shared a platform in Dublin's city centre during the 1983 referendum campaign on abortion. McCormack had visited Mary Robinson's office in Dublin and also knew Ann Lane well. McCormack had made the point then that the thousands of women who annually left Ireland for terminations in Britain were citizens; so if Ireland did not belong to them, it did not belong to anyone. A true democracy was one which allowed people on the margins to participate.

In contrast to the Republic, women held a fairly low profile in Northern political life. Not since Bernadette McAliskey (*née* Devlin) had there been a serving female MP representing the province in Westminster. This was not to suggest that they were not involved; but most women's activity tended to be channelled through community groups. By the close of the Irish President's sixth year in office, however, the 'Mary Robinson factor' was being cited as an ingredient in a new Northern Ireland Women's Coalition, which represented both religions and varying political persuasions – and which nominated seventy women for the Northern Ireland forum elections of May 1996.

But in early summer 1993, the President's international profile was only just beginning to rise and was matched only by her daunting work-rate. In the space of nine months her international schedule had ranged from Africa to Australia, New Zealand and Singapore; to Warrington, England, for a memorial service for two young boys killed by the IRA, to the United States for a humanitarian award, and to Spain, where the daily newspaper *El País* was impressed by this 'superwoman' with her 'beautiful caramel-green eyes'. The US visit had been particularly successful, coming at a time when senior Irish politicians had visited the White House to persuade the Clinton administration to take a benevolent interest in Northern Ireland.

In the early 1980s, Irish diplomats had endeavoured to curry favour with President Ronald Reagan, but, due to the strength of the Reagan-Thatcher relationship, only made an impact when interests did not conflict with Britain. Clinton, however, was different; here was a US leader who was not bound ideologically to Britain and who was interested in Irish affairs. Such was the warm reception given to Mrs Robinson – who wasn't even on an official state visit – that it was hinted that Ireland could be in a position to oust Britain from its warm seat in the Oval Office.

Then in late May came the confirmation that a gulf of over seventy years was to be bridged; President Robinson would pay a courtesy call on the British monarch, Queen Elizabeth II, at Buckingham Palace. Since 1921 and independence, no British monarch had made an official visit to the Republic, though visits by senior members of the royal family had increased in recent years. The establishment of the office of president by Ireland under the 1937 Constitution and the declaration of a republic in 1949 had severed any lingering links with the House of Windsor, and the assassination of Lord Louis Mountbatten in Sligo in 1979 had led the government to advise against British royal trips across the Irish Sea. In 1981 President Hillery had declined an invitation – on government advice – to attend the marriage of the Prince of Wales and Lady Diana Spencer.

The first meeting between a British monarch and an Irish president took place on 27 May 1993. Those seeking a comparable encounter had to make do with the exchange between Queen Elizabeth I and the sixteenth-century Irish pirate queen, Grace O'Malley. This time, the two heads of state drank tea, held 'wide-ranging' discussions in private, and the President gave her hostess a hand-turned wooden vessel by Liam O'Neill of An Spideal, County Galway; her gifts were always Irish-made. No invitations for official state visits were extended, with civil servants describing such speculation as 'premature'.

Afterwards, Mrs Robinson said that she believed that she had broken a 'psychological barrier', though she declined to give details about what subjects had been discussed and would not even say whether Northern Ireland had been on the agenda. Back at the Irish embassy, with the half-hour visit over, one moment was particularly sweet. The President's special adviser, Bride Rosney, was called to the phone. The first Irish mountaineering expedition to Everest had reached the peak's summit, by the more difficult northern route from Tibet. What's more, it had been achieved by a Belfast man, the cross-border expedition's leader, Dawson Stelfox. It was just forty years since the first ascent of Everest by Sherpa Tensing and Sir Edmund Hillery, the news of which had been held back for the Queen's coronation. In spite of several attempts, Britain had never reached the summit by the northern ridge. Rosney relayed the news to the Irish presidential party and there was a delighted outburst. The excitement was lost on one colleague, however, who seemed far more interested in asking the adviser if she could possibly pass the butter . . .

*

A month later came the final link in a chain of events which was to lead to renewed efforts to secure peace in Northern Ireland. It involved 'enormous risk and trust', according to trade unionist Inez McCormack who was very involved in its conception. McCormack had already helped to lay foundations, when the President was invited to a women's trade union conference in Dundalk, south of the border; she was also very involved in Mrs Robinson's first official visit to the North, which resulted in a lasting relationship with community groups.

McCormack's work on union issues made her a trusted figure in west Belfast. Her union represented staff working with the area's largest employer, the Royal Victoria Hospital. Though the work force was split evenly between Protestants and Catholics, the latter tended to be in the lower-grade jobs. In the 1980s, there were many attempts to cut back on services, and there was one four-month strike. It was characterised at the time as being backed by the Provisional IRA; hence the dispatch of the British Army and the police to break up peaceful pickets.

Similarly, on other human rights issues, McCormack found herself being smeared as a 'Provo sympathiser'. It was easy enough to tarnish those who did not have the access to the media or have the resources to fight back. When it was decided to invite the President to west Belfast, the invitation came from half a dozen community groups. 'Meeting the marginalised seemed to be very much a part of her agenda,' McCormack recalled. 'She wasn't bestowing herself on this constituency; it was being affirmed by her, and becoming an agent of its own change.'

In her inauguration speech in December 1990 the President had said that there were no conditions attached to the hand of friendship being extended across the border. To visit west Belfast was to visit a very republican community, and so it would have been insulting to attempt to screen who was going to attend. Naturally, Sinn Féin representatives would be in the room. It was up to the President to decide whose hand she would or would not shake.

When it happened it was no accident, though it was presented as such at the time and it led to the first full row between the President and the government. There had been much 'negotiation' between Áras an Uachtaráin and the government on her itinerary in the days beforehand. The Tánaiste and Minister for Foreign Affairs, Dick Spring – leader of the Labour Party to which she had once belonged – was under pressure from the British government to stop any such meeting taking place.

There were elaborate and heated exchanges with the British ambassador to Ireland, David Blatherwick. The Irish government felt that the timing was far from ideal, as the situation could be 'used' by the Provisional IRA during a sensitive period when there had been tentative attempts to open up dialogue; but Dublin also resented being pushed around by Westminster. There was, in addition, some confusion as to whether this was to be a 'foreign' visit or not.

If it was, this was implying that Northern Ireland was 'foreign territory'. If it was not, the President was presenting herself as representing all the island's people. Was there not an inherent contradiction here with her decision to resign from the Labour Party over lack of consultation with the unionists about the Anglo-Irish Agreement?

The Tánaiste decided to stop short of 'advising' the President owing to the constitutional implications, but informed her instead of the government's concerns. He did so on the morning of a trip to London for a meeting of the Anglo-Irish conference. The discussion was amicable, and Dick Spring left Áras an Uachtaráin with the impression that there would be further talks on the subject the following day. He flew to London and went to the Irish embassy in Grosvenor Place, where he was handed a note. Downtown Radio in Belfast had quoted a 'spokeswoman' for the President as saying that the west Belfast visit was to go ahead.

Spring was furious. He felt that he had been presented with a *fait accompli*, and it would not make for a good atmosphere at that morning's meeting. The talks overran, and there were veiled threats from British officials about withdrawing security. The next day, he returned to Áras an Uachtaráin; this meeting was 'far less amicable', as one official put it. He was told that no one had been authorised to speak to Downtown Radio; but the President did confirm that she intended to stick to her plan.

The response in Dublin and the Labour Party's anger can be gauged from a published account by former government press secretary Seán Duignan who was appointed to the Fianna Fáil-Labour coalition in February 1992. In his diary for 17 June 1993, he wrote:

> Dick [Spring] is livid with her. Albert [Reynolds] shakes his head too, but I know him . . . Dick goes up to Áras (again!). But the lady is not for turning. She insists she is going to go. Albert goes up around 5 p.m. She is still adamant. Dick furious. 'Some woman,' sez Albert. 'She is determined to make history,' sez Dick . . .
>
> [And the following day:] President goes North. Meets Adams and shakes the hand. Peter Robinson [deputy leader of the Democratic Unionist Party] goes ape. So too the SDLP. The NIO [Northern Ireland Office] say they raised their concerns 'at the highest level' with Irish government . . . . I tell pol[itical] corr[espondent]s that [British Secretary of State for Ireland Sir Patrick] Mayhew and Blatherwick pressed Albert and Dick at Downing Street to persuade her not to do it plus I tell them Albert

resisted Brit pressure to stop her, i.e. no question of Albert not giving her permission to go to Northern Ireland. Understandably, Dick's boys not amused – they let us know: 'She shouldn't be given permission to go to Disneyland.' Ouch!'[2]

She made her own ethical judgment. No press photographers were present when she shook hands with Gerry Adams, leader of Sinn Féin, the IRA's acknowledged political wing. Though she also met many other community leaders, there was widespread condemnation of her actions. It ran against official government policy towards the Sinn Féin, reflected in censorship in state broadcasting. Adams's voice was also banned from the British airwaves, and he was unable to get a visa to visit the US where his party had widespread support among Irish-Americans. To make such a gesture, then, was equated with supping with the devil himself.

Political correspondents were perplexed, and the Republic's government saw it as a setback to a nascent peace process. It was regarded within official circles as having put a severe dent in relations with Britain, and having sent a signal to the Provisional IRA that the government was not ready to express. The opposition howled. Fine Gael leader John Bruton said she was wrong, and asked if the government had advised her. It was 'possible to visit west Belfast without having contact with Sinn Féin', he said. Other members of his party also voiced their disapproval. 'If C.J. Haughey had visited west Belfast and shaken hands with Gerry Adams, all hell would have broken loose,' said Alan Shatter, spokesman on equality and law reform. 'Historical analogies would have been drawn. Conspiracy theories would have abounded. Calls for his resignation would have been made. The chattering classes would have been outraged . . . On an island where symbols are taken too seriously and are too often the cause of death and destruction, these handshakes, in present circumstances, are open to serious misrepresentation and could prove to be a tragic miscalculation by a president who has until now done us proud.'[3]

A Fine Gael member of the European Parliament and former Minister of Justice, Patrick Cooney, expressed 'outrage'. The handshake had alienated unionists, set back the day of reconciliation in the North and prejudiced her office and moral authority, he said. The next time the President proposed such a visit, the government should have 'more bottle' and stop her from going. The SDLP MP for West Belfast, Dr Joe Hendron, in contrast, acknowledged that it would have been difficult for her to travel to his constituency, meet community groups and then 'dictate to them who should be there or who should not be there'.

As time passed, however, the general view changed. It became obvious that Robinson's actions had helped to facilitate a visit by Gerry Adams to the United States. The same government officials who had been upset about what she had done then now regard her as having made a significant contribution to the overall weave in the peace initiative.

'It would have been so much easier for her to have done nothing,' Inez McCormack believes. 'She could have confined her visits to the North to collecting honorary degrees. Yet there was one of the toughest communities in Europe, pouring out its heart to her and she was listening and asking intelligent questions. No one had ever *listened* before.'[4]

The brief encounter proved to be prophetic. Three months later, Taoiseach Albert Reynolds shook Adams's hand. In time, so did President Clinton, once he had been effectively 'recruited' by a changing Irish-America. No longer confrontational, the new 'corporate' Irish-America of chief executives, company presidents and union leaders, led by strategists like Congressman Bruce Morrison and New York publisher Niall O'Dowd, preferred the diplomatic approach. Another link in the chain was a determined Irish-American on the other side of the Atlantic, the Clinton-appointed US Ambassador to Ireland, Jean Kennedy Smith. The politician given most credit was SDLP leader John Hume, who had begun formal talks with Sinn Féin back in 1988.

The following year, after many months of manoeuvring, the IRA announced a ceasefire. It was reciprocated by loyalist paramilitaries. A quarter-century of conflict and death was over, it seemed; or had paused – for 17 months, as later became bitterly clear.

Asked about the 'handshake' two months after the IRA ceasefire, the President admitted that she had been 'concerned' immediately afterwards as to whether she had 'done the right thing'. In an extensive interview with Olivia O'Leary of *The Sunday Tribune*, she effectively scotched the notion that it had happened by accident:

> It was a very difficult decision, one I thought deeply about. It was not easy to know whether you were doing the right thing. I was very keen to accept the invitation from the number of community groups in west Belfast who had invited me. I had a sense that it was important to build on the contacts that I had already established with those communities, having had many of them down here beforehand . . .
>
> In the difficulty, in the weighing it up, I underestimated what the media response would be afterwards. It was as though I had gone to Northern Ireland to shake Gerry Adams's hand. I tried to say that there was a story of local community vibrancy, of what was being done for young people, the drop-outs from school, the old people. There was no interest in that. Now that creates a lot of

pressure when you hold an office like mine because it's important
that you don't get drawn into political controversy.[5]

In contrast to the reported tension between Robinson and Haughey,
the new Taoiseach, Albert Reynolds, viewed the President with mild awe,
Seán Duignan recorded. She was untouchable – like Mother Teresa – and
almost a wonder of the world, like Australia's Ayer's Rock. 'He might
privately share some of Spring's reservations about her peripatetic tendencies, but he was also pleased that he got on well with her at a personal level,
and he assiduously avoided unnecessary friction between Merrion Street
[government buildings] and Áras an Uachtaráin,' Duignan wrote.

The Taoiseach would often draw his press secretary's attention to the
latest opinion poll, showing overwhelming public support for the
President on every issue. 'No arguing with that,' was Reynolds's comment.
'We walk around her.'[6]

If, a month after her first visit to the Queen in London, the single,
simple handshake contributed to the ceasefire, there were other helpful
gestures such as a goodwill meeting with independent loyalist leaders in
the Irish Consulate in New York in October 1994. Residents from the
loyalist Shankill area of Belfast were made as welcome as their nationalist
counterparts in Áras an Uachtaráin, in a series of reciprocal visits which
were as important, if not more so, than the President's journeys north.
Victims of the conflict, including representatives of those who died on
Bloody Sunday in 1972, and relatives of some of the 34 people who lost
their lives in the 1974 Dublin and Monaghan bombings presented her
with their requests for the right to justice.

Groups from both sides of the divide were eager to show her their
development plans. Inez McCormack, who took a step back once relationships had been established, witnessed a growth. Her most vivid memories
are of the simple, magic moments: the President paying tribute to the work
of the toilet cleaners in a local school; the small boy who approached, lifted
her face, kissed it and 'gave it back to her'. At all times, Mrs Robinson
followed protocol and was 'honourable', McCormack says, in response to
criticism by unionist politicians. 'Their criticism doesn't reflect the views
of the loyalist communities who have worked with her. Then those who
live a traditional political life are not able to grasp the implications of a
hand of friendship, with no conditions and no agenda.'

The President received an honorary law degree from Queen's University, Belfast, in the summer of 1995, and spoke periodically on her concerns for peace. In June 1996 she talked of how much happier Irish people
in Britain were with their identity, in contrast to the Northern Irish
nationalists who had been made to feel like second-class citizens. Irishness,

she noted, was no longer a 'territorial concept'. The Irish diaspora confirmed that fact.

The North was the cause of another altercation with the government during her term, though senior Labour Party officials now regard the incident as a 'spurious' confrontation. Following publication of a framework document on negotiations for the North's future early in 1995, the President was asked by *The Irish Times* for her response to it. At the time, she was on a state visit to Japan. Speaking in Osaka, she expressed concern about the 'genuine fears' of unionists who felt that the document could be seen to 'undermine' their sense of identity. 'The fear of the ground shifting, the fear of a takeover, is undermining a sense of identity,' she explained. 'If somebody said to us that Ireland should join the Commonwealth tomorrow, think of the ripples of fear that that would produce.'

Asked by the newspaper to compare her views now with her decision to resign from the Labour Party in 1985 over the Anglo-Irish Agreement, she said that this was a 'very different situation'. Yet there were parallels, journalist Joe Carroll noted – specifically, lack of consultation with unionists. She was not going to be 'drawn into a political context', she added, and hoped to 'remain in close contact in a much more informal way with those who are outside the political process but very politically aware – the community groups, church leaders and various others.'

If she were in Ireland, she said that she would be conscious that this was a 'particularly sensitive issue' and she would be 'very slow to comment' on it. 'But outside Ireland, when you are paying a state visit on behalf of your country, you can't not comment in an appropriate way and I gave a lot of thought to finding the appropriate language to do it.'[7]

It would be almost two months before the fallout. The occasion was a lunch for political correspondents, hosted by the Tánaiste, Dick Spring, in April 1995. In what Spring was to argue later was an off-the-record briefing, he responded to various questions about a recent rather controversial visit by the President to South America, and said that the media had treated her unfairly. He was also asked about her remarks on the framework document while in Japan, and made what one Sunday newspaper reported later as 'mildly critical' comments.

There was a row. Opposition parties accused Spring of 'double-speak' and 'divisive and unseemly conduct'. The Tánaiste countered with criticisms of the 'dishonourable' way off-the-record remarks had been reported. The 'long honeymoon' that the President had enjoyed was over, one correspondent judged, noting that Robinson had also created tensions when she was the first to visit flood victims in County Galway, before either the Taoiseach or the Tánaiste.

On 11 April it was reported that the Taoiseach, John Bruton, had held a confidential meeting with Mrs Robinson to 'mend fences'. Joe Carroll, who had conducted the initial interview in Japan, noted that one vital fact had been ignored in all the fuss: the President had made no criticism of government policy on the framework document. If she had, this would 'definitely' have represented a constitutional crisis, he said. The President had made it absolutely clear in the interview that she was not criticising the document, and had said explicitly that she supported successive Irish governments in the work that led up to its publication.[8]

'Our armoured door is closed. The wife's stomach is churning up with acid. Jesus, it's awful. I've loaded up again.' This was the gut reaction from a Northern nationalist politician to events almost a year later, in February 1996. Shortly after a highly successful visit to both parts of Ireland by President Clinton in December 1995, a massive bomb killed two men in London's Docklands. As well as the callous dynamic of terrorism, the political vacuum created by the British government's refusal to allow Sinn Féin to enter into dialogue was identified as the main cause for the IRA's decision to resume hostilities.

President Robinson was said to be personally devastated. Not three months before, on her third visit to the North since the ceasefire, she had made a veiled reference to the stalled peace initiative, when she acknowledged how 'precious and important' it was to build on the cessation of violence. During that visit to four counties – Donegal in the Republic, Fermanagh, Tyrone and Derry in the North – she was reported to be 'unperturbed' when a letter of protest from eight members of the Democratic Unionist Party was handed in to a hotel where she was holding a meeting. Outside, the delegation shouted: 'You are not welcome here.'

She was the first signatory to a peace initiative, Solidarity to Organise Peace (STOP), which was formed within days of the ceasefire breaking. The fragile British Tory government's heavy dependence on Northern unionists for its survival would ensure that decommissioning of arms would remain a precondition for any Sinn Féin involvement in all-party talks. The British opposition, Labour, remained silent, determined not to use the North to score political points. The reality was that the issue just wasn't of sufficient political significance to garner, or jeopardise, votes.

Loyalist paramilitaries continued to hold their peace, but the widening political vacuum had a disastrous effect on the work of local community groups. Had it all been an illusion, many commentators began to ask. After all, punishment beatings had continued right throughout the 17 months, earning the baseball bat 'a place in Irish history', in the words of Belfast writer Robert McLiam Wilson. And the extent of siege mentality on the unionist side was reflected in the provocation which nationalists had to endure during the traditional summer marching season.

There were continuous complaints from unionists about Robinson's cross-border trips. In March 1994, for instance, the Department of Foreign Affairs, Áras an Uachtaráin and the Northern Ireland Office took different views over the exact status of one such visit. The President's office at the Áras said it was 'official'; the Northern Ireland Office said it was 'private'; the Department of Foreign Affairs also said it was 'private'. The Áras acknowledged the dilemma for the British authorities, since they recognised only two categories: 'state' and 'private' visits. The Áras recognised three: 'state', when the visit was made to another country at the invitation of the head of state, and the expenses were borne by the host country; 'private', when the President left the state with the government's approval for a personal matter such as a holiday, and carried the expenses herself; and 'official', when the President left the country with the government's approval and undertook public engagements in another jurisdiction, at the invitation of community groups, universities, professional bodies and suchlike. Such visits were paid for from the President's official travel allowance.

In December 1995 *The Belfast Telegraph* had interviewed the President and asked her if she was deterred from travelling north by unionist complaints about the frequency of her visits. She was conscious of it, she said, and did bear it in mind at particular times. She didn't accept every invitation, she pointed out, and always tried to be even-handed, 'reaching out in different ways'. She also said that she would warmly welcome an opportunity to host a visit by Queen Elizabeth to the Republic, but state visits were 'matters for governments'.[9]

During the summer of 1996, President Robinson's frustration over the impasse was reflected in a show of tears. This was not the first time that she had allowed her emotions to show. Early on, there had been a perceptible change in her style. Mary Holland, Ireland correspondent for the British Sunday paper, *The Observer*, dated it to the election campaign of 1990, when 'a cool, formidably intelligent, slightly priggish lawyer' revealed another part of herself as she travelled the country. By the time she came to make her inauguration speech, she appeared to have 'deepened as a person, to be less cautious emotionally and to be looking for a language to communicate this'. She borrowed from poetry – which she had so loved at school – and, said Holland, 'it was a mark of how she had changed that it did not sound ridiculous'.[10]

She had been in the US in June 1996 when the IRA bomb blew the heart out of a Manchester shopping centre. Another bomb had almost blown a wedding apart in Enniskillen, County Fermanagh. The following month she visited Manchester, where she had opened an Irish festival the previous March, and criticised the IRA for its attack on a civilian population – an attack that was 'not in the name of any Irishness I represent as President of Ireland'. A few days later, she was opening a new residence for the homeless in Cork when she heard the news that an Orange march was to be allowed to go through the Northern town of Portadown in spite of the fears of local nationalist residents. When she came to the part of her speech dealing with the North, she started to cry, according to *The Cork Examiner*.

In September she made her fourteenth – but first unsuccessful – visit north when she addressed the European conference of Methodists. Following her address to the conference, she visited the nationalist enclave in the Short Strand estate of east Belfast to launch a local community partnership, and performed her first 'public' handshake with Sinn Féin leader Gerry Adams in west Belfast. However, there was a mixed reception in the loyalist Village area, where she arrived to open the Windsor Women's Centre. About twenty protesters hurled abuse – such as 'Go home, you Fenian bastard' and 'Get back to your own territory, you old cow'. Early the following day, the centre sustained severe damage in an arson attack. Inflammable liquid was poured through the roof and the building set alight.

The atmosphere deteriorated even further. In October 1996 a British soldier, Warrant Officer James Bradwell, died of injuries sustained in an IRA bomb attack on the Belfast suburb of Lisburn. Later that month, Robinson returned to mark the twentieth anniversary of the Northern Ireland Equal Opportunities Commission; she had chaired the commission's first conference in 1977. A unionist member of the new Northern Ireland forum was ruled out of order when he questioned her frequent visits and compared the Republic to Nazi Germany in its treatment of its Protestant minority.

The following month it was reported that the Windsor Women's Centre had experienced seven attacks in the eight weeks since the President's visit. Personal threats had been made against some of the 32 staff employed, and the repair bill for damage to the premises was set at £65,000.[11] To add to the gloom, it appeared that Northern Ireland had slid down the agenda for Bill Clinton's second-term presidential administration. Ambassador Kennedy Smith was set to be re-appointed to Ireland, but two key officials – Nancy Soderberg, deputy assistant to the President, and Tony Lake, National Security adviser – who had dealt with the Irish issue on a day-to-day basis, were tipped to be moved. The chairman of the Northern multi-party talks, former Senator George Mitchell, also looked as if he was going to be promoted out. Nothing could be guaranteed from a US President who no longer needed Irish-American votes, observed Niall O'Dowd, editor of *The Irish Voice*.[12]

On a BBC television programme documenting the impact of the President's visits to Northern Ireland – 16 by the end of November 1996 – the Ulster Unionist Party leader, David Trimble, accused her of promoting a republican agenda. She should stay away unless she was prepared to adhere to 'the proper protocol', he said. 'To come in this ambiguous manner, where it can be interpreted as representing Articles 2 and 3 being thrust down people's throats, is not welcome. If she cannot follow the normal courtesies towards Her Majesty, then she's better not coming.'

Responding, her office said that proper protocols were being followed. The President was usually greeted by the lord lieutenant for the area in which she arrived, and by a minister or senior official of the Northern Ireland office. On the same television programme, the President said that she had no political agenda. 'I would like to be genuinely believed for what is the core of my interests, which is one of friendship,' she said.[13]

She would not let the criticism pass. Speaking to the media at Coventry University in December during a three-day visit to Britain, she warned that politicians must be more careful with their language if a lasting peace in Northern Ireland was to be achieved. She declined to name names, but stressed that there was a responsibility to move the peace process on.

Early in 1997, Trimble and his fellow Unionist MP, William Ross, complained to the British Foreign Office about Robinson's visits. Ross asked officials how 'someone who claims jurisdiction over part of the UK can come in and unveil plaques as President of all Ireland'. The largely unionist *Belfast Newsletter* took a conciliatory, if somewhat patronising, view in the same week. Many unionists would readily concede that 'Éire President' Mary Robinson had 'some charming personal qualities', it said, but most took the view that she adopted too high a political profile on her frequent visits to the North 'which extend beyond that of a foreign head of state'. Mrs Robinson and her advisers in Dublin would 'hardly need reminding' that 'Her Majesty the Queen' was the sovereign head of the North. 'As the head of a foreign state, she is very welcome to visit Northern Ireland as long as the correct protocol is observed, and Ulster Unionist MPs were quite correct to relay their deep concerns to the Foreign Office over the nature of Mrs Robinson's jaunts across the border.' Ross, the East Londonderry MP, had observed that 'the Queen couldn't go to Dublin and open a school or unveil a plaque'.[14]

Ah, but couldn't she? After President Robinson's two visits to Buckingham Palace, and a successful return trip by Prince Charles, a formal invitation to Queen Elizabeth was always on the cards. It depended on the atmosphere in the North, however. As the British Tory government clung on to power and limped towards an election, a breakthrough in Anglo-Irish negotiations seemed remote. The 25th anniversary of Bloody Sunday passed in late January and early February 1997 with some of the largest ever marches in the North and demands for a British apology for the 13 deaths in Derry in 1972 at the hands of the First Parachute Regiment. The Irish government took up the relatives' case and exerted further diplomatic pressure. But the Northern Secretary, Sir Patrick Mayhew, would not be swayed.[15]

The British Labour Party sailed into government in May 1997, with a new Northern Secretary, Dr Marjorie 'Mo' Mowlam bringing a breath of fresh air. The election campaign, however, had been affected by IRA activity in Britain. Sectarian murders began to recur north of the border. It looked at that stage as if Queen Elizabeth would not be crossing the Irish Sea in 1997. There had been such high hopes. It would have been the 'cake icing' on a spectacular term in office, one observer put it. 'It almost feels as if we are settling for marzipan'.

If President Robinson's fifth province appeared to be surrounded by impassable mountains at home, her desire to be a symbol of reconciliation and healing remained untarnished throughout. Much of this was due to her own relentless energy and determination. By May 1994, as she turned 50, she was being lauded as one of the most popular leaders in the history of the Irish state. Not since Charles Stewart Parnell, former leader of the Irish Parliamentary Party, was in his prime in the late nineteenth century had any politician commanded such wide respect, *Irish Times* columnist Fintan O'Toole judged. 'Even the most potent figures in modern Irish political history – Eamon de Valera, Michael Collins – also created potent animosities,' he wrote. 'Yet Mary Robinson has achieved approval ratings of over 90 per cent, even in the most controversial periods of her presidency. And, what is most extraordinary, she has done so from a background not of balmy graciousness but of furious ideological struggle.'

As O'Toole recalled, she had come to the presidency on the back of 'two traumatic national dramas' and 'at the end of a decade in which the state had been more deeply divided than at any time since the civil war and its aftermath'. There was the presidential election itself. And there was the fallout from the 1983 abortion referendum, which had been described as 'the second partitioning of Ireland', he wrote. She had been one of the first public figures to express opposition to the constitutional amendment, with a passionate two-and-a-half-hour-long speech in the Seanad – 'one of the longest and most detailed Irish parliamentary speeches of recent times'.

'Such is the vigour of her presidency that it is hard to think of her as 50 years old,' O'Toole observed:

Such is the sense of her election in 1990 . . . that it is also hard to remember that she is, this year, 25 years in public life. Only two members of the Cabinet – Michael Smith and David Andrews – have been members of the Oireachtas for as long as she has. With literally half a lifetime in politics behind her, she represents a strange kind of continuity just as much as she stands for a dramatic break with the past. In retrospect, what makes her career distinctive and gives her access to the extraordinary degree of national and international regard she now enjoys is something that can go almost unnoticed amid the myriad causes she has espoused. Socialism, liberalism and feminism give that career its content, but it is another political philosophy which gives it its potency – democracy. While virtually all Irish politicians in the period in which she has been active have been democrats, no other politician has so consistently and so coherently tested the limits and the nature of democracy. What she has articulated above all is, paradoxically, a profound dissatisfaction with the nature of our democratic institutions. This, at a time when democratic politics is at a low ebb and its leaders internationally are held in low esteem, is perhaps her most valuable asset.[16]

If 'radicals' such as Mrs Robinson always regarded democracy as 'endangered and insufficient', as O'Toole put it, she had one of her first sights of this after her election when the island was convulsed in a tragic controversy over the painful issue of abortion. The year was young, in 1992, and Charles Haughey had been ousted as taoiseach, when *The Irish Times* reported that the state had applied for an order restraining a 14-year-old rape victim from leaving the jurisdiction of the Irish state under the terms of the Eighth Amendment to the Constitution. The girl was about six weeks to two months pregnant and had been the victim of a series of sexual assaults by a close friend of the family over a period of several years. She told her parents that she wished to have an abortion.[17]

The girl and her parents travelled to England in early February, but before the pregnancy could be terminated they heard some startling news. The family had inquired from the Irish police as to whether DNA evidence obtained after the abortion would be admissible in court. They were informed that it was not, because the procedure by which it would be obtained was illegal in Ireland. The office of the Director of Public Prosecutions had then contacted the Attorney General's office and an interim injunction had been applied for in the High Court, restraining the girl and her parents from procuring termination of the pregnancy in Britain.

The clinic appointment was cancelled and the family returned home. The day after the newspaper report, deputies in the Dáil demanded time to debate the case and the Attorney General issued a statement saying that he was acting 'in the discharge of his independent and non-governmental duties under the Constitution'. The outgoing Taoiseach, Charles Haughey, his partner in government, Des O'Malley of the Progressive Democrats, and Haughey's successor, Albert Reynolds, said that they had had no prior knowledge of the Attorney General's actions. On 17 February, the High Court granted the injunction restraining the girl from leaving the jurisdiction of the Irish state for nine months. Politicians on all sides expressed the hope that the family would appeal to the Supreme Court – which they did.

The country reacted with marches, speeches and public shock at what the abortion referendum had done. All the state's media were devoted to the issue, known as the 'X case'.

A few days later, on 19 February, the President intervened in a most dramatic fashion. Addressing south-east professional women's groups in Waterford, she said that she was very much in touch with 'the sense of frustration and the sense of helplessness' felt by Irish women and girls that week. Though the first to acknowledge that she had no role to play, she used the occasion to call for a positive response. 'We are experiencing as a people a very deep crisis in ourselves,' she said. 'I hope we have the courage, which we have not always had, to face up to and look squarely and to say this is a problem we have got to resolve.'

On 25 February she alluded to it again. By this time, the family had been forced to leave their Dublin home because of media pressure and controversy in their community over the case; and a Sunday newspaper opinion poll had found that 66 per cent of those questioned believed now that abortion should be allowed in Ireland in some circumstances. Delivering the Allen Lane Foundation lecture in Trinity College, Dublin, the President reflected what one newspaper described afterwards as 'the hurt, bewilderment and frustration, the helplessness and alarm' which she had sensed among the populace. Referring to the title of her speech, 'Striking a Balance', she said that she was acutely aware when she selected it that it might suggest 'an evasive or overly tactful approach to the issue of women's role and rights'. She wanted to emphasise that the balance she would like to see struck was 'not an awkward coming-to-terms of a last-minute compromise'. It must be 'a comprehensive re-assessment of the place and contribution of a woman in her society'. She went on:

> If the imbalances of the past came, as I believe they did, not simply
> from legislative injustice and economic inequality but from pro-

found resistances and failures of perception, then it follows that to right that balance we must do more than review our legislation and re-state our economic structures. We must also fundamentally re-appraise our view of who and what is valuable in our society. We must look with fresh and unprejudiced eyes at the work of women, the views of women, their way of organising and their interpretation of social priorities. To achieve this, we must, I believe, begin at the beginning and alter our way of thinking.

Equality between the sexes was perceived as a woman's issue, she continued. 'It is not.' It was perceived to be a marginal issue. 'It is not.' It was perceived to be a threat to the traditional structures of a society. 'It is not.'

> But because of these flawed interpretations, the approach to achieving equality has been similarly flawed. It remains an *ad hoc* approach. We make legislative changes and appoint women in response to organised insistence and the pressures of public opinion. Therefore the accounting of progress is recorded less through deep and generous shifts in established thinking, and more by listing laws or doing a number count of the women in public positions. This *ad hoc* approach ensures that the issue of women's equality is starved of reflective thinking and careful planning.

No, the 'elusive balance' required a more fundamental re-evaluation of women's role, worth and contribution to society, she said. She quoted Jane Austen, Virginia Woolf, Yeats, the Irish writer Mary Lavin and the nineteenth-century Chinese poet and journalist Qiu Jin. She gave practical examples of the way women organised, subverted existing structures and had shaped the voluntary effort worldwide.

> If we are to conserve our possessions, if we are to use our resources, we need to give some time and thought to an imaginative restructuring. I believe we need an imaginative re-assessment of our attitudes and needs as a community so that we can bring to the centre those energies which are still at the margin. Once and for all we need to commit ourselves to the concept that women's rights are not factional or sectional privileges, bestowed on the few at the whim of the few. They are human rights.[18]

The following day, 26 February, the Supreme Court lifted the injunction against travel. On 2 March, the girl, her parents and three gardaí went to St Mary's Hospital, Manchester, where the teenager suffered a natural and spontaneous miscarriage. DNA evidence was taken by the gardaí. In a full judgment on 5 March, the Supreme Court ruled by a four-to-one decision that abortion should be permitted in cases in which the mother's life was at risk, and held that the life of the girl in the 'X case' was at risk due to her 'suicidal inclinations'.

It would be almost six months before the 43-year-old man at the centre of the case was arrested and charged on nine counts of sexual assault, and unlawful carnal knowledge of a minor. In May he pleaded guilty on three counts. In June he was sentenced to 14 years' imprisonment and was released in 1997. The court had heard that the defendant had lived 'a few doors' from the girl's home and that there had been a very close relationship between the two families. On one occasion, the defendant had intercourse with the girl when her parents were away at the pilgrimage site of Lourdes.

So, nine years after one of the bitterest referendum campaigns in Irish history, the debate on abortion was reopened. The government chose to respond to the Supreme Court judgment with a referendum on abortion information. It was carried.

One unrelated event had an indirect bearing on that result. In May 1992 *The Irish Times* revealed that a leading member of the Catholic hierarchy in Ireland, the very popular Bishop of Galway, Eamon Casey, was the father of a child, and had borrowed money from diocesan funds to pay for the child's education. He left the country, amid claims that he had tried to persuade the child's mother, a young American and distant relative, Annie Murphy, to put the child up for adoption. The scandal was to have a devastating impact on the Catholic Church's moral authority.

As for Harry Whelehan, the Attorney General who had exercised the legislation in the first place in relation to the 14-year-old girl, he never shook off the stigma – though he was only doing his job. He was appointed president of the High Court but controversy was to dog him in relation to his office's handling of a separate case of child sexual abuse involving a member of the Catholic Church. It would lead to the downfall of a government.

The President's next direct involvement in the abortion issue would come three years later, when she referred a new Abortion Information Bill to the Supreme Court to test its constitutionality. It was the second Bill that she had referred to the court during her term of office, the first being the Matrimonial Home Bill in 1993, which was geared to pave the way for a divorce referendum, and which was declared unconstitutional.

The legislation ruled that the termination of the life of the unborn outside the state was permissible if it was established 'as a matter of probability' that there was a real and substantial risk to the *life*, as distinct from the *health*, of the mother. It also allowed for provision of information on abortion services outside the state – following successive court injunctions over the past decade which had prevented the supply of such information, to the extent that even certain editions of British women's magazines had been banned.

Yet there were several good reasons for Mrs Robinson to seek Supreme Court advice. Experienced family lawyer and Fine Gael backbench TD, Alan Shatter, had called for such a Supreme Court test. The Bill was 'constitutionally questionable and suspect', in Shatter's view. If a woman was entitled to a termination of pregnancy where there was a real and substantial threat to her life, she was also entitled to receive counselling, advice and assistance from her doctor or any pregnancy counsellor. Her doctor should also be constitutionally entitled to make any arrangements towards saving her life, he said, but the legislation made no distinction between mothers whose lives were at risk and those who were not.

On 12 May 1995 the Supreme Court ruled that the legislation was constitutional and represented a 'fair and reasonable balancing of conflicting rights'. 'Abortion information ruling a boost for divorce poll,' the newspapers proclaimed. The Taoiseach and his Minister of Health welcomed the findings, which effectively meant that the Bill could never be challenged in the future. That day, the President signed it into law.

The chapter was now closed. Or was it? In February 1997 it was reported that the gardaí were investigating a claim that a woman who had undergone an abortion in a Dublin clinic had developed medical complications. Such was the strength of the response – demands by anti-abortionists for another referendum outlawing abortions on Irish territory on the one hand, calls for legislation following the 'X case' judgment on the other – that the woman's own health and welfare were almost forgotten.

Coincidentally, a case was successfully taken in the Supreme Court by three student unions, appealing against restrictions on abortion information. Delivering the judgment, a leading member of the judiciary, Mr Justice Ronan Keane, criticised successive governments for failing to legislate. It was not the function of the court to 'supplement this governmental and legislative inertia', he said, nor to define the practical, moral, legal and political issues involved. In May 1997, when a general election was called, one of the first issues identified was . . . abortion.

If the abortion Bill referral indicated how carefully she had observed her constitutional role throughout, President Robinson did not escape criticism when that other great moral issue returned to haunt the Irish electorate, namely divorce. Following a commitment, the new centre-left coalition involving Fine Gael, Labour and the Democratic Left, which was formed after the collapse of the Fianna Fáil-Labour administration in late 1994, decided to hold a referendum on the issue. The poll was conducted in November 1995, six months after the abortion legislation had been found constitutional, and nine years after the first divisive divorce poll.

This was now a changed social and economic landscape, with the Catholic Church's influence steadily weakening. A month before the vote, the Catholic primate, Cardinal Cahal Daly, had been jeered angrily by a television audience when he tried to defend the Church's handling of sex abuse cases. Furthermore, changes in social welfare had made women less dependent on men. From 1989, when Fianna Fáil first went into coalition with the liberal Progressive Democrats, and from 1992 to 1994 with Labour, a whole raft of legislation had been put in place to ensure that there would be no repeat of the 1986 defeat. By 1995, some 18 pieces of supportive legislation were in place to close loopholes, dealing with division of property, succession rights, social welfare and pension entitlements.

The new legislation was carefully framed. It required couples to show that they had lived apart for four of the past five years, and that there was no chance of reconciliation. Adequate provision would have to be made for spouses and children. With an eye on Northern Ireland, the coalition government urged Catholic voters to be mindful of minority viewpoints. By this stage, some three to four hundred annulments were already being granted by the Catholic Church each year.

Despite support by all six political parties in the Dáil, the campaign was still bitter, with claims that the 'no' side had received funds from right-wing lay Catholic groups abroad, fears being whipped up again about the cost to the taxpayer, and threatening slogans like 'Hello Divorce . . . goodbye Daddy'. In late October 1995, with a bare three weeks to go, the President was questioned about the referendum in an interview on the satellite TV station NBC Super Channel: 'As President of Ireland I am guardian of the Constitution – therefore I do not get involved in issues of this kind,' she said. 'I am very aware of the extraordinary changes in marriage law and judicial separation that exist. So, in a way, the divorce issue has now become an issue of whether the Constitution will be changed to allow the right to remarry in Irish society.

'These issues have been discussed in a very open way, to continue to open up as a modern society while retaining the Irish qualities,' she went on. 'Looking back over the last twenty years, I'm much more impressed by the changes in Irish society than [with] identifying certain issues that still need to be addressed. What has happened since the issue was last before the people is a whole structure of reform of our marriage law, of various protections, of access to court remedies – a very thoughtful infrastructure – has been developed.'

She was rounded upon. The chairman of the No-Divorce Campaign, former High Court judge Rory O'Hanlon, challenged the view that the President's office was 'self-regulating' and said that Mrs Robinson was trying to interfere in breach of constitutional parameters. Such an interpretation would suggest that the President made up her own rules as she went along, he said. Yet seven months before, while still a judge, he had been liberal in his comments on the Abortion Information Bill.

As for her reference to 'very thoughtful legislation', O'Hanlon dismissed it as 'a massive, hastily cobbled-together body of law designed for the purpose of bolstering up a divorce campaign and making it more palatable to the Irish voter'. An examination of the legislation revealed it to be 'almost entirely concerned with cleaning up the wreckage of marriages that have broken down', he said, rather than providing support for couples who were trying to rear families.

The small Catholic-oriented Muintir na hÉireann Party, which tended to surface during such moral debates, accused the President of damaging her office. A former Fianna Fáil Foreign Affairs Minister, Michael O'Kennedy, also accused her of issuing 'misleading statements' and said that she had not fully reflected on the implications of the divorce referendum in her public comments. And another TD, Michael Noonan, who had been expelled from Fianna Fáil for opposing a referendum Bill, accused her of overstepping the mark.

The party's deputy leader, Mary O'Rourke, was more circumspect. She had not seen a full transcript of the interview, she said when asked to comment, but on the basis of what had been published she felt that the President had merely stated the facts.

The Christian Solidarity Party, which was urging a 'no' vote, said that it was 'singularly inappropriate' for the President to make any public comment on divorce. Even the Campaign for Fair Referenda was concerned, stating that her comments might be regarded as an 'unwarranted intrusion' into the divorce debate.

Robinson declined to respond. In a limited sense, her comments might be regarded as an intervention on one side in the referendum debate, commented David Gwynn Morgan, law professor at University College, Cork.[19] However, an *Irish Times* editorial noted that, while she might be on fair legal and constitutional ground, it would have been better had she avoided the matter altogether. Describing it as a 'presidential misjudgment', the newspaper said that Mrs Robinson had unwittingly 'given ammunition' to those opposed to divorce by 'appearing to weigh in quite inappropriately on the side of change . . . Her lawyers and advisers may state with confidence that she has not stepped outside the parameters of her office. But the judgment of common sense must be that this was an occasion on which she should have resisted the lure of the TV cameras and stayed mute.'[20]

The referendum result was so close that it was the subject of a court challenge. Many people believed that the atrocious weather in the west of Ireland that day, where a large turnout of elderly and conservative voters was expected, actually determined the end result. It was not until June 1996 that the Supreme Court upheld the referendum result in favour of divorce. By this stage, the backlash had already been felt. And it was directed against a significant part of the Robinson constituency: women.

CHAPTER 13

Acts of Imagination

'With the big battles won what's to keep us interested?' Such was the cry at the close of 1995, as peace appeared to have broken out between liberals and conservatives, between Church and state, in the new 1990s' Ireland.[1]

With divorce and some form of access to abortion on the statute books – and the North outside her control anyway – had the former Mayo senator and academic who had been elected first woman head of state played her hand? Not according to her own manifesto or inauguration speech. It had listed other priorities, including community empowerment, human rights, the Third World, the position of women and what it meant to be Irish at the close of the second millennium.

Many felt that the change in Irish identity dated from a game of football; though one commentator traced it back to a U2 rock concert in Madison Square Garden, New York. Militant republicans had hijacked definitions of 'Irishness', in an echo of the late nineteenth-century trend of 'reactive patriotism' which, as one commentator, Declan Kiberd, has noted, 'saw Ireland as not-England'.[2] Mary Robinson was a part of that movement which was attempting to redefine it in more active terms.

Identity and image were issues that extended far beyond her own presidential wardrobe – a wardrobe of Irish design put together by Cecily MacMenamin, a director of and buyer for the large and very fashionable Dublin department store, Brown Thomas, who contributed to the President's ranking on international 'best dressed' lists early on in her term. But in the year of her election, a gruff Geordie was the Republic's most popular 'native': Jack Charlton, manager of the Irish soccer team, which qualified for the World Cup. If the players had been refugees seeking jobs in Ireland's hard-pressed economy, they mightn't have been so readily adopted. But when international sporting prowess was at stake, second- and third-generation nationals could sport English accents, coloured skin and still be accepted as first-rate 'Paddys'.

'These are great days for those of us, citizens of this fair land, who have

Czech or Italian or Nigerian fathers to go with our Irish passports and our Irish mothers,' Andy Pollak wrote in *The Irish Times*. 'The Irish soccer team, with its extraordinary collection of polyglot Irish pedigrees, has given us a new pride in our multi-cultural Irishness, and put one more nail in the coffin of the old, exclusive . . . GAA-supporting, Fianna Fáil-definition of 'real' Irishness. I'm sure Leopold Bloom is up there cheering along with the rest of us half-breeds.'[3]

In April 1994 yet another definition displaced the Charlton factor. Irish television was hosting the Eurovision Song Contest, an annual exercise in middle-of-the-road pop which normally aroused little more than derision among the many with a genuine interest in contemporary music. During the intermission between competitors and results, the host country took its showcase piece to the stage. By the time it had reached its breathless conclusion, the performance known as *Riverdance*, backed up by vocals from Anúna and a score composed by Bill Whelan, had the audience cheering on its feet. As a piece of choreography, it was a masterpiece. Irish traditional dancing was no longer an almost puritanical exercise in skilled footwork. *Riverdance*, led by an Irish-American from Chicago, combined movement, speed, skill, adrenalin and, yes, sex. Whereas Irish America had already influenced music on both sides of the Atlantic, it had now infiltrated another medium, which had in turn been influenced by polkas, sets, jigs and reels from the other side of the Irish Sea. Almost before the dancers left the set, contracts for the video and the tour had been drawn up.

The Irish language was already experiencing something of a revival, partly as a reflection of the worldwide 'roots' phenomenon which had been under way for several decades. It seemed as if the greater the magnetic pull on Ireland's allegiance to a single Europe – a Europe which was giving significant financial boosts to the Irish economy – the more a search for identity was beginning to yield some fruit. While the minority of between 40,000 and 80,000 native Irish speakers in peripheral areas was dwindling, there was an increasing demand among parents in urban areas for Irish language schools, known as *gaelscoileanna*. In 1996, after a campaign lasting over a decade, a new Irish language television station, Teleffs na Gaeilge, was funded by the government.

Her commitment to learning and speaking the language, her constant references to Irish literature and her recognition of the Irishness of those emigrants abroad had linked the President to the new identity debate. For some, her very election had initiated it. Interviewed in June 1991 by arts critic and journalist Paddy Woodworth, she spoke at length about the role it played in her life and in Irish society. Her strong personal interest had been awakened in her teens as a student at the annual Yeats Summer

School in Sligo, where she had 'endured horsehair mattresses by night to enjoy the delights of the lectures by day', she said.

At university, she had abandoned the Stanislavsky Method of acting after 'failing to imagine herself as a briefcase', but had enjoyed the friendship of Eavan Boland and other rising literary figures, she told Woodworth. Her lasting love of the cinema had begun as a young student at finishing-school in Paris, when she had discovered that she could go to the pictures at the 'scandalously early hour' of 10 a.m. Irish film-makers should make their films in Ireland with 'creativity and artistic expression', she said; this sort of approach was preferable to imitating the larger film producers and trying to 'put together these multi-million-pound packages'.

The Irish language had a very important place in national culture, although it was 'endangered', she felt. She had grown up with good Irish in Mayo, and was best at it in boarding-school in Dublin, she said. There was a 'downhill pattern' after that, however, but she had realised through her involvement 'as a lawyer and culturally' at European level the significance of 'reinforcing ourselves as a separate and ancient and rich cultural tradition' as 1992 approached – a key date for the single European market.

She had intended to refresh her Irish for years, and had spent her first Easter as president in the Connemara Gaeltacht in Spiddal, County Galway. 'I want to get away from the politician's *cupla focail* [few words] in Irish,' she said. 'I want my Irish to be good enough to say what I want to say, confidently and with pleasure, in the middle of a speech.'

As president, she was keen to take up opportunities to broaden the sense of Irishness, she went on. 'I have a sense that we are coming to a kind of maturity about ourselves, we are coming to it at a time when there is great creativity and vitality, and it is replacing a worrying uncertainty and self-deprecation which, I think, comes from a kind of post-colonial hang-up about ourselves. I think we have to pull the different threads together.'

The arts as a medium for tolerance and pluralism could help to broaden public horizons, she agreed – on Northern Ireland, gay rights, the position of travelling people. She alluded to space being made available in Áras an Uachtaráin for artistic events and confirmed that there were plans to set up a visitor centre in the house. She was still 'reading' her way into the office, she said, but had thought a good deal about the concept of Irish identity in the 1990s. She intended to seek and take advice. 'My skill as a lawyer is in taking a briefing, and in advocating,' she explained. 'In a way I think what I'm doing at the moment is taking a broad briefing with a view to using the office to advocate, both within Ireland and, hopefully, outside.'[4]

She would rarely draw comparisons with her predecessors, but she did speak of how her inclusive, rather than exclusive, view of Irishness had set her apart from one former office-holder. Speaking in May 1992 at the 400th anniversary celebrations of Trinity College, Dublin – which had bestowed an honorary doctorate on her some months before – she referred to the 'man for all seasons', Ireland's first president, Dr Douglas Hyde. She had many experiences in common with him, she said, alternating between English and Irish as she spoke. Both came from the west of Ireland, both had graduated from Trinity with law degrees, both had received honorary doctorates, both had served in the Seanad and both had recognised the importance of the Irish language to the Ireland of their time.

Hyde had accepted his doctorate after something of a battle with the college authorities over the rejection of his application for a professorship in 1896. He had lacerated them in return – hitting out at 'that Stygian flood of black ignorance about everything Irish which, Lethe-like, rolls through the portals of my beloved Alma Mater'. But whereas he had championed the de-anglicising of Ireland and the exclusive promotion of the native tongue, Robinson's emphasis was firmly on a 'pluralist, open' state within Europe, where those who did not speak Irish were not criticised, and where there was a wider concept of identity that embraced all shades of opinion and belief.

Her campaign extended to sport and to the Gaelic Athletic Association which fostered the games of Gaelic football, hurling, camogie and hand-ball, and which had originally imposed a ban on its members preventing them from participating in or even observing certain specified 'non-Gaelic' activities such as rugby. Speaking in December 1991 at the presentation of the association's annual 'all-star awards', she expressed some disappoint-ment that the contribution of women was not honoured at the banquet, and urged the GAA to embrace 'new ideas and cultures' openly and positively. While Ireland had much to contribute, it also had much to gain from other cultures and traditions, she said.

In 1992, during a successful state visit to France, she had spoken of her 'moral authority' to the French daily, *Libération*, and had charmed the late President François Mitterrand. Her visit, on the eve of the signing of the Maastricht Treaty agreement on Europe, was praised as a most valuable diplomatic and political exercise, in presenting to the French public an alternative image to that of an Ireland torn apart by violence. Four years later, Mitterrand's successor, Jacques Chirac, kissed her hand outside the Elysée Palace as she arrived to open the six-month-long Irish cultural festival in Paris, *L'Imaginaire Irlandais*. Though she was credited with having instigated it, some commentators preferred to believe that Charles Haughey, who never failed to command a presence among European leaders, was the real mastermind.

She wanted France to become familiar with the 'cultural renaissance' which had taken place in Ireland in recent years, the President told Chirac. The festival was a reflection of a modern, dynamic and creative Irish society. For his part, Chirac professed to having visited Ireland about ten times, mostly as a youth-hosteller. The island had found its own identity in the European Union, he said; an identity which had not been diluted in any way and which was 'respected', he said, by all other EU member states.

Not everyone would agree. Before membership of the European Union, and since Ireland had acceded to the Maastricht Treaty on EU convergence in 1992, there had been a continuing, if sporadic, debate on neutrality and on Ireland's attempts to retain traditional 'non-military' involvement while still being a member of one of the world's most powerful economic blocs.

Yet there was no point in talking of 'traditional neutrality' as one talked about Irish corned beef and cabbage, the Labour Party's Michael D. Higgins had said in the lead-up to the Maastricht referendum. Nor should it be invoked to shield an absence of any foreign policy – a fact which often made for a 'sticking-plaster' approach to European diplomacy.

'Ireland alone is a nation deaf and dumb – a nation so preoccupied with its own internal purity that it is unprepared to risk contagion by intervening in the international scene to effect real change,' the UCD philosopher Dr Richard Kearney, had observed in 1987. 'Today, such an Ireland is neither desirable nor feasible.'[5] One of the shortcomings of Irish discussion on membership of the European Union was the almost exclusive emphasis on economic matters. He wasn't the first to remark on this. Belonging to Europe – and exporting Ireland's unemployed – was not just an economic matter, but involved political and cultural citizenship, he said. It also involved adopting a sense of positive neutrality and forging new affiliations with other neutral states, which could make a contribution to international fora and present an alternative view to 'the hegemony of the geo-political power blocs (and their military offshoots, NATO and the Warsaw Pact)'.

In a postmodern Europe, the national preoccupation with emigration and immigration should be replaced by a positive view of migration, he said: mobility nurtured ideas. 'The days of uniquely Irish solutions to uniquely Irish problems are over. If we are to make the migratory model effective, if we are to create a climate to which the Irish abroad would wish to return, it is necessary to recognise that people leave Ireland for two main reasons: economic – they cannot earn an adequate living here; and cultural – Irish society today is simply not dynamic and liberated enough.'

The image of a postmodern Europe as an open frontier community of communities required that Ireland's view of itself and others needed to change, he said. 'In this respect, perhaps the "identity crisis" which has dominated Irish cultural debates in recent years should be seen in a new light: not as a self-obsessive quest for a lost national essence, but as a basic dissatisfaction with the inherited ideologies of identity which sufficed up to now.'

Kearney had touched on a complex issue. In the late 1980s, no longer did many young emigrants regard themselves as victims of an Irish economy oppressed by the legacy of the British colonial system. These new emigrants had skills; they laughed at the mythical view of home expressed by the older generation in London pubs and Irish bars in New York – and at the musical odes to sweet Cavan lakes which were, in reality, now polluted beyond all recognition owing to intensive EU-supported agriculture.

The President had appealed to that vast community abroad, promising a welcoming candle in the window, in her inaugural speech. Now, just as she promoted a different Ireland to that marketed abroad by the IRA and loyalist paramilitaries, so she began to present a more positive view at home of the diaspora, numbering about 70 million of Irish descent worldwide.

In July 1992 she took up the option under Article 13.7 of the Irish Constitution to deliver an address to both houses of the Oireachtas; the only precedent had been Eamon de Valera in 1969, when he marked the fiftieth anniversary of the first Dáil, and spoke in the Mansion House. The title – 'The Irish Identity in Europe' – was touched on by her a few days before, when she paid the first official visit by an Irish head of state to the 'home from home' across the water, Scotland, and accepted yet another of the many honorary degrees which would be conferred upon her, this time from St Andrews University.

She spoke of the ties that bound: of peripherality and identity. 'We are very comfortable with each other, Ireland and Scotland', she said. James Connolly, socialist, a leader in the 1916 Rising and a major figure in Irish history, had been born of Irish parents in Edinburgh; John Ferguson, Irish home rule radical and land activist, had become the first Irish Glasgow councillor. Wounds inflicted by the ongoing conflict in Northern Ireland were felt in Scotland also, through close economic and social ties. And there were literary links with Scots writers such as Sorley MacLean and Liz Lochhead.

Her timing was carefully chosen, shortly after the referendum on the Maastricht Treaty which had been carried, in spite of fears among opponents about the implications for Irish neutrality. In an address which she wrote herself, and which was vetted by the government, she emphasised inclusivity, and spoke not only of the European Union but of a Europe beyond it and of Ireland's instinctive sympathy for the Third World. She urged that there be an honest debate on neutrality, and said that there should be no fears that such discussion might be interpreted as 'un-European'.

She spoke of emigration and the unemployed and the changing role of women; but her most direct appeal was to the people of all traditions in Northern Ireland, recalling that some of the most moving moments of her presidency to date had been passed there, or during reciprocal visits by Northern groups to Áras an Uachtaráin. Her direct predecessor, Dr Patrick Hillery, was among the large audience present. The absence of former Taoiseach Charles Haughey was noted.

The speech was generally well received, although one Sunday newspaper columnist criticised her for delivering 'easily digested, feel-good, heart-warming mush in place of hard-edged reasoning and tough decisions', and another said it was 'a banal procession of new-age clichés' by a 'would-be Mother of the Nation'.[6]

In early February 1995, as preparations were well under way to mark its 150th anniversary, the Irish famine was the theme of Robinson's second address to both houses of the Oireachtas. The cabinet had agreed earlier that week to hold a constitutional referendum on the right of emigrants to vote in Seanad elections, where three of the sixty seats would be reserved for their representatives. Skilfully, she used the occasion to transmit subtle messages on nationality and nationalism, on emigration and on the North. Speaking in both Irish and English, she did not seek to rewrite history, but recalled her visit the previous year to the graves of Irish famine victims who had ended up at Grosse Ile on the St Lawrence river in eastern Canada:

> I arrived in heavy rain and as I looked at the mounds which, together with white crosses, are all that mark the mass graves of the five thousand or more Irish people who died there, I was struck by the sheer power of commemoration. And as I stood looking at Irish graves, I was also listening to the story of the French-Canadian families who braved fever and shared their food, who took the Irish into their homes and into their heritage. Indeed, the woman who told me that story had her own origins in the arrival at Grosse Ile. She spoke to me in her native French and, with considerable pride, in her inherited Irish.
>
> The more I have travelled the more I have seen that the Irish language since the famine has endured in the accents of New York and Toronto and Sydney, not to mention Camden Town. As such it is an interesting record of survival and adaptation.

She had met young people from the entire island of Ireland who had felt they had no choice but to emigrate, and the grief of seeing a child or other family member leave would always remain sharp, and the absence would never be easy to bear. However, modern communications had wrought a dramatic change. Even she could recall the 'joy' at seeing a copy of her local Mayo newspaper in a newsagent's shop while a student in Boston.

Although emigration from Ireland had been experienced over centuries as a chronicle of sorrow and regret, it was also one of contribution and adaptation to new host societies, she said. Irishness was not simply territorial, but was at its best when reaching out to everyone on the island, and when it could honour those whose sense of identity and cultural values might be 'more British than Irish'.

Ireland had been shaped by change over more than five thousand years – by Celts, Vikings, Normans, Huguenots, Scots and English settlers, she said, and 'whatever the rights or wrongs of history, all those people marked this island'. History should be kept in perspective. At the start of the famine anniversary, people should look to the background 'with a clear insight which exchanges the view that we were inevitable victims in it, for an active involvement in its present application'. Humanitarian relief then could be examined in detail, related to such relief now, and the inadequacies of both assessed.[7]

There was little obvious response. The speech was 'too intellectual' for 'Irish labourers in Kilburn', one politician was quoted as saying afterwards. And, as a turn in the economy stemmed emigration, a referendum on the emigrants' right to vote was deferred in October 1996. A month after the address, a philosophy lecturer, Dr Noreen O'Carroll, wrote of her astonishment at the cool reaction. 'Far from being a matter of little national importance, as her critics would have us believe, the President's recent address to the Oireachtas is, in my view, the most significant speech made by any public figure on this island for years.' The President's simple insight had enormous implications, she felt, in gently challenging every person on the island to 'reflect anew on Irish identity and to do so by applying the concept of "diaspora" not only to Irish emigrants and to those of Irish descent, but also to our very origins on the island of Ireland'. Such an exploration revealed what it was to be truly Irish, 'to be tolerant of, and understanding of, a diversity of peoples, traditions and influences'.[8]

Not everyone was impressed with this concept of confidence-building, though there was money to be made from it as 'Celtic' music became a marketable commodity. 'Nowadays it's impossible to question the hype that surrounds Irish achievement without getting denounced as a killjoy,' arts journalist John Boland wrote in August 1995. 'This new middle-class

Éire Nua even absorbs the hitherto-unfashionable Irish language into everyday Irish life . . . We're told, too, that Van Morrison and the Cranberries and Sinead O'Connor are not merely musicians but are mystically and mysteriously Celtic in their visionary insights, that diasporas are joyfully peculiar to this island (tell that to the Italians for starters), that Irish theatre and film-making are uniquely exciting, and that Riverdance is not just a skilful mélange of Broadway and bodhrans, but says something profound about the Irish character.'

This 'ersatz' image of Ireland bore no relation to reality, in Boland's view. Butter was linked with a sense of national identity as if it were produced nowhere else. 'Irish aid volunteers get praised by our President as being uniquely caring, as if aid volunteers elsewhere don't care enough.' Yet, critics were dismissed as if they were somehow 'un-Irish' and unpatriotic. 'As a nation, are we so insecure that we have to keep asserting our superiority?' he asked, demanding that the once familiar Irish habit of begrudgery be restored to its 'former honoured status'.⁹

His words did not go astray. *The Irish Times* published the following letter in January 1996:

> We were an elderly couple, one of the 150,000 such, bidding farewell to a loved one, sadly on her way back into exile. In the harrowing mass grief, all around us, we saw something of the obverse of President Robinson's roseate black-tie, Waldorf Astoria, Dorchester Hotel expatriate Irish diaspora, those well prepared for it by their élitist education and professional status in our unjust society.
>
> In the pent-up love, pain and tear-stained faces of those leaving and those of us left behind etched in all its human reality, was 'our' diaspora, those of us with little else but our bare hands driven into exile by hunger, joblessness and poverty. We are among the second-highest ethnic group sleeping rough in London's cardboard city, in the prisons, the jails, the mental hospitals, the alcoholic wards, the brothels, the kitchens of cheap-labour hotels, the building sites, the dole queues and skid rows of the world, too poor to come home for Christmas.
>
> It is said that, with our fertility rate, our population should be between 11 and 14 million. Who cares for those millions of us dumped on the charity of the nations of the world? 'You had to come here to be fed, Paddy.'
>
> For those of us who have survived the cynical ethnic cleansing of the last 70 years by a succession of political leaders, there is that same small, self-indulgent, post-colonial wealthy millionaire, first-generation peasant, propertied, privileged few families, uncon-

cerned for the tens of thousands of our unemployed fellow citizens, their children, their elderly dependants. At least one-third of our people live below the poverty line, and go to bed hungry every night. What a shameful mockery for those of 'our' diaspora is our free, egalitarian, independent, democratic Republic.

May one grieving Irish family, among those bidding farewell and those left behind, tell our roving President her fatuous low-watt, low-powered, 'cheapest available, warmly welcoming electrical' candle in her window brought no comfort to our diaspora and could now, permanently, be switched off.[10]

The author was Dr Noel Browne, potential Labour candidate for the presidency in 1990 who was, as another correspondent noticed, 'continuing to tilt at windmills'. A responding letter to the newspaper preferred to compare him to Thomas Merton – 'a man crazed with caring about the human condition, crying forever into the north wind of indifference and despair'.[11]

Ireland's link with international aid and the Third World was another dimension to this new badge of identity. It had been from the outset of the Robinson presidency, partly through the influence of Professor Enda McDonagh, her chaplain. Indeed, 'Development Day', when returned aid workers were invited to Áras an Uachtaráin before Christmas, had become one of the office's most successful annual events.

She had, the Maynooth College theologian observed, always been so concerned about women, about the travelling community, about deprivation at home, while her legal interests had been international. The two 'fused', in his view, when she began to take an interest in development – and took a second look at European integration and the exclusive and exploitative threat posed by a powerful capitalist bloc.[12]

And so developing countries with Irish links had taken priority on the President's international itinerary from early on. The government had conceded an increase in her budget to allow for more foreign travel, with itineraries reflecting imaginative ideas. During her first, and very successful, presidential visit to the United States in the autumn of 1991 – when she gave five major lectures over a gruelling ten days on subjects ranging from feminism to AIDS and world poverty – she set the agenda. A stronger United Nations was vital, to help relieve 'the crushing burden of armaments and the diversion to war' of 'energies and resources which should go instead to development and human need', she insisted. The international community needed to renew and increase its support for the UN, she said, speaking at the presentation of the Berkeley Medal to her at the University of California. 'Three-quarters of the world's traffic in conventional arms goes to the Third World,' she said. Control and reduction of this trade in armaments could help to stabilise African economies and release vital development resources. As for the complex issue of financial obligations and transfers, terms of trade shifted to the disadvantage of primary producers in the Third World. 'By some accounts, the gap between the developed and the developing world appears to be widening, not narrowing.'

Referring to the Cold War, she said that the reduction of tension between the superpowers had only clarified the severity of other world problems, like poverty, lack of human rights, regional and national conflicts, ethnic and religious differences between and within nations. 'Let us remember how small the world seemed when we feared that it might be destroyed. Let us not forget that it is no bigger now that we need to reconstruct it. In this small world there are no safe distances.'

The President appealed for 'acts of imagination' and told the American students about Ireland's direct experience of famine which had decimated the population in the 1840s. There was an old folk saying in Ireland: 'it's easy to sleep on another man's wound'. The bleak statement had emerged out of the past and out of Irish people's own memories of struggle and oppression.

She quoted American writer Edward R. Murrow, Irish poet Patrick Kavanagh, Ghanaian playwright Efua Sutherland and Ugandan poet Oko p'Bitak, drawing particular attention to Bitak's and Sutherland's own continent of Africa. 'What makes the imaginative faculty so valuable is that it can unite apparently disparate events and occasions and make sense of them,' she stressed. 'If we use our imagination we can see that the suffering of individual African people, the complex balances of power and supply, and the survival and strengthening of democracy in our world and theirs are all part of a single equation, not separate parts of separate problems.

'We need to consider them together,' she continued. 'And there are always temptations, as we live in the midst of progress and plenty, not to consider them.' She reminded her audience of the opening lines of Ralph Ellison's novel, *Invisible Man*: 'I am an invisible man . . . I am invisible, understand, simply because people refuse to see me.'

In the time of Bishop Berkeley – whose home was Ireland – such problems would have been too remote to know about, let alone to contemplate, she said. 'We have no such excuse.' And she finished with a story about the links between Ireland and other cultures in her part of Mayo, and how such links were strengthened by an annual walk across the local countryside. 'Last year, representatives of the Choctaw Indians of

Oklahoma were there. What makes this so memorable is that during the Irish famine, this tribe – who had themselves been forcibly removed from their homeland – raised 710 dollars, an enormous sum in those days, for the relief of Irish famine victims. Across a much larger, more distant and remote world than ours in the nineteenth century, they used their own experience to make an imaginative understanding. They chose not to sleep on our wound . . .'[13]

In May 1992 the President was made an honorary Chief of the Choctaw Nation of Oklahoma at a ceremony in Áras an Uachtaráin.

No one would have said that she was job-hunting way back then, but the role of the UN in tackling debt and development issues would continue to feature in her speeches abroad, as would the Irish famine. In August 1992 famine in the East African state of Somalia prompted David Andrews, the Irish Foreign Minister, to visit. It was a gruelling trip, amid tight security. A small group of Irish officials and two reporters – Roisín Boyd of RTE and myself – were facilitated by Irish aid agencies, using hired gunmen for protection, in the capital, Mogadishu. Relief agencies, some of them Irish, were spending up to 50 per cent of their budget on protection for food distribution and staff. On his return, Andrews made a heartfelt plea at the UN.

Within weeks, the President had announced her intention to travel to the Horn of Africa also. She would, she promised, follow up her visit with a personal report to the UN Secretary General, Dr Boutros Boutros-Ghali, in a bid to focus world attention on the beleaguered nation, which was one of many casualties of the global arms race. Ironically, the very Europe which she was always so keen to promote had been a huge contributor to this conflict through the arms trade and through its trade policies and approach to Third World debt.

An army of some thirty Irish reporters and photographers was mustered to accompany the presidential party, which included the President's husband Nicholas and special adviser Bride Rosney. The schedule drawn up reflected the pressure that aid agency officials had exerted prior to her departure. In some cases, less than fifteen minutes was earmarked for stops at various Irish-associated food projects, and the entourage frequently had to break into a run on the ground. The drivers were Somali 'security men', touting machine-guns and chewing qat, the leaves of which suppress the appetite and act as an intoxicant. Throughout the heat and dust and distress, a quiet-spoken Algerian diplomat, the UN special envoy to Somalia, Mohamed Sahnoun, stayed at the President's right-hand side.

Sahnoun had nothing but admiration for Irish non-governmental organisations (NGOs), particularly for their less bureacratic approach to starvation and illness. Inter-agency competition was taken to extremes at times, however. One early morning, I saw the head of one of the NGOs erecting his signs outside an orphanage in Mogadishu. The Somali orphanage director was a little bemused at this instant 'partnership', but certainly wasn't going to object if there was the prospect of some funding or food aid. The same agency head was witnessed later in the day telling one of his Irish volunteers to stick out her chest: the logo on her T-shirt couldn't be seen clearly enough by the television cameras. As for the T-shirts, they reflected what some agencies were accused of – a neo-colonialist approach to intervention.

The President was moved to tears by what she witnessed on her three-day trip; not in Somalia itself, but in the Kenyan capital, Nairobi, shortly after she walked down the red carpet into the hotel to give her press conference. 'It has been a very difficult three days . . . very, very difficult,' she began, her voice quivering. 'I found that when I was there in Baidoa and in Afgoi and in Mogadishu, and this morning in Mandera, I had no difficulty in remaining calm and in not letting my emotions show, and I am sorry that I cannot be entirely calm in speaking to you because I have such a sense of what the world must take responsibility for . . .'

The anger and emotion were deeply moving; so dramatic that when it was the turn of the Minister for Foreign Affairs to speak, he responded in the way most men do. Castigating the UN for inaction, his hand was repeatedly striking the table.

She had had to make it 'personal', Mary Robinson said afterwards when she called for a new vision of Africa and expressed her feelings of shame. She had to embrace the women, caress children who were little more than sacks of brittle bones, and cuddle the lucky ones whose plastic feeding tags were becoming too tight on chubby wrists.

In spite of carping and bickering behind the scenes, the visit represented a significant moral boost for Irish aid workers. 'We are not missionaries, we are trained professionals and we are tired of being told how good we are – only to go home and find that there is no recognition of our experience when we try to re-enter the work force,' Mary Sweeney, one of the Irish development workers there for the long haul, told me. 'You go away for two years, you work bloody hard in the toughest conditions, and yet you return home to find an employer asking you why you opted out. There is a complete lack of understanding about the value of what we in long-term development do here, in partnership with local people.'

Some of the agency personnel made forceful points about the need for long-term (as distinct from emergency) support. 'Don't forget the rest of the continent,' one of the officials had pleaded with the President.

International response to her visit – the first of its type by a western head of state since the Somali crisis – was muted. The big television networks were more interested in the movements of the svelte Iman, the Kenyan-born Somali model and spouse of rock singer David Bowie, who was in Somalia at the same time. Film stars Sophia Loren and Audrey Hepburn, the latter an envoy for UNICEF, had also made visits.

The President stopped off in New York on the way home to make an appeal to the UN Secretary-General, and it was here that the first major US news coverage of the trip was recorded. She gave an early-morning interview on ABC television's *Good Morning America*, and described movingly how an emaciated boy had wanted to shake her hand, but had winced with the pain of his sores when he did. 'He held it up again,' she recalled. 'It was more important to be touched.' There was a minor upset, reflecting the hazards of live television interviews. Halfway through quoting the poet Seamus Heaney – 'history says don't hope on this side of the grave, but then once in a lifetime' – her voice was cut off, and replaced by that of a man advertising paper towels. The show's three million viewers later heard an apology and the full quote, which finished with 'the longed-for tidal wave of justice can rise up and hope and history rhyme'.

She would not allow the government to nominate her for the Nobel Peace Prize, it was reported at the end of that year. Though she was 'refusing to comment on the matter', it was known that she felt such a move to be inappropriate. Her view was that the award should be 'made on the basis of a lifetime's work for peace rather than on a single effort'.[14]

The US announced that it was seeking a UN mandate to send 28,000 troops to Somalia to protect food aid. This was a move which certainly could be defined as the sort of 'international action' sought by her, but in fact elicited a mixed response from international agencies, and would prove to be a costly and devastating mistake for the people of Somalia. As guns bred guns, so the whole militarised atmosphere was to cost aid workers' lives; in February 1993 Valerie Place, an Irish volunteer with the agency Concern Worldwide, was killed. The President had met her during her visit.

In December 1992 she published a diary of her visit, entitled *A Voice for Somalia*, which was illustrated with photographs taken by the Irish media. Much of the account was a personal record of the three days in East Africa, with little by way of background detail; names, when mentioned, tended to be Irish, rather than Somali. She described how her inner sense of justice and equality had been offended by what she witnessed, and, interestingly, recalled her feelings after her press conference in Kenya:

> In the event, because I was hit by a wall of emotion, of frustration and anger . . . I thought I had blown the opportunity. That part of

me that was a barrister – with the training and discipline of my profession, based on the ability to take a briefing and to advocate a case – knew it was not appropriate to let emotions break through . . . However, I wasn't just a barrister pleading a case. I was the President of Ireland giving a personal witness and responding to the people of Somalia. Above all, I was a human being devastated by what I had seen. In that context, it was impossible not to show emotion.[15]

The visit may have produced limited results for the Somali people, but it represented a watershed as far as the Irish presidency was concerned – none of her predecessors had visited a humanitarian disaster on this scale before. If she was trying to develop a Mother Teresa image, the President scotched that notion firmly the following year on a state visit to India, New Zealand and Hong Kong in late September and early October 1993. The journey itself was eventful: the air-force jet carrying the presidential party lost altitude suddenly in an electrical storm as it began its descent into Calcutta. Hours later, the state of Maharashtra was struck by an earthquake. The Robinson jet was requested to 'fly low' over the devastated area – an apparently facile gesture which drew a somewhat embarrassed response back home, where the government pledged £100,000 towards emergency relief.

After her meeting in Calcutta with Mother Teresa, then 82, the President spoke of her veneration for Mahatma Gandhi as someone who had been a major inspiration to her. She also admired the nun greatly for her work, and for challenging society's perception that girls were less valuable than boys, and that street children were almost without worth. Unlike the nun, however, the President believed in the option of family planning and in a woman's right to prevent unwanted pregnancy.

There would be more journeys to Africa, as a bitter civil war tore Rwanda apart. The twin themes of UN reform, and the lessons to be learned from the Irish famine experience, would be constants in the President's speeches. For instance, failure to consider ways of preventing human rights violations could deepen public scepticism of the role of the UN in this area, she warned at a major conference in Strasbourg in February 1993.

In early summer 1994 she opened a famine museum in the eighteenth-century Palladian mansion, Strokestown House, in County Roscommon, next to her home county of Mayo. It was the first of its type. Located in the stable yards, it was a privately funded restoration project by an enlightened local businessman, Jim Callery, in co-operation with a dynamic young relative, arts administrator Luke Dodd. Strokestown held a particular place in Irish famine history: the landlords, the Mahons, were among the most active in clearing their property of people, by assisted passage to Canada and by eviction. In November 1847 the estate owner, Major Denis Mahon, was shot dead.

In her introduction to the museum's guidebook, the President wrote about the importance of how history was recorded. 'More than anything else, this famine museum shows us that history is not about power and triumph nearly so often as it is about suffering and vulnerability,' she said. 'As we look at these artefacts and open our minds to these stories, we can feel again that it is an Irish strength to celebrate the people in our past, not for power, not for victory, but for the profound dignity of human survival. We can honour that survival best, it seems to me, by taking our folk-memory of this catastrophe into the present world with us, and allowing it to strengthen and deepen our identity with those who are still suffering.'

Not everyone agreed with the idea of reviving painful memories. There was still a collective amnesia about the reality behind the Irish famine. Historians warned that those planning the commemoration must be aware of sensitivities, and of attempts to subvert the truth. Kevin Whelan, bicentennial research fellow of the Royal Irish Academy, pointed out how Britain had viewed the Irish famine as an opportunity for Ireland's economic and social development; the potato was regarded as a 'lazy root grown in lazy beds by lazy people'. Such a viewpoint, influenced by prevailing evangelical and *laissez-faire* economics, led to an extreme reluctance to intervene as one million people died.

But some Irish had also benefited: landlords, merchants and farmers who exploited their weaker neighbours. And the Catholic Church which was able to step in as the sole representative national organisation, filling the cultural void left by those predominantly Irish-speaking peoples who had died or had emigrated. In such circumstances, it would be 'all too easy' to descend into 'maudlin sentimentality', Whelan wrote, wallowing as 'vicarious victims' rather than as beneficiaries. 'The one million dead left few descendants,' he pointed out. The bulk of those were scattered across the globe; and it would also be 'too facile' to 'blame every Irish ill, from schizophrenia to alcoholism, on the famine'.[16]

If the famine was considered a sensitive subject among the populace, President Robinson's interest in UN reform appeared to tread on toes within official government circles. It was to mark the second substantial confrontation with the administration. In December 1993 the government declined to allow her to co-chair a Ford Foundation-Yale University group set up to map out the role of the UN over the next fifty years, which had been established at the invitation of the UN Secretary

General. The Ford Foundation had loose links with the Trilateral Commission, from which Mary Robinson had resigned some years before. The government relied on advice from the Attorney General, who said that she was not within her constitutional powers to accept. Early the following year, it emerged that she had taken her own legal advice on this, and disagreed with the interpretation. Government sources said later that it was a policy problem, rather than a constitutional one, although a sentence in a letter intimating constitutional difficulties to the President may have indicated otherwise.

Such invitations were normally considered by the Taoiseach's department, the cabinet office and the Department of Foreign Affairs. The last-named department feared that a series of recommendations which might become known as the 'Robinson report' would compromise Ireland's own stance on UN reform and its position as an EU member. A letter was sent by Brian McCarthy, deputy secretary to the government, to Peter Ryan, the President's secretary, pointing out that it appeared that the invitation, had it been accepted, would involve the performance of presidential functions not envisaged by the Constitution or by law.

The President replied that she was required to act on the government's advice in relation to the Constitution, but not in relation to other functions such as those of a personal nature. When the government's real anxiety – about policy – emerged, she deferred immediately. 'It was a difficult issue,' she later said. 'The government altered ground and said it would constrain future governments. I accepted that there was a viewpoint: I didn't share it but I respected it.'[17]

When her decision to take legal advice was reported in the press, she wrote the Tánaiste an angry letter, convinced that he had leaked the information. Once again, it gave the impression that she and Dick Spring were at loggerheads and left, some sources say, 'a couple of sour tastes'.

There would be other opportunities to address UN reform. In March 1994 she delivered what was described as a 'major speech' on the UN's future at Harvard University, which was followed up by an address in New York to the UN Commission on the Status of Women. The latter had been organised as a preview for the UN's fourth world conference on women in Beijing in 1995. Commenting afterwards, the UN Secretary General, Dr Boutros Boutros-Ghali, encouraged speculation when he forecast a UN role for her and invited the President to maintain her high-profile interest in the organisation's various activities.

The first hand Robinson shook in 1994 'set the international agenda for the year', the *Phoenix* annual noted.[18] She had invited US senator Ted Kennedy and his sister, the US Ambassador to Ireland, Mrs Jean Kennedy Smith, to tea. Ted was a 'useful ally', now that he was back on Capitol Hill, the magazine remarked. As far as *Phoenix* was concerned, she had an agenda that included cultivating a 'regal image', further boosted by the purchase that year of Massbrook, a large country house in Mayo, formerly owned by the de Ferranti family, for some £350,000. A new top-of-the range BMW was also acquired, which was reported in the *Irish Independent* and resulted in legal proceedings over its tone.

The writ was unprecedented in the case of an Irish president; central to it were comments made in a letter to the newspaper about her taste in cars. There was also concern about a report in the same newspaper the same day to the effect that two gardaí had been transferred from their duties as the President's personal security detail at Áras an Uachtaráin, following complaints from the President's office. Five members of the security detail and drivers had been transferred the previous year. The President's office said that the moves followed professional advice from the police; the newspaper quoted the Garda Commissioner as making it clear that the transfer had been taken to facilitate a request from the President. The case was settled out of court and the newspaper made a donation to charity.

Certainly 1994 was hectic, with journeys to the inauguration of Nelson Mandela as President of South Africa, to Poland, to Canada for the Commonwealth Games, to the African countries of Zimbabwe, Tanzania, Zambia and Rwanda. The following year, international travel was to prove more controversial, however. In March 1995 she left for a series of state visits to South America, taking in Argentina, Chile and Brazil. This was not uncharted territory; there were close Irish historical links with all three countries, particularly Argentina where some 300,000 could claim Irish ancestry. A Mayo man, Admiral William Brown, had founded the Argentinian Navy. Many of the nineteenth-century Irish emigrants had become wealthy estate owners. In Chile, the country's liberator, Bernardo O'Higgins, was renowned as the son of the Sligo-born viceroy of Peru. Yet Ireland had only one resident ambassador in the whole of Latin America.

This could not have explained the diplomatic gaffes which surrounded the two-week trip. In both Argentina and Brazil, rows erupted over her failure to visit areas where Irish missionaries were working with the poor, and there was criticism of her shaking the hand of Chile's brutal military dictator, General Augusto Pinochet. There was nothing that the President could have done, as a guest, it was explained afterwards. This was a state visit, rather than a personal one. She had been 'absolutely surprised and dismayed' when she heard that Pinochet was present at the dinner held in her honour, she said. 'I did not show any pleasure in shaking his hand.'[19]

In the case of her failure to meet the Dominican nuns in Argentina, the itinerary had been decided by the Argentinian government; her office felt that the status of the trip as a state visit had been misunderstood and that the media coverage became 'single-focused'. She even earned criticism from that long-time supporter of her every move, *The Irish Times*. The newspaper's Washington correspondent, Conor O'Clery, who had accompanied her on the South American trail, had asked her directly if her future lay with the UN. 'The President's reply was suitably bashful. No one would take it as a denial,' the newspaper's leader writer said afterwards in an editorial which went on to question whether she really had enough experience, or international support, for the UN job. It referred to 'inherent stresses and tensions' with the government, which had not improved with the passage of time.

The South American tour had been characterised by 'a sequence of sour moments and rather transparent attempts at buck-passing as one embarrassment succeeded another', the writer said. 'Sympathisers of the President speak with concern about attempts to cramp her style and her vision of the office. Others in contact with her activities speak of her sense of restlessness and claim to recognise a growing tendency to hauteur and stiffness about her.'[20]

The controversy continued, with former presidential candidate Brian Lenihan rallying to her support. An Irish priest working in São Paulo said that the ambiguity surrounding the visit began with the planning, which did not involve consultations with the large number of Irish lay and religious organisations working with the marginalised. 'This pre-emptive setting of the agenda gave the whole visit a primarily commercial colouring,' Father David Regan wrote, clearly misunderstanding the protocol involved in a state visit. Had the President changed, or was she being used to do the work of the Irish Export Board? In another shot from the west, Dr Noel Browne sarcastically wondered why she had so far failed to visit the US-blockaded island of Cuba to shake hands with its socialist leader, Fidel Castro, on the Irish people's behalf.[21]

It was to get no easier. In August 1995 the UN world women's conference was due to open in Beijing, and it was expected that the President would lead a strong Irish delegation of both officials and NGO representatives which had received significant state funding to travel. This was not to be. The very able equality minister, Mervyn Taylor, led the party instead. The President was to be invited as a guest of the UN, then? Most of the other female world leaders would be there, and it would certainly assist in the UN secretary general campaign, if such a campaign existed.

No. Robinson was not on the UN list, but there was a separate list of invitations issued by the Chinese government, a UN spokeswoman told me in Beijing. The US First Lady, Hillary Rodham Clinton, was on it, as was the Icelandic President, Vigdis Finnbogadottir. A third list comprised guests with special expertise, including Queen Fabiola of Belgium and British Labour politician Baroness Shirley Williams. Normal protocol would have involved informal contact before issuing of an invitation. That none was received in Dublin suggested that President Robinson could not participate in what would have also become a state visit – and a difficult one, given her record on Tibet, the Dalai Lama and human rights.

If the President did not want to travel because of the impact on her human rights record, the Minister of State for Foreign Affairs, Joan Burton, also had reservations; and the chairwoman of the National Women's Council, Noreen Byrne, confirmed that she would not go because of her views on China's strict population policy. Undeterred, Mervyn Taylor led the large Irish government delegation, only to find himself distracted by preparations for the approaching divorce referendum at home.

Much of the official conference was taken up with politicking over the official platform for action which had moral, rather than legal, standing. Still, such was the fear about what it could produce that it engendered an 'unholy alliance' involving the Catholic Church, right-wing US congress-men, Islamic fundamentalists and the Chinese government. The network-ing took place in corridors and in and around tents hosting the NGO forum in the Beijing suburb – a safe 30 miles out – of Huairou. Women from both sides of the Irish border who had travelled with the support of the Irish government exchanged views and addresses; from Bangladesh to Tanzania and Tullamore to Belcoo, the impact of isolation, poverty, environmental degradation and domestic violence was very much the same.

Leaders like Benazir Bhutto of Pakistan and Hillary Clinton stole the headlines – the latter's line about 'human rights being women's rights' sounded as if it had come straight out of a Mary Robinson speech. But perhaps no other woman aroused as much fascination as the female leader of the Vatican delegation, Professor Mary Ann Glendon. The slight, blonde 56-year-old Harvard law professor matched no stereotypes. With a background in civil rights in Mississippi and an interest in new economic approaches to Third World issues, she was a feminist and a radical, but not a radical feminist; she was also half Irish and half American, but not typically Irish-American. She had met Mary Robinson on several occa-sions, she told this reporter, and felt that the Irish President was a role model representing 'the feminism of the third millennium', the sort of feminism that both she and the Pope could identify with.

The law professor was well aware that Ireland was two months away from a referendum on divorce. With its history of maintaining an intellec-tual tradition when Europe was in ruins, the Republic ought to 'pull up its socks' and 'get intellectual about Catholicism again', she said.[22]

The final Beijing document was far from perfect. The Vatican dodged and weaved on the issue of condoms in relation to AIDS. The Platform for Action did have three tangible results, however, according to US feminist writer Charlotte Bunch. It may have been the fourth for women, but it was the first world conference to involve participants at all levels and to relate international to national needs. It was an invaluable experience for those involved. And it produced a document to which governments had to be accountable. The President's presence would not have influenced the outcome one whit; for those Irish women present, however, it would have been symbolic.

'As for becoming secretary general of the United Nations, I would say she has not got a chance. Every big-time politician in every small-time country in the world fancies just that job. Why should the men from the jungles and the deserts give it to her?' wrote Mary Ellen Synon in an Irish Sunday newspaper in April 1995, shortly after the South American débâcle.[23] Not everyone agreed. If there was mud, little of it was going to stick. Just as frequent references to the Trilateral Commission had failed to halt her career in the Seanad, or dent her presidential campaign, so Mary Robinson was able to shake off controversy once again, even as it was confirmed in the Dáil that the cost of the presidency in 1993 amounted to two million pounds.

'President not to seek UN post' was the newspaper headline in October 1995, as she responded to questions in New York following an address to the UN General Assembly to mark its fiftieth anniversary. In her speech she had said that the future of the UN was in question, and had put forward a four-point renewal plan. So, if she had declared herself to be out of the race for the big job, could she not opt for one of the UN agencies, like human rights commissioner?

Still the speculation continued, with much of the eulogising about her credentials appearing in the international press. By April 1996 she had received favourable nominations from such US publications as *The Nation* and *US News and World Report*, and from British newspapers like *The Independent*, *The Guardian* and *The Observer*. However, moves by US Senator Ted Kennedy to have her address the joint houses of the US Congress during a state visit there in June came to naught when it emerged that the Taoiseach, John Bruton, was to speak instead.

The Democrat senator and close associate of Bill Clinton was now widely acknowledged to be a key Robinson supporter for the UN job, as were former UN diplomats Erskine B. Childers and Sir Brian Urquhart. Indeed, in March 1995, Childers (the son of the late president of the same name), had referred several times to the next UN secretary general as 'she' in his keynote address to a consultative seminar on Irish foreign policy in University College, Cork.

There were inherent dangers in the Kennedy support, however. Was the US hoping to appoint someone it could manipulate? Its well-publicised decision to veto any bid by the current incumbent to seek a second term had already alienated some member states, particularly since America had not paid its UN dues. Yet the speculation continued, even as Robinson undertook the first official visit (as distinct from the courtesy call in 1993) to Britain.

'Compare and contrast the two ladies who will lunch at Buckingham Palace on 6 June,' the weekly *Economist* wrote. Both were heads of state, both were popular, but there the resemblance ended, it said. 'Whereas Queen Elizabeth is a remote figure, Mrs Robinson is a woman of the people. Where Queen Elizabeth's contribution to national unity is simply to be there, Mrs Robinson has worked ceaselessly to reconcile Ireland's warring identities. Whereas Queen Elizabeth's unhappy family amuses half the nation and bemuses the other half, Mrs Robinson has an exemplary domestic life, not least because she is a Catholic married to a Protestant.' Whereas the Queen's watchwords were 'restraint and caution', Mrs Robinson was prepared to take risks, such as shaking the hand of Sinn Féin leader Gerry Adams before the IRA ceasefire, it said. 'Where it is hard to imagine Queen Elizabeth in any job but the one she does, Mrs Robinson is now being widely touted as the next secretary general of the United Nations.

'There is one other difference between the two ladies,' the article continued. 'Queen Elizabeth got the job because her father had it. Mrs Robinson got the job because she was elected to it. Could these facts – inheritance versus election, figurehead versus nation-builder – possibly be related?'

CHAPTER 14

A Touch of Witchcraft

May 1996. Cherry blossoms. A riot of gorse. Sheets of rain, drenching the 'garden of Ireland', County Wicklow. British-registered cars crawled into a tiny village on a river to photograph the set for the latest Irish film.

This production was actually a television series, made by the BBC and named *Ballykissangel.* It wasn't exactly 'oirish' paddywhackery, but did have a slightly improbable plot. Even as the Irish Catholic Church was staggering from one child abuse scandal to the next, an Irish-born scriptwriter had penned a story about an English curate who had been transferred to a small Irish country town. Naturally the curate caught the eye of the young female proprietor of the local pub.

The series had received a dubious reception at home, but in Britain it had been a hit. With fourteen million viewers recorded every week, it had reached the top 5 per cent in ratings before the end of its first six-week run. The parish priest of the real Wicklow village, Avoca, was far from offended. Fr Dan Breen was delighted at the show's success. The tourist pressure might have its downside, but most of the candles lit that week in his church of St Mary and St Patrick had been paid for by English visitors. The church had been built by local miners, at a time when copper was extracted from a local seam. When the world price of the metal collapsed, the mine closed down with the loss of many jobs in 1983.

The series was 'whimsical, light-hearted' and the cheroot-smoking, leather-jacketed Fr Breen did not fear any censure from his superiors. Hadn't the Church enough on its plate to be worrying about, without losing sleep over a television soap? He was slightly annoyed at the lack of support from the state broadcasting service, RTE, which did not participate during the programme's commissioning, but bought into the series later. 'It has lost its sense of humour,' he said. 'It has become like the Catholic Church in the 1950s – autocratic and abusing its powers. As for this so-called liberalism in the media, it is more autocratic than the Church was at its worst,' he said. 'The press is worse than the Church, you know!

Look at the President, Mary Robinson, and Dr Noel Browne. Both canonised. Noel Browne did not do away with tuberculosis in Ireland, and Mary Robinson is not a world leader like Helmut Kohl. This is *Beano* and *Dandy* stuff! It is immature to canonise her. She is a failed politician – a product of the law library which is no nursery for saints. Nothing personal – I admire her. She is a great ornament for Ireland. But I'd say the same about Brian Lenihan or Charles Haughey if either of them were proposed as world leaders. The worst thing is, you can't say any of this. We are told that this is what we must think, and we are expected to believe it. Like the Dark Ages. A touch of witchcraft!'

'Witchcraft.' An emotive term, and one which reflected a small but perceptible change in public attitudes towards the Irish President. Much of it was not directed at her, or even at her office, but reflected a maturity – this woman was not a god, after all – and a growing sense of frustration, confusion and bewilderment about changes in Irish society, and the moral vacuum created.

There was a rising crime rate, with a series of particularly savage attacks directed against women. As for liberalisation, this social change could not have come about without some backlash. When it hit, it did so from an unexpected quarter. In December 1995, as the President and government hosted a visit to Ireland by Bill Clinton – still during the IRA ceasefire – a row erupted over a speech given by the Taoiseach's wife, Finola Bruton, at a function where the keynote speaker was Hillary Clinton. 'Now is the time to recognise that the notion of equality does not necessarily give a natural primacy to a professional career over other choices a woman may make,' Mrs Bruton told the audience. Much of what she continued to talk about appeared inoffensive on paper, stressing the importance of the woman in the home. Yet it was her tone of voice, her attempts to castigate guests – many of whom had worked long, hard voluntary hours over the years to set up women's refuges and such like – that jarred. That the spouse of a taoiseach should take the opportunity to wag her finger at Irish feminists was just too much to take. Two junior ministers went on record to criticise her, with one describing her words as a 'rather smug little speech'.

As someone who appeared to represent a power base of marginalised women's groups, the President could have been the target of Mrs Bruton's speech. But she was not; rather it was aimed at a movement perceived to be dominated by middle-class, educated, urban women. And, as shrewd political commentators noted, it may also have been a carefully calculated attempt to win back some support for Fine Gael after the close-run divorce referendum. If so, it struck a chord. The criticism it aroused – and the genuine hurt felt by many who had toiled on behalf of battered wives and single mothers – was matched by overwhelming support among ordinary women, many of whom felt it was an exact reflection of their own thoughts, and not at all a crafty strategy on the part of Fine Gael.

The President had been aware of the dangers of exclusivity back in 1991, in the text of her Ogden Lecture to Brown University in the US. There had never been a more exciting time for a woman to offer her abilities to society, she had said then. Yet, there were dangers. Quoting Mary Wollstonecraft, who said that she did not wish women to have power over men, but over themselves, she warned against a 'too narrow' interpretation of feminism which excluded women who described themselves as 'just housewives': 'No ideology can dètermine vision, no set of precepts can prescribe contribution. Whether a woman is in the home with young children, or on her own, or with her chosen companion, or in the workplace, we must know that on each and every occasion her life can speak out to us out of its power and self-possession if we will listen to it.'[2]

October 1996: Maya Angelou was upset. It wasn't the bag of chocolate truffles on each chair. Nor was it the lavish setting, the ballgowns, the black ties that annoyed her. The hyperbolic – almost embarrassingly bombastic – welcome to the night's dinner in the Boston Marriott Copley Place Hotel was not new to her.

Pat Mitchell, 1996 Mistress of Ceremonies for the International Women's Forum, and president of Turner Original Productions (a media company owned by CNN magnate Ted Turner), was uninhibited. She talked of courage (mostly her own) and power – the power she felt on walking into a room with over a thousand successful women. It was when she begged the audience to reach out a hand to the sisters round about that a male official with the Irish president's party blanched. Charismatic prayer meetings and girl scout sing-songs were not part of the Irish President's protocol . . .

They were lawyers, accountants, architects, marketing managers. Everyone seemed to be a vice-president of something or other; at one table, a US state attorney chatted to a sales representative for pet fish food. Founded in 1982, the International Women's Forum aimed 'to assist women to achieve new and greater leadership roles in every sphere', with 51 affiliates in 16 countries throughout North and South America, the Caribbean, Europe, Asia and the Pacific Rim. Previous 'inductees' to their hall of fame ranged from Eleanor Roosevelt to Wilma Mankiller, the first woman elected chief of the Cherokee nation, to Margaret Thatcher – mention of whom elicited loud applause.

Corporate sponsors of the night flashed their logos: Gillette (all those lady shavers), Cadillac, Cigna Life Insurance ('in the business of caring') and AT&T. Several approaches had been made by the organisers to the

Irish President before this event, but there was a genuine apprehension on her part about participating. Would it be a re-run of a similar women's ceremony the year before, where the initial programme for award-winners involved walking up on stage with Mickey Mouse, and the planned finale had them standing in a circle singing Disney's 'It's a Small World'. Though changes were made at the last minute, it had earned the nickname of the Rocky Horror Picture Show.

As for Angelou, author of *I Know Why the Caged Bird Sings*, she was gracious in her acceptance of an award that should have been bestowed on her years before. Gracious even with the embarrassing format: a Caucasian introducing a Caucasian – the US ambassador to Ireland, Jean Kennedy Smith, and the Irish President, Mary Robinson; and an African-American heralding an African-American – Coretta Scott King and Angelou.

Mrs King was forceful, a solid tower of strength, as she had been following the death of her husband, the civil rights leader, Martin Luther King in Memphis, Tennessee, in April 1968. Together with Maya Angelou, who had worked with the Kings during the civil rights campaign, her presence was enough to fill the room. Mary Robinson rose to the occasion, straight off the plane from Dublin and after a hectic few days in Frankfurt where Ireland's diaspora was the theme of the international book fair, and where she had touched again on her current theme – a more generous concept of Irish identity that honoured the Britishness of the unionist community in Northern Ireland. The programme for the gala dinner described her as 'president of one of the world's most conservative, patriarchal countries' who 'ran and won in 1990 on a platform for change' and who had, by working for such change from within, 'stood conventional feminism on its head'.

The description raised a lot of eyebrows back at home. Ireland was not, after all, Iran. Under the Marriott ballroom lights and with an eye on the clock, the US ambassador to Ireland then zipped through an impressive speech. 'President Robinson's dynamic public presence has helped propel Ireland – a nation of three and a half million people – into a place of pride and prominence on the European stage,' Mrs Kennedy Smith said. She went on:

> She is the modern face of her country – vibrant and expressive. But she also stands as its conscience. During her term, President Robinson has reshaped the greatest sorrow of Irish history – the Irish famine – into a catalyst for ensuring that no other people suffer the same anguish. I am among the many who have turned on the evening news to see images of the President walking the alleys of Somalia, Rwanda or Zaire, comforting near-lifeless children,

listening to tribal leaders, and imploring the nations of the world to stand up to their duty to all humankind. The belief that all of us are members of a human family, that we all share common origins and a common destiny, is embraced and articulated by President Robinson wherever she goes. She has carried it with her to Northern Ireland, where she has talked to community groups of both traditions, encouraging them in their search for peace.

The US ambassador quoted from the President's 1995 address to the United Nations: 'Those of us who exercise leadership at this time will have to understand and accept this enormous responsibility. Hope and vision will not be enough. Concern and compassion must be translated into action in the real world.' And Kennedy Smith referred to Robinson's inspiration for the seventy million Irish abroad: 'Irishness is not simply territorial . . . the men and women of our diaspora represent not simply a series of departures and losses' but 'a precious reflection of our own growth and change'.

Then she brought her audience home: 'Each night in Dublin during the winter months, when the trees are bare and the darkness comes early, I drive by President Robinson's house on the way home, and through the branches, I see a simple light shining in her window.' The candle for the diaspora. The famous low-watt bulb.

The Irish President recalled her election campaign, talked of the honour of receiving this recognition, appealed for women to be 'written back into history', paid tribute to Maya Angelou, and elicited a laugh. In the early days of her election, her aide-de-camp had told her that she had 'everything in crisis'. He had gone home for his tea and his wife had said that 'things have changed around here . . .'. She was followed by the Irish singer, Mary Black, one of the many women of Ireland to whom she dedicated her IWF award, and a champagne toast.

'Ireland comes to Boston', the *Globe*'s social column had warned the day before. But she had made time to meet members of Boston's Irish diaspora, it said. She would be guest of honour at Sunday's annual Irish Immigration Center awards dinner at the Boston Park Plaza. Monday, she would feast on sliced roast duck. 'The President is also special to the UN association, since Senator Edward Kennedy has been a prime supporter of Robinson to replace UN Secretary-General Boutros Boutros-Ghali at the election in December,' the column continued.

Such support was on the President's mind for different reasons. Asked at a Saturday-night press briefing what she intended to say at two of her functions – addresses to the UN associations in Boston and New York –

she said that she would pay tribute to Erskine B. Childers, former UN diplomat and one of those most keen on her bidding for the UN job, who had died suddenly at the end of August.

Two months later, three years of speculation came to a grinding halt. It was confirmed that a Ghanaian, Kofi Annan, would take the UN top job. Other so-called front-runners, like Norwegian prime minister Gro Harlem Brundtland, had not made it either but were being tipped for other posts. Though some close to her said that President Robinson had never considered herself a serious contender, there was some disappointment. Was the government to blame for not canvassing more actively for her?

Impossible, claims one senior Labour Party official. Even if there had been a realistic opportunity – and China would surely have objected to her views on Tibet, while the US never really felt that the UN was in need of a feminist link – Ireland could not even have tested the water when Robinson was steadfastly declaring that she had no interest. Ambassadors could not have been given a mandate. The Tánaiste and Foreign Affairs minister, Dick Spring, had made an informal approach to her 18 months before, the source said, but it was 'terribly inconclusive'. She had given no indication of a serious interest.

Instead, UN High Commissioner for Human Rights was the job mentioned for President Robinson, as 1997 and the final year of her term of office dawned. She confirmed that she would make an announcement one way or another about her intentions by the end of March.

Annan's selection confirmed what many diplomats had been trying to point out all along: selection of a UN Secretary General is not like a White House campaign, where one candidate is pitted against another. Rather, it has more in common with the 'smoke-filled room dark-horse candidate' era which preceded television; a bit like a papal conclave, which can produce unexpected results. The five permanent members of the UN Security Council hold veto power over selection within the council, while the General Assembly has the theoretical right – never exercised – to override the council's decision by failing to give the nominee the necessary majority vote. The emphasis on a broad consensus has led the council to conduct straw polls, in which members vote anonymously before the formal balloting on a list of acceptable candidates.[3]

Ireland's contribution to international diplomacy was not on the minds of some of Robinson's compatriots by then. If she was worried about her future, there were women experiencing a searing physical pain. A number had been mistakenly infected by the National Blood Transfusion Service with blood contaminated with the Hepatitis C virus. A member of the lobby group formed to fight their case, Brigid Ellen McCole of County

Donegal, herself infected, had died in hospital shortly after she had agreed to a settlement of £175,000 from the service's board. She had refused the same sum five months before, and had been hounded by legal representatives for the state. One of her most treasured possessions, reproduced in Irish newspapers that day, was a photograph of her shaking hands with President Robinson, when the group visited Áras an Uachtaráin in November 1994.

Had there been any improvement in the lot of the women Mary Robinson had pledged to represent? Not for the Hepatitis C sufferers, certainly. Not for the women who found themselves victims of violent street crime. Not for the working mothers who were still unable to claim tax relief on child care, most of which was privately run. Not for those at the bottom of a two-tier society.

An Irishman, Peter Sutherland, had been head of the World Trade Organisation, which had helped to shape a new economic order for better or worse – the latter in the case of developing countries. The former Irish Attorney General and European Commissioner was appointed chairman of the Overseas Development Council, an international think-tank on trade and development, in 1997.

A speech that Mary Robinson had made in Galway in 1978 when still a senator could have come back to haunt her, if she had let it. A woman's self-realisation was thwarted in a capitalist society, she had said then. The feminist movement should 'demand a radical planned alternative to the free enterprise society in which we live, and should examine the potential of a genuinely socialist Ireland'.[4]

Almost twenty years later, no mention by the President of socialist alternatives; violence and inequality were still on the agenda, even with twenty female deputies in parliament. But the women from all walks of life who had been represented at the UN conference in Beijing in 1995 were empowered by it, and by the President's office, rather than by parliamentary representation in a male political system. Housewives, rather than feminists, had given depth to women's movements through community action, and had moulded that action into a political force.

As journalist Carol Coulter wrote in 1993, the very nature of the presidency and its largely symbolic role was a major influence:

> The fact that the President does not engage in governmental decisions allows Mary Robinson to use the institution to talk about universal aspirations, to use symbols and the language of inclusiveness, as she does in a manner no male politician has been able to do since the foundation of the state. She is thus able to relate to a popular memory of a kind of politics which was about the common

good, about general emancipation, about ideals, which has more
resonance among the public than the sclerotic system of party
politics – which came into being with the foundation of the state –
allows. The very exclusion of women from this system enhances her
distinctness from it.[5]

The availability of divorce, if expensive and tortuous, and some form of
access to abortion were positive steps, though the figure for Irish women
seeking abortions in Britain had risen to 4,500 by 1995 – and that only
accounted for those who gave an Irish address. In 1997 there was still
limited access to family-planning services outside Dublin. But the new
Ireland of the 1990s could only open up a little more with a visit by the
President to Pope John Paul II in 1997.

Having just returned from Rwanda, where she spoke at a Pan-African
conference on peace, gender and development, she discussed the African
state and the Irish peace process at a private audience with the Pope in the
Vatican in March. One daily newspaper had predicted that she would be
'snubbed' because she would not be offered Papal honours. Another
reminded readers that the last time a female head of Ireland, the British
monarch Elizabeth I, had come into direct contact with the Pope, she had
been excommunicated. The same publication reported afterwards that
church officials had been shocked at the casual nature of the President's
dress. There was a strict Vatican protocol, after all. This was 'misleading',
both *The Irish Times* and *The Sunday Tribune* responded. No such awards
are made during private audiences, the former said.

'Although the President has no executive powers, the Pope is under no
illusion as to her moral and spiritual influence in Ireland,' the feminist
theologian Mary Condren commented in the London *Independent*. 'Her
message to the Pope might be as follows: if Catholicism is not part of the
solution, then it may be part of the problem. The choices are stark.'

Traditionally, she said, Irish Catholic mothers could be relied on to pass
on the faith. 'However, in the light of Ireland's political and social history,
where children have been sacrificed to maintain a façade, and where
political violence is underpinned by sacrificial motifs, many are now
simply turning away in search of a life-giving spirituality – one that will
serve to empower their search for new ways of living with integrity. Once
content to act as handmaids of the Church, Irish women are demanding a
voice and, in some cases, full ministerial authority,' she went on. 'One of
the last straws grasped at by St Thomas Aquinas to refuse priestly ordina-
tion to women was that women (like slaves) could "not signify eminence".
President Robinson is proof that they can, and a compelling example of
why they must.'[6]

Speaking to reporters after her meeting with the Pope, the President said that issues like divorce and abortion had not come up in her discussions with either John Paul II or the Vatican Secretary of State, Cardinal Angelo Sodano. The exchange had been 'very good' and frank, she said, and they were on the same wavelength on many issues, such as the developing world. She had also expressed her pleasure, she emphasised, on visiting him on International Women's Day. She had worn a sprig of mimosa to mark the day, and no mantilla. And she had worn green, rather than the traditional black.

The visit was to spark off a debate which ran and ran in the letters pages of Irish newspapers. It reached a climax in mid-April, following a letter from Fr David O'Hanlon, a 28-year-old student at the Irish College in Rome, who described her presence, 'bedizened in Kelly green, showy jewellery and – to boot! – a sprig of vegetation' as 'cheap'. Rebutted by a chorus of bishops and priests, the criticism was expanded upon in an article in which O'Hanlon stood by his view. It was countered by a report that the Vatican regarded it as a 'private' visit and no offence had been caused. The Catholic Press Office in Dublin also reiterated that Mary Robinson's dress was 'of no concern' to Irish bishops; the suggestion that the Pope should be concerned was 'a bit ridiculous', spokesman Jim Cantwell said.[7]

If there was a tendency to dismiss Fr O'Hanlon as a mere student, others felt differently. His criticism was a manifestation of all that was wrong with the Catholic Church in its view of women, Dr Noreen O'Carroll said. Medb Ruane took on the patristic theology student on his own terms. So obsessed was this particular school of theology, as practised by Jerome, Ambrose or Augustine, with the female body that it recommended virginity to all women as the only possible solution to their sorry state, she pointed out.[8]

For Robinson's chaplain, Professor Enda McDonagh, the debate revealed a strand in Irish life that was 'partly begrudgery and partly mistaken piety'. The President had engendered enormous admiration within the Irish Catholic Church for her work on the Third World, though she had been characterised as hostile in the past. Certainly, she had become more sympathetic to the work of nuns and priests. She had become a model figure when the Church was going through a crisis, and had offered moral leadership – as a president of the people, rather than of women only, though this might have disappointed some feminists. Time would tell her influence, he felt. In helping both politicians and Church people to leave disintegration in their wake, she had provided an opportunity for Irish society to move into a more humane and moral phase.[9]

John Cooney in *The Sunday Tribune* put the debate into context. A government minister had recently referred to Ireland as a 'post-Catholic country'. This had been given official recognition by the Holy See in the decision not to confer a papal honour on the Irish President, he said. Far from being interpreted as a snub, it should be seen as a 'normalising' of Ireland's relations with the Vatican, which, he said, 'since independence in 1922 had been conducted on the basis of this country's spiritual servility to Rome'. The supreme example of this 'over-reverential attitude' to Rome was the way in which Eamon de Valera had tried to secure the Holy See's blessing sixty years before for the Constitution, which he had not yet submitted to the Oireachtas or to the Irish people for their approval.

'Whatever her own private religious feelings,' wrote Cooney, 'President Robinson had become the first Irish head of state to meet a pope as an equal, and she has no papal medal to prove it!'[10]

That fifth province appeared to be on the horizon at last.

CHAPTER 15

The Sun Shines On

Snapshot: a room in Trinity College, Dublin; many women, a few men. A sunny afternoon in April 1997, the talk is political. Anticipation is in the air: about a hot summer; about the impact on Northern Ireland of the May Day British general election; about the date for a similar election in the Republic; and about a successor to President Mary Robinson, who had announced the previous month that she was not running for a second term.

'Different voices, different agendas' was the theme of the discussion. One voice was that of a 38-year-old from Belfast, who described how she had never experienced democracy. Another voice agreed. In fact, democracy was so poorly served in Northern Ireland that there had not even been a public debate about abortion.

There was discussion about the 'time warp' in which established political parties were caught on both sides of the Irish border, and their reliance on outworn nineteenth-century models which had 'passed their sell-by date'. The culture of contemporary politics was scrutinised; the system was still 'incredibly hierarchical', observed Fine Gael TD and former National Women's Council chair-holder Frances Fitzgerald, who had attended the UN women's conference in Beijing in 1995. A national executive member of the opposing party, Fianna Fáil, appeared to agree, but said it was 'up to women themselves' to change the system. There was 'nothing stopping women' from running for office in her party, she said confidently.

Not everyone agreed. It was no coincidence that, in a state where child-care had never been regarded as an election issue, women's representation was still only 13 per cent of the total in parliament, Fitzgerald continued. It seemed as if Irish society was experiencing a 'fallow period' in relation to stamping the women's agenda on the political system. Yet the credibility and recognition afforded by the President, Mary Robinson, to the voluntary and community movement had nurtured a much more dynamic relationship between community politics and that formal system, she said.

It was a revealing statement, and one which reflected an understanding of Mary Robinson's language. Not everyone comprehended it, even after seven years, when on 12 March 1997 she announced her decision not to run again. She had just returned from the Vatican, amid the risible debate over her dress. A couple of weeks before, she had been in Rwanda. If she was serious about pursuing a position in the United Nations – commissioner for human rights, for example – she required government support. That support could not be forthcoming unless she declared her intentions for the future.

It was unfortunate that the tightly controlled announcement dominated the news on the very day of publication of a report on the Hepatitis C scandal, affecting hundreds of women. There had been no contact with any government or party official before the President's meeting with the Taoiseach to inform him of her decision, said Bride Rosney. In a statement, Positive Action, the group representing the infected women, said that it felt 'in no way hurt or upset' by the publicity surrounding the President's decision. The organisation had become 'very familiar with media attention that has diverted from our issues to other matters'. Mrs Robinson had demonstrated a 'quiet support' by meeting some of the group in November 1994.

Certainly, the media response to her announcement was overwhelming. It consumed acres of newsprint the following day. For *The Irish Times*, it was the only story on the front page. Throughout that issue of 13 March, there were repeated tributes. 'People power' had been the secret of her success; she had brought the sun out in France; the Pope had been much impressed by her humanity; her courtesy call on Queen Elizabeth in 1993 – one of 15 visits to Britain during her term – had helped to thaw Anglo-Irish relations and raise the status of the Irish community there. In the US, the newspaper told its readers, she had left a lasting mark of grace and compassion and knew how to make use of her 'bully pulpit' during her 13 visits there. The two public occasions on which she had wept – in Nairobi, for Somalia in 1992, and in Cork when she heard news of the end of the IRA ceasefire – had given the lie to the 'ideal of the stiff upper-lip'. Her constant visits to places normally shunned by politicians could have become a joke, but didn't; instead, they empowered those whose existence the establishment had scarcely noticed. She had made herself head of a state that had no 'formal, institutional existence', but extended to the 'D' sector – the disadvantaged, disaffected, disabled and the Irish diaspora.

There was even an account of her radical transformation in style from 'someone to whom clothes meant little' to someone who featured regularly on the world's best-dressed lists. 'Best of all,' the readers were told, she had avoided 'the kind of clothes favoured by most female politicians who tend to follow the example set by Margaret Thatcher when she was Britain's prime minister'. Not for her the 'royal-blue suits with sensible knee-length skirts and a pussy-cat-bow blouse'; she had instead represented the best of Irish fashion design.

The woman who might have opened 'abortion referral clinics in Áras an Uachtaráin', according to the wild propaganda, had transformed an office that seemed the wrong shape for her, the newspaper's columnist Fintan O'Toole wrote. 'She has helped us to re-imagine Ireland.' The newspaper's editorial went a little further; paying tribute to Labour leader Dick Spring who had sensed the mood in 1990, it said that Mary Robinson was about to step down from the presidency of a state which was 'more confident, more caring, more honest, and more open than when she took her oath of office in 1990'. The phenomenon that is Mary Robinson would 'fascinate the chroniclers and the sociologists' when the history of these times came to be written.[1]

Amid such tributes, it is small wonder that the President reportedly remarked that she thought she had 'died'. That day – coincidentally the day the first divorce decree under the new legislation was granted in her home county of Mayo – she planted yet another of at least a hundred trees which had been given her presidential spadeful of soil. Recalling some of these occasions, she described a tree that had not survived, on the windswept Aran island of Inis Oirr which had given her such a tremendous vote of support almost seven years before. The islanders had built a wall around the tree to protect it. It had been nicknamed *mná na hÉireann*, 'women of Ireland', she quipped.[2]

She got on with business as usual with a state visit to Sweden. On 1 April she summoned her Council of State for the seventh time to seek advice on the constitutionality of another piece of legislation, the Employment Equality Bill. It was agreed to refer it to the Supreme Court – a wise decision, given that some parts relating to people with disabilities were deemed unconstitutional. The following month, another piece of legislation, the Equal Status Bill, was also referred; it mirrored the Equality Bill, in prohibiting discrimination on nine grounds, including race, colour, religion, sexual orientation and membership of the travelling community.

A sense of perspective had been restored in the interim with some more critical analysis in the media of her role as well as references to controversies. Amid the continuing debate about alleged payment to politicians by the supermarket magnate, Ben Dunne, *The Sunday Independent* questioned the Dunnes' £15,000 contribution to her presidential election campaign in 1990. It was a contribution of which she had claimed to have no direct knowledge, and one which she would not have accepted had she known. The newspaper examined the cost of her office and the substantial increase in her budget – failing to point out that the former Fianna Fáil leader, Charles Haughey, had pledged to expand this very budget during the Lenihan election campaign. By the close of the presidency, the office was estimated to have cost just over £4 million in seven years.

The Sunday newspaper also reminded readers of the problems with her immediate staff and with the gardaí assigned to protect her; the little 'spat' with the Defence Forces over the 'Big Bird' remark; her purchase of an 'elegant Victorian mansion', complete with indoor swimming-pool and 'a double jacuzzi in her bedroom' on 120 acres in County Mayo and the 14 days' notice to quit given to the caretaker; 'squabbles' with the government; the South American visit; tensions between her and Dick Spring; the satellite television interview during the divorce referendum campaign; and her recent visit to the Pope.[3]

The editor of *The Sunday Business Post*, Damien Kiberd, felt that Robinson was far too young for beatification or canonisation. True, she had been able to reach out to the excluded voices in society, but for those primarily impressed by wealth, power and influence, she could appear like some 'do-gooder, a politically correct lay version of Mother Teresa of Calcutta', he wrote. Her speeches in office had, of necessity, been 'bland and predictable' and in physical terms she possessed 'certain robotic qualities', he judged.

It was also unfair to dismiss her predecessors completely, he felt. Cearbhall Ó Dálaigh would have been 'more than a match for her in terms of learning and scholarship', as would de Valera, the only man in Ireland, apparently, who fully understood Einstein's theory of relativity. As for the 'style stakes', had not Patrick Hillery been voted the 'handsomest head of state in western Europe' by women readers of the German magazine *Der Spiegel*?[4]

The indefatigable *Irish Times* journalist Kevin Myers also took a different view to that of most of his colleagues. He had welcomed Mary Robinson's election, and in his view she had been a 'refreshing departure'. But she had also indulged in 'our almost infinite appetite for Good Eggism', particularly where 'simple piety' took preference over 'complex solutions to complex problems'. One such unresolved issue was that of the travelling community, he said. On the very week that she had announced her decision to stand down, the Galway town of Tuam had been in 'uproar' over a court case involving travellers accused of various offences. The affray, reportedly between travellers themselves, had involved over a hundred people with various weapons and had lasted for two nights. The judge had been receiving threatening phone calls.

'The truth is, the *bien-pensants* quite like the Good Egg approach to problems,' he wrote. 'The problems don't go away, but we feel better. And that is not necessarily a good thing.'[5]

But was this not asking too much of a non-executive head of state? Her presidency had been 'worth every penny', remarked one senior Labour Party figure, who had had to deal with many of the difficult moments. Even if there were 'two Mary Robinsons', one of whom was less well liked within the party, there was nevertheless a 'huge admiration for her style'.

Her language was still misunderstood, the Belfast trade unionist Inez McCormack also observed during the week of the announcement. The events behind the scenes, such as the reciprocal visits to Áras an Uachtaráin by Northern community groups on all sides of the divide, were in many ways more interesting than the initial contact which inspired them. It was significant, she claimed, that community centres in Ireland and abroad had hung her photograph on the wall.

She always knew what questions to ask; in her previous legal capacity, she had often covered the same ground. 'The listening process that she has been engaged in is still not understood within the existing political system,' McCormack said, 'but it has produced an enormously sustainable trust.'[6]

Her special adviser, Bride Rosney, was relieved that the President had decided against running again. Just as she had planted a lot of trees, she had also planted many seeds. 'Part of the test of success will be to see what happens afterwards,' Rosney said. This presidency was recognised as the 'third string' in the Oireachtas. She had delivered on promises made in her inaugural speech. Yet Rosney could also understand the tensions created among elected politicians, because the head of state had the 'glory moments' and did not have to tackle the 'hard issues'.[7]

Had the trappings of office changed her? Yes, said some of those close to her, who felt she had become colder, more aloof, less sensitive to those upon whom she depended the most. Press photographers said that she had become more wooden, more formal, and less spontaneous. No, in the view of her old colleague, Senator David Norris – low on the list of several names tipped in the initial public debate over her succession. 'The qualities she always possessed were simply revealed,' he said. That reserve of the early years had been broken down during her election campaign by the immense wave of warmth shown towards her. The emotion she had displayed in Somalia in 1992 had not only set a precedent for a head of state, but also revealed a 'rigorous intellectual honesty and terrific human compassion' which could identify the human rights issue in every situation, Norris believed.

Such was Mary Robinson's wide range of interests that she could never be labelled a fanatic. She had never indulged in clichés, preferring to bring some fresh ideas to every public occasion, however 'small'. She had empowered those by whom she had risen to power, he felt. But one could not expect too much of her. Certainly, she had laid the legal groundwork for radical social change. But a 'post-Catholic Ireland' with a booming economy was in danger of swinging from an 'unthinking Catholic country to an unthinking materialistic country', unless its population was mature enough.

There was some doubt as to whether it was. Abroad, Ireland's concern for humanitarian affairs had been given a backhanded boost by Beijing, which objected to Danish and Irish support for a UN resolution criticising China's human rights record. Yet at home there was a row over the morality of a vasectomy clinic in County Donegal, and over 60 per cent of respondents in a newspaper poll favoured another referendum, rather than legislation, on abortion.

An increase in illegal immigrants attracted by the country's economic success had precipitated front-page reports with a semi-alarmist tone in the press. The Minister of State at the Department of Justice with responsibility for overseas development, Joan Burton, was quoted as being 'very worried' that agents were targeting Ireland as 'an easy country to smuggle people into'. It would have raised a smile among some of those who had been and gone. Her own department had never made entry easy for immigrants, many of whom had found in the past that their Irish 'welcome' amounted to a few nights in jail or, at best, the first flight out. As the Irish Refugee Council pointed out, the Republic still had far fewer asylum-seekers than other European countries.

The travellers issue was, as Kevin Myers pointed out, still unresolved, but this was as much to do with a failure to appreciate the rights of self-determination as about a changing economy in which their role, even as natural recyclers, had been dismissed. The location of a halting site in Galway summed up the public attitude: it was right next to the city dump.

Mary Robinson was right to seek new challenges, Senator Norris remarked. 'One hardly gets seven years for manslaughter. Fourteen years up in the Park? A mass murderer wouldn't be given that!'[8]

And how did she feel? Interviewed a month after her announcement, the President said that it was time for her to leave Ireland and start a new career elsewhere. Not running for office again had been 'the most difficult decision', she told me as she sat sipping sparkling mineral water in the Áras drawing-room with its french windows tempting the eye out to the manicured gardens and the Dublin mountains beyond. Peat briquettes were stacked neatly in the fireplace. Here, hundreds of groups had taken tea over the last seven years in china cups imprinted with gold harps.

'It wasn't made easily or quickly or in a straight line,' she said, as Bride

Rosney sat with a tape-recorder and an eye to the clock. 'I even made the joke that my mind is very clean – I'd changed it so often since Christmas! I think I was gradually recognising that the issues I cared most about had, in fact, not only a life of their own but that I had to break a dependency which worked both ways. It was better for me to move into another sphere. And just when I had made my mind up about that, the unexpected possibility of doing something very concretely in the area of human rights arose. I had recognised that I would have to get out of Ireland, realistically, and I had already faced that. People think there are wonderful options for an ex-president. There aren't necessarily!'

One of the strongest influences in making the decision about standing again had been Northern Ireland, she said. She was optimistic, despite signs of escalating violence and the continued absence of an IRA ceasefire. She had been 'inspired and encouraged and invigorated' by the women she had met in the North over the years, particularly those working-class women with no resources who were building their own networks and who were 'compellingly practical' at a community level.

Cross-community links had not 'retrenched' in spite of the continued political tension, she felt. Many return visits to Áras an Uachtaráin were better for having taken place 'out of the public eye', though. Just the week before, she had talked to 70 people from a Catholic and a Presbyterian parish in one room; on the same day, Irish daffodil bulbs had been planted in the Áras garden which had been produced by Northern Irish breeders. There were 135 varieties, and it was a 'wonderful Northern Ireland day'. The breeders were aware that they had made a lasting contribution, she said. 'Their sense of being in a place of friendship was very strong.'

Her perspective as a woman was 'very important' in relation to her office, and the role she now sought to play in the United Nations. 'I see it almost as a seamless web in relation to the conference in Rwanda on peace, gender and development,' she continued, referring to the gathering she had been asked to address there the month before. 'That was a great initiative within Rwanda of the women's organisations, the women's minister, the Rwandan government, with backing from the Organisation of African Unity and the Organisation for Economic Development in Africa. The fact that you had women from 15 other African countries coming to Rwanda for this conference on that particular issue was front-line commitment. It was saying: "We are meeting in a place of some of the most difficult issues" and that kind of practical, problem-solving deter-mination was there in a way that, again, I found very inspiring,' she said. 'I made the remark – it's a kind of cliché – that "I have seen the revolution and she's working". Africa is changing . . . The confidence is there.'

In a broad review of her seven-year term, she said that she had at all times been 'very happy' about working within the constitutional limits of the presidency – a framework she regarded as sacrosanct – rather than trying to change those limits. Her involvement in public life and her training as a constitutional lawyer had helped but it was not imperative, she said. The fact that she had sought legal advice over one particular clash with the government (the bar on her chairing the committee on reform of the UN in December 1993) had set a precedent and had helped to 'stretch the office' for those who came after, she said.

Other clashes had been distorted in the media, she felt, like the ban on the Dimbleby lecture in 1991: 'I felt that it was important that the presidency would work well with the government in a very even-handed, fair, non-political way. When there were, as there always would be, certain difficult issues, my own disposition was to try to resolve them, if necessary to compromise, but at times to stand firm. Because I had the training of a constitutional lawyer, I think I had more confidence about standing firm in the early days on a number of issues, some of which didn't reach the public press – which I must say I was very happy about at the time.'

The Dimbleby lecture controversy was part of 'a gradual recognition that just because a presidency is non-executive, it doesn't mean it doesn't have things to say that are, in fact, very well worth saying and serve the office well by being said'.

The controversy following her comments in 1995 on the Framework Document for Northern Ireland reflected the difficulty of being interviewed out of Ireland (she was in Japan at the time). 'I make speeches on government policy and I say things I wouldn't say back in Ireland and it's a more difficult context.'

Yet she was very well aware of certain fears, which had to be voiced. 'That again is an area where, potentially, at any stage a government can feel annoyed if it is in a very delicate policy-making role. I don't think that that's something that can totally be resolved. It's just an area of potential difficulty.'

One issue about which she had no regrets at all was the Adams hand-shake of 1993. This was also 'one of the most difficult decisions', which had not been taken lightly or without a great deal of 'thought and agonising beforehand'. She had had a lot of contact with groups from west Belfast and had met some of them on an earlier visit. 'They had been urging and urging me: "Come into west Belfast, come and meet our community." I waited until there was a very broad range of invitations – I think there were six different groups. It was evident that they wanted me to come so that I could see the reality of west Belfast, and I had to accept the community as it is, which meant that I would meet Gerry Adams and Joe Hendron and others in the room.'

She had weighed all this up, and was also aware that the discussions would be with community leaders, rather than those representatives of Sinn Féin and the SDLP. 'It wasn't easy and it wasn't that kind of black-and-white line where you know what you are doing was right. I took a risk and knew I was taking a risk, and I was, I must say, a little bit dismayed at the extent of the political focus on the handshake with Gerry Adams. Nobody was interested in west Belfast, the vibrancy of the community and their sense of isolation. It wasn't a story!'

Yet even when she received critical letters from members of the Northern unionist community who had felt betrayed by the handshake, there was 'no moment' when she regretted having taken the risk. 'On the other side, I could see the opening up of a community. And I don't say that the visit necessarily did it all, but I think it was very significant that people felt that they were respected, that somebody cared. The very fact that I took a risk was all part of the debate and dialogue,' she said. 'And after that, communities in west Belfast were linking with people in Galway, linking with people of Ballymun. And everything changed somehow at grass-roots community level. And at a political level, which is not my direct concern, there also seemed to be an opening-up.

'But it is at that other level, that is of very little interest unless you are interested, that I felt a great deal had happened,' she went on. 'The self-belief of people changed. They began to say "at last we are being recognised" as a community with great vibrancy, very caring, doing a great deal for young people who are involved in joy-riding, for children who have grown up with 25 years of violence, for a whole system that had to find strength to survive within itself because of the double isolation of being ignored within Northern Ireland and by this part of the country.'

Highlights for her to date? The 'smell of wet paint' in local community centres, that great pride in local involvement which she felt she had inherited from her father, and which was reflected in Patrick Kavanagh's poem, 'Epic', on the sense of place. The humanitarian visits, which represented a genuine Irish concern that was part of the country's history, namely the famine. The state visits, which were a very important part of projecting the modern image of Ireland abroad. There was much prejudice towards Ireland that Irish people were not aware of, she claimed. 'We think we're much better known than we are and that people think very highly of us,' she said, referring to a recent survey in the Netherlands which had shown that this was not necessarily the case. 'We're a little smug about our image abroad.'

And the low points? The inevitable demands on her family, living in the presidential apartments above, and her children's determination to keep their lives private to the extent that they would not attend functions with her – and 'they're right'. Even when the former manager of the national football team, Jack Charlton, had visited the Áras, Aubrey had said that he would look at him out of the window rather than come down to the main event.

She didn't mention another disappointment – perhaps because she still held out some small hope that before her term of office ended she would host a historic first state visit to Ireland by the British Queen. In mid-May, after the British Labour Party swept to victory, the new prime minister, Tony Blair, appeared to offer a ray of hope, even as the loyalist ceasefire looked to have disintegrated with the murder of a prominent GAA man in County Derry. On a visit to the North, Blair injected momentum into the peace process by offering Sinn Féin inclusive talks if the IRA called an unequivocal ceasefire, and by reassuring unionists on the principle of consent.

If she could have changed anything in her life, she would have wanted to be a writer, she said. The elderly nun who had taught her, Sister Joan Stephenson, was right: she had been torn between poetry, which formed the basis for her close friendship with poet Eavan Boland in college, and her legal studies. 'I don't like being in the public eye,' she said simply. 'I prefer to be at the back of a church.'[9]

The government threw all its weight behind her in her bid to become UN Human Rights Commissioner, a relatively new and undeveloped post hitherto held by Latin America, and one which had been criticised by human rights groups for lacking resources and teeth. There was at least one rival – Sonia Picado-Sotela, the Costa Rican ambassador to the US. Mary Robinson was to be presented as a 'non-western western candidate', someone from a small country with no record of colonisation and a high profile on development issues.

There was some confusion over reports in April 1997 that Mexico and Chile intended to support the Irish candidate, after their Foreign Ministers had met the Irish counterpart, Dick Spring, at an EU/Latin American meeting in Holland. Later that month, however, both countries threw their weight behind the Costa Rican, saying that there had been a 'misunderstanding' over support for Ireland. It was perceived as a setback. A final decision was expected by July, five months before Mrs Robinson was due to leave office.

There was continued speculation about her successor. One suggestion was her husband, Nicholas, since he had 'the formal wardrobe' and 'no political baggage'. The Progressive Democrats party, which proposed that the Constitution should be amended to allow for a presidential nomination by popular wish, warned that the electorate was concerned that the office might relapse into a retirement post. 'We do not need a Val Doonican presidency – in which rockers, carpet slippers, cardigans, log fires and golf games are the public image of the job,' the Progressive Democrats leader, Mary Harney, said.

There appeared to be an emerging consensus that there should be an election, and that candidates should not be retiring politicians, but young, energetic public figures like the determined campaigner for the children of Chernobyl, Cork woman Adi Roche, or the hospice movement pioneering fundraiser and labour lawyer, Dr Mary Redmond. Other possible candidates included former European Commissioner and former head of the World Trade Organisation, Peter Sutherland, who was appointed chairman of the Overseas Development Council, an international think-tank, in early 1997; politicians such as former Fianna Fáil leader and Taoiseach Albert Reynolds, former foreign minister David Andrews, and a Fine Gael MEP, Mary Banotti; Dick Spring, the Labour Party leader who had nominated Mary Robinson, was not ruled out either.

Speaking at the 1997 Labour Party annual conference, which was held just a month before the Fine Gael-Labour-Democratic Left coalition called a general election for 6 June, the man who had 'invented' the Mary Robinson presidency promised that there would be a plebiscite if he had anything to do with it. 'Seven years ago, I stood in the Royal Dublin Society beside a woman who had made a lot of promises,' Dick Spring opened his televised keynote speech, reminding delegates that they had never sought to 'politicise' the office of president and would not do so now. Still, the temptation to conjure up the 'magic' of 1990 – a magic, a spontaneity, which many felt could never be repeated – was too strong to resist if there was political gain to be made: 'I can still remember the feeling I had that night. A feeling of exhilaration. A feeling that we had delivered. A feeling that things would never be the same again. And they haven't been. The woman who spoke to the whole of Ireland that night went on to keep all her promises,' he said.

'She didn't just transform the office she'd won. She tranformed Ireland. She transformed our image abroad – and she transformed our perception of ourselves. She didn't just make changes or lead the way. She had personified change.'[10]

For weeks, her name appeared in letters pages of the newspapers, before the general election took over. That election was to reveal a hard face of a changing Ireland. Vulnerable sections of society, like Romanian refugees and single mothers on lone-parent allowances, were targets for cheap political shots. The one female leader of a political party, Mary Harney of the right-wing Progressive Democrats, proposed a saving in state payment of lone-parent allowances if young single mothers could be persuaded to stay at home with their parents. She was to qualify this by referring to family support – feeding into myths about teenage pregnancies and failing to acknowledge that there had always been more tolerance for such things in working-class urban areas than among the middle classes.

It was as if the independent woman had to come under attack. Only a week before the election was called, a new-born baby had been found dead in a midlands graveyard. A 16-year-old girl came forward after a garda appeal.

Harney's 'mother-and-child scheme', for all its flaws, was to receive support in opinion polls. Ironically, in the first week of the election campaign, the original architect of a welfare system providing free medical care for mothers and children to the age of 16, Dr Noel Browne, died in Connemara. Obituaries made little of his criticism of President Robinson, or of the fact that he could have been the Labour Party candidate for the presidency back in 1990. Described as 'one of the few', and as an idealist, he had never ceased to be a thorn in authority's side. Even the Catholic Church, which he had grown to hate for its opposition to his welfare scheme, paid tribute to his 'consistent concern for the poor and the suffering'.

'An outstanding Irishman . . . with a deep commitment to the health and welfare of the Irish people,' President Robinson said in a simple statement.

The 'Robinson factor', which many said had helped the Labour Party to sweep into a coalition government in 1992, was not enough to help it this time round. Labour fared badly in 1997, dropping from 19 per cent of the vote and 33 seats to just over 10 per cent and 17 seats. It would not be enough to hold together the so-called 'rainbow' coalition of Fine Gael, Labour and Democratic Left, which had been in power since 1994. Fianna Fáil, which had used its time in opposition under the new leadership of Bertie Ahern to regroup and re-organise, gained 39 per cent of the vote and 77 seats – not enough to form an overall majority, but enough to enter coalition with the Progressive Democrats which returned only four seats. It appeared that independents would hold the balance of power, while Sinn Féin returned a deputy who polled over 11,000 first-preference votes in the border constituency of Cavan-Monaghan.

As talks were held with a view to forming a government before the end of June, the North boiled over. Two police officers were shot dead on 16 June by the IRA in Lurgan, County Armagh, throwing into a spin British and Irish efforts to include Sinn Féin in peace talks, and to avoid violence during the loyalist marching season.

Four days earlier, on 12 June, the UN Secretary General confirmed that he had nominated Mary Robinson for the post of UN High Commissioner for Human Rights. She was an 'extraordinary leader' who would 'bring dynamism, credibility and leadership' to the post, Mr Annan said, adding that he hoped that she would be able to take up the vacant post based in Geneva in September, although her term as president was not due to expire until December. The intensive lobbying campaign by Irish diplomats, which had carefully avoided presenting her as a 'western candidate', had paid off.

Ratification by the UN General Assembly within the week was a mere formality. Statements of praise and congratulations poured in from political leaders, while it was noted that 'discreet' US backing had helped her to secure the job. However, at the general assembly sitting on 17 June, the Costa Rican ambassador criticised the appointment for failing to reflect a proper geographical balance or the interests of the Third World.

'Daunting' was how she described the appointment at a function hosted by the Irish Refugee Council the following day, when she warned that racism could rear its 'ugly head' in Ireland unless people learned to deal with the issues surrounding refugees and immigration, and were 'true to their history'. In the last century, Irish emigrants to North America had received a mixed reception, with some Americans less than welcoming of the 'desperate, disease-ridden' immigrants who had crossed the Atlantic, she said. Others, such as the Québecois in Canada, had shown courage, and one mayor of Quebec had died of cholera after working with Irish immigrants.

An Amnesty International critique of her new post confirmed that it would be no sinecure. In a report which was scathingly critical of her predecessor, the Ecuadorean, José Ayala-Lasso, the human rights organisation argued that a chasm had developed between expectations and delivery. The budget for the post was a mere £30 million, to cover 450 staff, compared to £80 million for the UN High Commissioner for Refugees. The shortage of resources was compounded by the fact that half the finance came from voluntary contributions. This meant that member states who preferred a 'cosmetic approach' could refuse to pay.

There was also a marked difference of interpretation about the nature of the post, Amnesty International warned. 'Human rights' to western member states was synonymous with free speech, freedom of conscience, fair trials and eradication of torture, while Asian and African member states placed more emphasis on the rights of community and social and economic development. China, in particular, had taken a firm stance against any attempt to interfere in its internal affairs. Divisions within the Geneva office and Mrs Robinson's perceived lack of management experience would mean that she would be relying heavily on Kofi Annan for support.

UN sources warned that she would need 'eyes and ears', another Bride Rosney. Otherwise, she could find herself resigning early from the four-year job in sheer frustration. Commenting on the appointment, the *Phoenix* magazine said that Mary Robinson's Trilateral Commission connections, forged during her time on its executive from 1973 to 1980, had helped her to secure the job. *The Sunday Independent* was true to form. RTE television news bulletins had been treating the news as worthy of the kind of coverage usually reserved for 'moon landings', columnist Gene Kerrigan wrote. However, she was now 'moving from the harmless fantasyland of the Áras to a world where thousands get their throats cut because the people with armies find it not in their interests to protect the helpless', he warned. It was time to stop believing in the 'huggy-wuggy' myth.[11]

There was some criticism in newspaper letters pages of the likelihood that she would stand down early. Was she simply using the Irish presidency as a stepping-stone? What was even more telling was that within days of the confirmation that she would not be seeking a second term in office, Ann Lane, who had been with her for 28 years, and Laura Donegan, who had been with her for 16, were looking for new jobs. They had not been asked to travel to Geneva.

On 19 July 1997, some 18 months after the resumption of hostilities, the IRA declared a renewed ceasefire in Northern Ireland. It was 'unequivocal', it said in a statement. There was no mention of the word 'permanent'.

'Such a small person. Such a little country. Such a big world. Such a massive contribution. Thank you, Mary,' wrote one newspaper reader, as Robinson faced her final weeks at home. Another reader asked the *Irish Times* meteorological correspondent to explain a curious phenomenon: 'Despite the grim foreboding surrounding the President's announcement not to seek a second term, the sun continues to rise each morning . . .'[12] And it did.

Notes

1. The Long Shadow
1. *Vanity Fair*, July 1992
2. Tim Pat Coogan, *De Valera: Long Fellow, Long Shadow* (London, 1993)
3. John Bowman, *The Sunday Times*, 12 August 1990
4. Jim Duffy, *The Irish Times*, 25 September 1990
5. Bowman, *The Sunday Times*, 12 August 1990
6. Jim Duffy, *The Irish Times*, 26 September 1990
7. ibid.
8. Professor John A. Murphy, *The Sunday Independent*, 30 September 1990; Professor Ronan Fanning, *The Sunday Independent*, 21 October 1990; Jim Duffy, *The Irish Times*, 27 September 1990
9. Duffy, *The Irish Times*, 27 September 1990
10. Dr Mary Hayden, *Irish Independent*, 7 May 1937
11. Doris Kearns Goodwin, *No Ordinary Time* (New York, 1994)

2. The Right Stuff
1. Brendan Behan, *The Hostage* (Dublin, 1958)
2. Roy Foster, *Modern Ireland, 1600–1972* (London, 1988)
3. 'Castle' refers to Dublin Castle, seat of the British administration in Ireland until independence
4. Terry Reilly, *Dear Old Ballina*, introduction by President Robinson (Ballina, 1993)
5. Foster, *Modern Ireland, 1600–1972*
6. Michael O'Sullivan, *Mary Robinson: The Life and Times of an Irish Liberal* (Dublin, 1993)
7. ibid.
8. The Anglo-Irish Treaty of 1921 was agreed after a truce in Ireland's war of independence with Britain between January 1919 and July 1921. As president of the Irish Republic, Eamon de Valera accredited five members of his government to open negotiations with Britain on the treaty terms in October. However, when the eventual text was signed, under threat of a resumption of war by British prime minister Lloyd George, de Valera refused to accept it.

Under the treaty's term, southern Ireland was to become a free state with full dominion status within the British Commonwealth, but the six counties of Northern Ireland would remain with Britain. A bitter civil war followed, which split Irish families – and politics – down the middle. The two largest political parties, Fianna Fáil and Fine Gael, still reflect this civil war divide; there is little difference in their essentially right-wing policies.

9. *Elizabeth Ham By Herself, 1783 to 1820*
10. Kevin Whelan, bicentennial research fellow of the Royal Irish Academy, 'The famine as a lesson to feckless Irish', *The Sunday Tribune*, 4 December 1994
11. ibid. and Kevin Whelan's essay in Cathal Porteir (ed.), *The Great Irish Famine* (Dublin, 1995)
12. ibid.
13. ibid.
14. O'Sullivan
15. Reilly
16. *Man Alive*, Dublin, 1974
17. Dr Aubrey Bourke, interview with the author, February 1997.
18. Caroline Walsh, *The Irish Times*, 21 December 1990
19. ibid.
20. Joseph McDonnell and Michael Durcan interviewed by Michael O'Sullivan, ibid.
21. Dorothy McKane, interview with the author, 29 April 1997
22. Adrian and Henry Bourke, interviews with the author, February 1997
23. Henry Bourke, *The Sunday Tribune*, 16 September 1990
24. Mary Robinson, *Harper's and Queen*, March 1994
25. *The Sunday Tribune*, 16 September 1990
26. *The Irish Times*, 21 December 1990
27. ibid.

3. We Expected Anything of Her

1. Kate Shanahan, 'The girl who was top of the class', *The Irish Press*, 21 May 1994
2. ibid.
3. ibid.
4. ibid.
5. ibid. and Gemma Hussey, *The Irish Times*, 13 November 1993
6. J.V. Luce, *Trinity College, Dublin: The First 400 Years* (Dublin, 1992)
7. Interview with the author, March 1997
8. Henry Bourke, *The Sunday Tribune*, 16 September 1990
9. Dr Barbara Wright, Dean of Arts (Letters),TCD, *Trinity Today*, 1995–96
10. Luce, p.199
11. Luce, p.142
12. Interview with Paddy Woodworth, *The Irish Times*, 24 June 1991
13. Professor Enda McDonagh, interview with the author, April 1997
14. Mary T.W. Bourke, 'Law and Morality in Ireland': inaugural address to the Dublin University Law Society, 3 February 1967

4. Direct Action

1. Eleanor Kerlow, *Poisoned Ivy* (New York, 1994)
2. ibid.
3. 'Tribute to Archibald Cox', *Harvard Law Bulletin*, February 1992, p.17
4. Kerlow, *Poisoned Ivy*
5. Mary McCutchan, *Irish Independent*, 22 August 1969
6. Christina Murphy, *The Irish Times*, 26 February 1977
7. *The Chicago Tribune*, 16 December 1990
8. Jacqui Dunne, *The Sunday Independent*, 15 June 1980
9. Mary Maher *The Irish Times*, 16 October 1989
10. *The Harvard Crimson*, 11 June 1968
11. *The Irish Times*, 26 February 1977
12. Fergus Finlay, *Mary Robinson: A President with a Purpose* (Dublin, 1990)
13. *Irish Independent*, 22 August 1969
14. *The Irish Times*, 13 August 1969
15. *Irish Independent*, 22 August 1969
16. *The Irish Times*, 26 February 1977
17. Adrian Bourke, interview with the author, February 1997
18. ibid.
19. Two women had stood on the TCD panel before but had been unsuccessful. Charlotte Lane McClenaghan stood in both 1954 and 1957, and Frances Jane French in 1957.
20. The proposed merger of the two universities had been mooted by the late Minister for Education, Donogh O'Malley, who introduced free secondary education among other initiatives, and who died suddenly at the age of 47 in 1968
21. *The Irish Times*, 12 August 1969
22. *Irish Independent*, 22 August 1969

23. Michael O'Sullivan, *Mary Robinson: The Life and Times of an Irish Liberal* (Dublin, 1993)
24. John Healy, *The Irish Times*, 7 November 1969
25. *The Irish Times*, 7 November 1969
26. Mary Kenny, *The Irish Press*, 30 April 1970
27. ibid.

5. Pills and Bills

1. June Levine, *Sisters: The Personal Story of an Irish Feminist* (Dublin, 1982)
2. Kate Millett, *Sexual Politics* (1970)
3. Levine, p.142
4. *The Irish Times*, 11 December 1970
5. *The Irish Times*, 16 October 1989
6. *The Irish Press*, 9 March 1971
7. Levine, pp.159–70
8. Later renamed the Women's Political Association
9. Liam McAuley, *The Belfast Telegraph*, 5 April 1971
10. The means test was significant because this was a form of national health which had not been provided for in Ireland and might deprive doctors of an income. (Archbishop McQuaid of Dublin, a key figure in the affair, was a doctor's son.)
11. J.J. Lee, *Ireland 1912–85: Politics and Society* (Cambridge, 1989)
12. *The Belfast Telegraph*, 5 April 1971
13. J.J. Lee, p.498
14. *The Belfast Telegraph*, 5 April 1971
15. ibid.
16. Levine, p.181
17. Seanad record, 7 July 1971
18. *The Irish Times*, 7 August 1971

6. Making an Impact

1. *The Irish Times*, 30 December 1995
2. *The Irish Times*, 28 October 1972
3. *The Irish Times*, 23 January 1973
4. Speech to Cork Literary and Scientific Society, reprinted in *The Irish Times*, 9 November 1973
5. *The Irish Times*, 1 and 5 September 1972
6. *The Irish Times*, 13 February 1973.
7. J.J. Lee, *Ireland 1912–85: Politics and Society* (Cambridge, 1989), p.479
8. *The Irish Times*, 31 October 1973
9. *The Irish Times*, 28 November 1973
10. *The Irish Times*, 5 December 1973
11. Dr Aubrey Bourke, in an interview with the author, 7 February 1997
12. W.D. Flackes and Sydney Elliott, *Northern Ireland: A Political Directory, 1968–93* (Belfast, 1994)
13. *The Irish Times*, 14 February 1974
14. *The Irish Times*, 25 March 1974
15. J.J. Lee, p.479

7. It Will Be Hard to Stop Her

1. R.F. Foster, *Modern Ireland 1600–72* (London, 1988), p.514
2 J.J. Lee: *Ireland 1912–85: Politics and Society*

(Cambridge, 1989), p.240

3. *The Irish Times*, 9 November 1990
4. *The Irish Times*, 19 April 1974
5. *The Irish Times*, 17 May 1974
6. *The Irish Times*, 3 July 1974
7. RTE, *This Week*, as reported in *The Irish Times*, 28 October 1974
8. *The Irish Times*, 28 October 1974
9. ibid.
10. RTE, reported in *The Irish Times*, 30 October 1974
11. *The Irish Times*, 7 December 1974
12. *The Word*, June 1975
13. *The Belfast Telegraph*, 16 June 1975
14. Senator Mary Robinson, 'Women and the New Irish State': Thomas Davis Lecture, 30 November 1975
15. Senator Mary Robinson, speech on divorce to the Irish Association of Civil Liberty, 5 December 1974
16. *The Sunday World*, 12 September 1976
17. *The Irish Times*, 4 June 1977
18. Only in 1962 was provision made for free legal aid in Irish criminal cases, but Ireland had to be forced to provide a similar system of free legal aid in civil cases by the European Court of Human Rights ruling. Mrs Josie Airey wanted to apply for a judicial separation from her husband, but wasn't entitled to state-funded legal assistance. She had to fight all the way to the European Court in Strasbourg, with the support of barrister Mary Robinson, to secure this. The case was won on the grounds that the Irish government was in breach of the European Convention on Human Rights. In 1979, finally, a legal aid board was set up to provide civil legal aid, subject to a means test. It has been undermined by a lack of state resources.
19. *The Irish Times*, 26 September 1977
20. *Trinity News*, 24 November 1977
21. *The Irish Times*, 28 July 1979
22. *The Irish Press*, 9 August 1977
23. The Lomé Convention is an agreement between the European Union and countries in sub-Saharan Africa, the Caribbean and the Pacific on financial aid, institutional co-operation and trade preferences, essentially designed to prop up the former colonies of Britain, France, Holland and Belgium. Some 46 states were associated with the EU when the first convention was signed in 1975, but it has now expanded considerably to 70 states. Under the first agreement, almost all the products from Africa, the Caribbean and the Pacific (the so-called ACP countries) could enter the EU without tariffs or quotas, with the exception of certain products covered by the Common Agricultural Policy. The renegotiated convention continued duty-free access to European markets for a range of goods, but some EU states wanted to cut back on their aid contributions – amounting to over £12 billion over five years. There are fears that the agreement might not survive beyond the year 2000 as guilt for a colonial past subsides.
24. *The Irish Times*, 9 November 1990

8. Bruising Battles
1. *The Irish Times*, 15 January, 1983
2. *The Irish Times*, 26 March, 1982
3. ibid.
4. *The Irish Times*, 26 February 1977
5. Senator David Norris in an interview with the author, 16 April 1997
6. *The Irish Times*, 18 September 1982
7. *The Irish Times*, 31 August 1983
8. ibid.
9. *The Irish Times*, 1 September, 1983
10. *All in a Life: Garret FitzGerald: An Autobiography* (Dublin, 1991), pp.445–46
11. ibid
12. Sam McAughtry, *The Irish Times*
13. Madeleine Reid, *The Impact of Community Law on the Irish Constitution* (Dublin, 1990)
14. *The Irish Times*, 19 November 1985
15. ibid.
16. *The Irish Times*, 21 November 1985

9. President and Purpose
1. The Irish National Caucus, an umbrella group for most of the Irish-American organisations, includes the Gaelic Athletic Association and the Ancient Order of Hibernians, Irish county associations and many local bodies. In 1978 its three-man inquiry team, led by its national co-ordinator, Fr Seán McManus, had talks in Northern Ireland with the IRA, UDA, UVF and some other loyalist groupings. It urged for the inclusion of paramilitary organisations in any search for a solution to the Northern conflict. In the same year, it was attacked by the Irish Taoiseach, Jack Lynch, for supporting the Provisional IRA, but spokesmen for the caucus have said that it has no connection with any organisation outside the US, and it had been cleared by the FBI of any support of violence.

   Noraid, also known as the Irish Northern Aid Committee, was established in 1969 for the stated purpose of providing funds for the relief of families affected by the struggle against Britain. An estimated $5 million raised by 1987 has been handled in Ireland by people associated with Provisional Sinn Féin, and there have been constant allegations that it is being used for purchase of arms for the IRA. (W.D. Flackes and Sydney Elliott, *Northern Ireland: A Political Directory 1968–93*)
2. 'Family Law in Ireland': summary of address by Senator Mary Robinson, SC, to 18th Triennial Conference of the Association Countrywomen of the World, 27 May 1986
3. 'The Status of Children Bill and Succession

Rights': summary of speech by Senator Mary Robinson, SC, to a meeting organised by Cherish, Dublin, 17 June 1986

4. 'Divorce Referendum – a Watershed for the Country': summary of contribution by Senator Mary Robinson at Divorce Action Group meeting, Coolmine Community School, Dublin, 5 June 1986

5. Garret FitzGerald, *All in a Life: An Autobiography* (Dublin, 1991), pp.630–31

6. *The Irish Press*, 8 August 1990

7. *The Sunday Tribune*, 15 December 1996

8. Interview with Jonathan Philbin Bowman, *U* magazine, July 1990

9. ibid.

10. Interview with May Clinton, *Irish Farmers' Monthly*, June 1990

11. The Pale is that area of Dublin and surrounding parts of Leinster which for many centuries was the traditional seat of administration during British rule. Now referred to as that area of the capital which is sometimes out of touch with the mood of the rest of the island.

12. *The Derry Journal*, 6 July 1990

13. *The Enniscorthy Echo*, 10 August 1990

14. *The Clonmel Nationalist*, 11 August 1990

15. *The Clonmel Nationalist*, 1 September 1990

16. *The Sunday Times*, 12 August 1990

17. *Irish Independent*, 8 September 1990

10. Rocking that System

1. It had been implied that the secretary to the President, Mr Michael O hÓdhrain, was not present and that the Fianna Fáil leader, Mr Haughey, had called an emergency front bench meeting in the interim. In fact, the events were taking place 'long after normal office hours', the solicitor said, and his client, Mr O hÓdhrain, had gone to the Peacock Theatre with his wife – only to return to Áras an Uachtaráin, when contacted immediately, at about 8.45 p.m.

In the course of his series in *The Irish Times* on the presidency, Duffy had referred to a particular episode in May 1982 when Fianna Fáil politicians in opposition, including Mr Lenihan, had tried to exert undue influence on the then president, following the fall of a coalition government. Lenihan subsequently denied that he had been involved, when asked to respond to a question on the events of that night posed by a Fine Gael 'plant' in the audience for the popular RTE television political programme *Questions and Answers*. The research student disputed this, said that Mr Lenihan had told him as much, and played a tape of the interview at a press conference convened by *The Irish Times* on 25 October to prove it.

2. Emily O'Reilly, *Candidate: The Truth Behind the Presidential Campaign* (Dublin, 1991)

3. ibid.

4. Henry Bourke, interview with the author,

February 1997

5. *The Irish Times*, 6 November 1990

6. Jim Farrelly, *Who's Who in Irish Politics* (Dublin, 1991)

7. O'Reilly, ibid.

8. Henry Bourke, ibid.

11. Dangerous Nonsense

1. Paul Durcan, *The Evening Herald*, 9 November 1990

2. Mary Maher, *The Irish Times*, 11 November 1990

3. Translates as 'a thousand thanks to you all'; from the President's inaugural address, 3 December 1990

4. *The Irish Times*, 4 December 1990

5. President Robinson in an interview with the author, 10 April 1997

6. *The Times*, 10 November 1990

7. *The Chicago Tribune*, 16 December 1990

8. *Dallas Times Herald*, 30 December 1990

9. *Vanity Fair*, July 1992

10. *The Sunday Tribune*, 9 December 1990

11. ibid.

12. Dr Richard Kearney, 'Letters on a New Republic' in Dermot Bolger (ed.) *Letters from a New Island* (Dublin, 1991)

13. John Walshe, *The Irish Times*, 29 November 1990

14. Geraldine Kennedy, *The Irish Times*, 1 December 1990

15 Joe Carroll, *The Irish Times*, 10 November 1990

16 *Phoenix* annual, 1990

17. *The Irish Times*, 19 June 1991

18. *The Guardian*, 12 September 1991

19. Renagh Holohan, *The Irish Times*, 24 June 1991

20. *The Irish Times*, 10 November 1990

12. Celtic Tiger

1. Jennifer Foote, *Newsweek*, 28 October 1991

2. Seán Duignan, *One Spin on the Merry-Go-Round* (Dublin, 1995)

3. Alan Shatter, *The Irish Times*, 21 June 1993

4. Inez McCormack, interview with the author, 20 March 1997

5. Interview by Olivia O'Leary, *The Sunday Tribune*, 13 November 1994

6. Duignan, *One Spin on the Merry-Go-Round*

7. Joe Carroll, *The Irish Times*, 28 February 1995

8. Joe Carroll, *The Irish Times*, 15 April 1995

9. *The Belfast Telegraph*, 20 December 1995

10. *The Observer*, 3 November 1991

11. *The Irish Times*, 14 November 1996

12. *The Irish Times*, 7 November 1996

13. BBC Northern Ireland, *Spotlight*, 26 November 1996

14. *The Belfast Newsletter*, 5 February 1997

15. At the time, there was considerable pressure on the British government to reopen an inquiry into the events of Bloody Sunday on 30 January 1972, on foot of new evidence

which emerged after the Widgery report into the shootings of April 1972. The shootings had occurred during an illegal march organised by the Derry Civil Rights Association, and were condemned by civil rights leaders as 'another Sharpeville'. In response, the British Embassy was burned down by demonstrators in Dublin.

The Widgery report found that the British soldiers had been fired on first, though none of the dead or wounded were armed. The report also said that the march might have passed off without incident if the British Army had maintained its low-key attitude. The controversy surrounding the deaths is regarded as decisive in Britain's decision to impose direct rule on Northern Ireland from Westminster.

16. Fintan O'Toole, *The Irish Times*, 21 May 1994
17. *The Irish Times*, 12 February 1992
18. President Robinson, 'The Allen Lane Foundation Lecture', 25 February 1992
19. *The Irish Times*, 31 October 1995
20. ibid.

13. Acts of Imagination

1. *The Irish Times*, 29 December 1995
2. Declan Kiberd, *Inventing Ireland* (London, 1995)
3. *The Irish Times*, 30 July 1990 – the *fainne* was a symbol of ability to speak the Irish language, while GAA stands for the Gaelic Athletic Association which had a reputation for frowning on 'foreign' games
4. Paddy Woodworth, *The Irish Times*, 24–25 June 1991
5. Dr Richard Kearney, *The Irish Times*, 31 December 1987
6. Mary Ellen Synon, *Sunday Business Post*, and Gene Kerrigan, *Sunday Independent*, 12 July 1992
7. President Robinson's address to the Oireachtas, 2 February 1995
8. Dr Noreen O'Carroll, *The Irish Times*, 3 March 1995
9. John Boland, *The Irish Times*, 21 August 1995
10. Noel Browne, Letters to the Editor, *The Irish Times*, 13 January 1996
11. Bill Long, Letters to the Editor, *The Irish Times*, 29 January 1996
12. Professor Enda McDonagh, in an interview with the author, 24 April 1997
13. 'A World Grown Smaller', address by President Mary Robinson on the occasion of the Berkeley Medal, University of California, 18 October 1991
14. Quidnunc, *The Irish Times*, 28 November 1992
15. Mary Robinson, *A Voice for Somalia* (Dublin, 1992)
16. Kevin Whelan, *The Sunday Tribune*

magazine, 4 December 1994
17. President Robinson, interview with the author, 10 April 1997
18. *Phoenix* annual, 1994
19. RTE, 18 April 1995
20. *The Irish Times*, 1 April 1995
21. Fr David Regan, Letters to the Editor, *The Irish Times*, 8 April; Dr Noel Browne, 11 April 1995
22. *The Irish Times*, 9 September 1995
23. Mary Ellen Synon, *The Sunday Tribune*, 2 April 1995
24. *The Economist*, 1 June 1996

14. A Touch of Witchcraft

1. Fr Dan Breen, Avoca, County Wicklow, in an interview with the author, May 1996
2. President Mary Robinson, *A Hundred Years – Facing the Challenge*, Ogden Lecture, Brown University, 19 October 1991
3. United Nations Association, USA Factsheet: 'Electing a UN Secretary General'
4. Senator Mary Robinson, University College Galway Labour Party meeting, 10 February 1978
5. Carol Coulter, *The Hidden Tradition: Feminism, Women and Nationalism in Ireland* (Dublin, 1993)
6. Mary Condren, *The Independent*, 7 March 1997
7. Fr David O'Hanlon, Letters to the Editor, *The Irish Times*, 8 April 1997; and *The Irish Times*, 19 April 1997
8. Dr Noreen O'Carroll, *The Irish Times*, 23 April 1997; and Medb Ruane, *The Irish Times*, 26 April 1997
9. Professor Enda McDonagh, interview with the author, 24 April 1997
10. *The Sunday Tribune*, 9 March 1997

15. The Sun Shines On

1. *The Irish Times*, 13 March 1997
2. *The Irish Times*, 14 March 1997
3. Jody Corcoran, *The Sunday Independent*, 16 March 1997
4. *The Sunday Business Post*, 16 March 1997
5. Kevin Myers, *The Irish Times*, 15 March 1997
6. Interview with the author, 20 March 1997
7. Interview with the author, 10 April 1997
8. Interview with the author, 15 April 1997
9. Interview with the author, 10 April 1997
10. Address by the Tánaiste, foreign affairs minister and Labour Party leader Dick Spring to the Labour Party National Conference 1992, University Concert Hall, Limerick, 12 April 1997
11. *Phoenix* magazine, 6 June 1997, and Gene Kerrigan, *The Sunday Independent*, 15 June 1997
12. Ailish M. Nic Pháidin and T.O. Connor, *The Irish Times* letters page, 18 and 20 March 1997

Appendix: presidents and political parties in power

PRESIDENTS OF THE IRISH REPUBLIC

Dr Douglas Hyde	1938–45
Seán T. O'Kelly	1945–59
Eamon de Valera	1959–73
Erskine Childers	1973–74
Cearbhall Ó Dálaigh	1974–76
Patrick Hillery	1976–90
Mary Robinson	1990–97

IRISH GENERAL ELECTIONS 1923–97

Year	Government	Taoiseach
1923	Cumann na nGaedheal	William T. Cosgrave
June 1927	»	»
Sept 1927	»	»
1932	Fianna Fáil	Eamon de Valera
1933	»	»
1937	»	»
1938	»	»
1943	»	»
1944	»	»
1948	Inter-party	John A. Costello
1951	Fianna Fáil	Eamon de Valera
1954	Inter-party	John A. Costello
1957	Fianna Fáil	Eamon de Valera to 1959
		Sean Lemass
1961	»	»
1965	Fianna Fáil	Sean Lemass to 1966
		Jack Lynch
1969	»	»
1973	Fine Gael-Labour coalition	Liam Cosgrave
1977	Fianna Fáil	Jack Lynch to 1979
		Charles J. Haughey
1981	Fine Gael-Labour	Garret FitzGerald
Feb 1982	Fianna Fáil	Charles J. Haughey
Nov 1982	Fine Gael-Labour	Garret FitzGerald
1987	Fianna Fáil	Charles J. Haughey
1989	Fianna Fáil-Progressive Democrats	Charles J. Haughey to Feb '92
		Albert Reynolds
1992	Fianna Fáil-Labour to Nov '94	Albert Reynolds to Nov '94
	Labour-Fine Gael-Democratic	John Bruton from Nov '94
	Left from Nov '94 (no election)	
1997	Fianna Fáil-Progressive Democrats	Bertie Ahern

Glossary

Áras an Uachtaráin: the presidential residence, Phoenix Park, Dublin
Dáil: parliament of the Irish Republic
Gardaí/Garda Siochána: the Irish police force
Oireachtas: the legislature
Seanad: senate or upper house of parliament
Tánaiste: deputy prime minister
Taoiseach: prime minister
TD: Teachta Dála, member of the Dáil

Index

abortion issue, 111-14, 122, 184, 213, 221; information, 132-3; referendum, 1983, 143, 161, 163, 175, 179; 'X' case, 176-9; information bill, 179-81
Action Group on South Africa, 40
Adams, Gerry, 166-9, 173, 205, 223-4
adoption, 79
Adoption Act, 1952, 79, 87
Ahern, Bertie, 158, 227
Airey, Mrs Josie, 101, 106, 129
Alderdice, Dr John, 148
Alexander, Mother, 32
Alliance Party, 162
Allihies, Co. Cork, 11-13, 124-5
Amnesty International, 228
AnCO, 97
Anderson, Mary, 60
Andrews, David, 176, 195, 226
Angelou, Maya, 208, 209-10
Anglo-Irish Agreement 1985, 115-17, 118, 137, 154, 162
Annan, Kofi, 211, 227-8
Aquinas, Mother, 29, 63
Aquinas, St Thomas, 213
Aras an Uachtaráin, 147, 159, 169, 220, 222; staff, 154, 157; visitor centre, 186; security, 201
Argentina, 114, 201-2
Armstrong, Fergus, 49, 50, 51
Arnold, Bruce, 133-4
Australia, 163
Ayala-Lasso, Jose, 228

Ballina, Co. Mayo, 17, 22, 26-8, 31, 150; Amana raided, 23-4
Ballykissangel, 206
Banotti, Mary, 226
Barnes, Monica, 142
Barrett, Patrick, 19, 20, 25

Barry, Peter, 118, 131
beef tribunal, 154
Beere, Dr Thekla, 64
Behan, Brendan, 19
Beijing women's conference, 202-4, 216
Belfast, 165-9, 173; Adams handshake, 223-4
Belfast City Council, 154
Belfast Newsletter, 174
Belfast Telegraph, 66, 68, 95-6, 172
Bhutto, Benazir, 153, 203
Binchy, William, 113
Black, Mary, 210
Black and Tans, 23-4
Blair, Tony, 225
Blatherwick, David, 165, 166
Bloody Sunday relatives' group, 162, 169, 174-5
Boland, Eavan, 56, 148, 151, 186, 225
Boland, Dr Freddie, 96
Boland, John, 191-2
bombs; Dublin, 79, 80, 169; Enniskillen, 148; Warrington, 163; Monaghan, 169; Canary Wharf, 171; Manchester, 172-3; Lisburn, 173
Bord Fàilte, 159
Bord Iascaigh Mhara, 74
Boston Women's Health Collective, 61
Bourke, Adrian, 27-8, 30, 34, 38-40, 42, 109, 122; Senate campaign, 54-5; Presidential campaign, 137
Bourke, Aubrey, 27, 34, 39
Bourke, Denis, 25
Bourke, Dorothy, 25
Bourke, Dr Aubrey, 20, 24-7, 29, 41-2, 43, 50; visits Dr McQuaid, 37-8; Senate campaign, 54; Robinson marriage, 63; contraceptives issue, 84
Bourke, Hal, 25
Bourke, Henry, 26-30, 34,

37-42, 54, 82, 144; First Confession, 28; Senate campaign, 55; Presidential campaign, 139-40, 144
Bourke, Henry Charles, 21-2, 23-4
Bourke, Ivy, 25, 38, 84
Bourke, John, 20
Bourke, John Paget, 22, 34
Bourke, Mary. *see* Robinson, Mary
Bourke, Oliver, 34, 39
Bourke, Lt-General Oliver Paget, 21
Bourke, Paget, 24-5, 25, 102
Bourke, Paget John, 21
Bourke, Robert Paget, 22
Bourke, Roddy, 25
Bourke, Tessa, 25-6, 28, 37, 38-9; Senate campaign, 55; Robinson marriage, 63; death of, 81
Bourke, William, 87
Bourke, William Orme Paget, 20-1
Bourke family, 19-26
Boutros-Ghali, Dr Boutros, 195, 200, 210
Bowman, John, 15, 133
Bowman, Jonathan Philbin, 129-30
Boyd, Roisin, 195
Boyle, Hilary, 62
Bradwell, Warrant Officer James, 173
Brandt Commission, 105
Brazil, 201
Breen, Fr Dan, 206-7
Britain; Robinson visits, 158, 163
Broadcasting Act, 1960, 92
Browne, Dr Noel, 67, 81, 82, 85-6, 99, 192-3, 202, 207; and Presidency, 123, 124-5, 131, 133; death of, 227
Browne, Nora, 64
Browne, Phyllis, 124
Browne, Vincent, 153-4
Brundtland, Gro Harlem,

108, 211
Bruton, Finola, 207-8
Bruton, John, 143, 167, 170-1, 204
Buchanan, Revd A.D., 56
Bunch, Charlotte, 204
Burton, Joan, 127, 203, 221
Butler, Rt Revd Arthur, 56
Byrne, Ann, 128
Byrne, Dr, Archbishop of Dublin, 35
Byrne, Frankie, 64
Byrne, Gay, 65-6
Byrne, Noreen, 203

Callaghan, Mary Rose, 31, 32
Callery, Jim, 198
Campaign for Fair Referenda, 182
Canada, 190, 201, 228
Cantwell, Jim, 214
Carrington, Lord, 96
Carroll, Joe, 171
Casey, Dr Eamon, Bishop of Galway, 179
Castle, Barbara, 61
Catholic Church, 19-20, 135-6, 199, 214, 227; in Constitution, 42, 77-8; scandals, 155, 161, 179, 181; role of women, 214-15
Catholic hierarchy; contraception, 67-8, 82-3, 84, 88; New Ireland Forum, 108, 114-15; abortion referendum, 113; divorce, 119-20
censorship, 82, 92-5
Centre for Strategic and International Studies, 160
Chains or Change, 62-3
Charles, Prince of Wales, 17, 164, 174
Charlton, Jack, 184, 225
Cherish, 79, 112, 128, 130, 132
Chicago Tribune, 153
Childers, Erskine, 15, 123,